German and Italian
Lyrics of the
Middle Ages

D1281488

FREDERICK GOLDIN is a member of the department of English at the City College, and of the Doctoral Program in Comparative Literature at the Graduate School, of the City University of New York. He has written previously on the medieval lyric in *The Mirror of Narcissus* and in several articles.

German and Italian Lyrics of the Middle Ages

An Anthology and a History

TRANSLATIONS AND INTRODUCTIONS BY

Frederick Goldin

ANCHOR BOOKS
ANCHOR PRESS/DOUBLEDAY
GARDEN CITY, NEW YORK

The Anchor Books edition is the first publication of *German and Italian Lyrics of the Middle Ages*
Anchor Books edition: 1973

PT1421
G6

ISBN 0-385-04617-0
Library of Congress Catalog Card Number 72-97264
Copyright © 1973 by Frederick Goldin
PRINTED IN THE UNITED STATES OF AMERICA
ALL RIGHTS RESERVED
First Edition

To my wife *Dione*

08180

Preface

Many people helped me in different ways as I was working on this book. I want to thank my friends and colleagues for their encouraging and helpful response to many of the translations and introductions: Renata Karlin, Joan M. Ferrante, George D. Economou, Hella Somogyi, Alfred Kracher, Saul N. Brody, Esther Casier Quinn, Robert W. Hanning.

I was also helped by other friends, in other ways: this book would have been much harder to complete, and would have been completed in a far less happy mood, if these persons had not been true friends: Frieda Huth, and the late George Johnson, George and Adeline Berglund, Axel Krigsman, Frank Nucci.

The three editors I worked with at Doubleday—Susan Burchardt Watt, Judith Dollenmayer, and William Whitehead—believed in this book and went along with me every step of the way, from the first tentative proposal to the galleys I scarred with blue. And I am grateful to William Strachan for his patience and precision.

I was also helped by my children. I thank my two daughters, Lisa and Cheryl, for helping with the manuscript, and for bringing me their German homework faithfully in Vienna, and for always wanting to help. My son, Paul, had a devouring interest in these pages that made me eager to increase their number.

The best help of all came from my wife, Dione, in this as in everything.

April 1, 1973

Foreword

The two bodies of lyric poetry represented here are related as descendants from the same source. The new lyric poetry created by the troubadours toward the end of the eleventh century spread in all directions throughout Europe and caused a new beginning in the literature of every nation. The greater number and the most important of these new songs were love songs; and so, in German-speaking areas, those who composed in this new vein were called Minnesänger, those who sang on the theme of courtly love.

These songs extolled the dignity, and even the spirituality, of passionate love as a means of accomplishing their main purpose. For these songs were composed to please a courtly audience, and their message was less about love than about the audience: only in this class, among these noble people, could such love even be imagined. The troubadours, in pursuit of this purpose, developed sophisticated techniques of versification, and equally sophisticated performance techniques aimed at intensifying the audience's experience of intimacy, exclusiveness, and privilege. In general, the Minnesänger kept their rhymes and meters simpler, but they equaled the troubadours in the skill of playing to their audience.

The Sicilians composed their lyrics in similar conditions, though they did not take as their supreme principle the effect of their verses in performance. But as Italian poetry developed, it moved out of court, and it had to find a new language that could speak to a new audience and be adequate to a new poetic aspiration. These later poets, the stilnovisti, free of the demands of a courtly audience and able to look beyond the limits of courtly life, devoted themselves to the exploration of figurative language, looked into language for the meaning of experience.

Thus both the Minnesänger and the Italian poets began with the same material, and in response to different needs they developed two great and distinctly different bodies of lyric poetry. But, along with the poets who first inspired them, they described the secular possibilities of passionate feeling in a language that is still the substratum of much of our poetry and our private thoughts.

The history of the lyric in German-speaking areas and in Italy is traced from poet to poet through the introductory notes. Readers who do not like introductions but want to know something of a poet's life need not go beyond the first few paragraphs.

F. G.

Contents

PART II *Italian Lyrics*

PART I

German Lyrics

Guide to the Pronunciation
of Middle High German

The circumflex accent (ʌ) in the texts that follow signifies a long vowel. Vowels without this mark are short. Both long and short vowels should be pronounced as in modern German.

ae signifies modern German long *ä,* as in *Fähre,* English "hare."

oe signifies modern German long *ö,* as in *schön,* Goethe, French *peu.*

iu signifies modern German long *ü,* as in *für,* French *menu.*

Note that *ae, oe, iu* are not diphthongs.

In the diphthongs, each letter retains its value and the first letter is stressed. Thus, for example, *ei* is pronounced as in English "say"; *ie* somewhat as in English "pier"; *ou* as in English "know."

ch is always pronounced as in modern German *Bach, noch,* even when it follows *i* or *e.* (It never has the modern German squeezed-*h* sound, as in *ich.*)

h is pronounced like *ch* before and after a consonant: *naht-nacht.* Otherwise it is pronounced as in modern German *haben;* but it was always pronounced between vowels, as in *sehen* (*se-hen*), unlike modern German.

r was trilled.

st and *sp* are pronounced more as we would pronounce them than as in modern German. Thus *stein* ("stone") was pronounced approximately like our word "stain."

w is pronounced as in English.

Otherwise, be guided by modern German.

DER von KÜRENBERG

(mid-twelfth century)

Through his reference to himself in no. 2 below, "the one from Kürenberg" is the first German lyric poet whom we call by some sort of name. This designation appears as a rubric in the one manuscript that contains his poetry. Although Kürenberg cannot be definitely localized, it is certain that the poet flourished in the Danube area–in southern Germany or in Austria. Otherwise, nothing is known about him.

Most of his lyrics consist of one strophe, a few have two. The four-line strophes are made up of two rhymed couplets; each line consists of two four-beat half-lines, with a pause in the middle. The fact that this is also the structure of the *Nibelungenstrophe* has led to the very dubious suggestion that Der von Kürenberg was the author of the epic.

Apart from the ubiquitousness of spies and the consequent need for secrecy—inevitable themes in any literary work set in a court—there is no resemblance either in subject matter or in versification between these lyrics and those of the later poets. It is clear that Der von Kürenberg wrote before any Romance influence was felt.

All of his lyrics are objective in the sense that they are represented as the utterances of characters in specific situations: the poet never speaks of his own experience, nor does he ever address the audience. In the later courtly lyric the point of view will become much more complicated, and the poet will use his own person as the subject. Der von Kürenberg's lyrics have traditionally been separated into *Frauenstrophen* and *Männerstrophen,* according to who is speaking.

Every reader will admire the poet's art in drawing out of a single detail, or gesture, or phase so many consequences that are surprising and "right" at the same time. Within the tight limits of his strophe he thus conveys the sense of an intense and manifold experience. Another remarkable feature of his poetry is the way the last line suddenly transforms the initial effect of all the other lines.

Text: Carl von Kraus, ed. *Des Minnesangs Frühling* nach Karl Lachmann, Moriz Haupt und Friedrich Vogt neu bearbeitet. 30th ed. Leipzig: S. Hirzel, 1950.

1

Leit machet sorge   vil liebe wünne.
eines hübschen ritters   gewan ich künde:
daz mir den benomen hânt   die merker und ir nît,
des mohte mir mîn herze   nie mêre frô werden sît.

2

Ich stuont mir nehtint spâte   an einer zinnen:
dô hôrte ich einen ritter   vil wol singen   I
in Kürenberges wîse   al ûz der menigîn:
er muoz mir rûmen diu lant,   ald ich geniete mich sîn.

Nu brinc mir her vil balde   mîn ros, mîn îsengwant,
wan ich muoz einer frouwen   rûmen diu lant.   II
diu wil mich des betwingen   daz ich ir holt sî.[1]
si muoz der mîner minne   iemer darbende sîn.

3

Swenne ich stân aleine   in mînem hemede,
und ich an dich gedenke,   ritter edele,
so erblüet sich mîn varwe   als der rôse an dem dorne tuot,[1]
und gewinnet daz herze   vil mangen trûrigen muot.

[1] *Holt* denotes the relationship between lord and vassal.
[1] In the MF edition this line reads: *als der rôse in touwe tuot,* like the rose under dew.

1

Bad luck brings sorrow, good luck rejoicing.
Once I got to know a lordly man:
the busybodies and their envy took him from me then.
Because of that my heart will not rejoice again.

2

Late at night I stood on a battlement:
then I heard a knight singing well   I
a melody of Kürenberg amidst the crowd.
Let him clear out of my land, or let him be mine.

Now bring me my horse and armor, fast,
for I must clear out of a lady's land: II
she wants to make me bow and serve.[1]
She will have to live without my love.

3

When I stand alone in my shift
and think, noble knight, of you,
my color flowers up like the rose on the thorn,[1]
and my heart gathers sorrows.

4

Ez hât mir an dem herzen   vil dicke wê getân
daz mich des geluste   des ich niht mohte hân
noch niemer mac gewinnen.   daz ist schedelîch.
jone meine ich golt noch silber: ez ist den liuten gelîch.

5

Ich zôch mir einen valken   mêre danne ein jâr.
dô ich in gezamete   als ich in wolte hân   I
und ich im sîn gevidere   mit golde wol bewant,
er huop sich ûf vil hôhe   und floug in anderiu lant.

Sît sach ich den valken   schône fliegen:
er fuorte an sînem fuoze   sîdîne riemen,   II
und was im sîn gevidere   alrôt guldîn.
got sende si zesamene   die gerne geliep wellen sin.

6

Der tunkele sterne   sam der birget sich,
als tuo du, frouwe schœne,   sô du sehest mich,
sô lâ du dîniu ougen gên   an einen andern man.
son weiz doch lützel iemen   wiez undr uns zwein ist getân.

4

It has often caused my heart great pain
that I craved a thing I could not have
and can never get. That hurts.
Now I don't mean gold or silver: this thing looks like people.

5

I trained me a falcon, for more than a year.
When I had him tamed the way I wanted him   I
and set gold among his feathers,
he rose up high and flew away to wildness.

Since then I have seen the falcon in lordly flight:
he bore silken jesses on his legs,   II
and gold and red in his feathers.
God bring together all people who want to be lovers.

6

The morning star goes under cover.
Beautiful and high born, do the same when you see me
and let your eyes turn to another.
No one will guess what we have together.

7

Aller wîbe wünne   diu gêt noch megetîn.
als ich an si gesende   den lieben boten mîn,
jô wurbe ichz gerne selbe,   wær ez ir schade niet.[1]
in weiz wiez ir gevalle: mir wart nie wîp alsô liep.

8

Wîp unde vederspil   diu werdent lîhte zam:
swer si ze rehte lucket,   sô suochent si den man.
als warb ein schœne ritter   umb eine frouwen guot.
als ich dar an gedenke,   sô stêt wol hôhe mîn muot.

[1] That is, if he were seen courting her, it would harm her reputation.

7

The joy of all women still goes a maid.
When I send my dear messenger to her,
I'd gladly bring it myself, if that would not injure her.[1]
I don't know how she likes it: no woman was ever so dear before.

8

Woman and falcons—they are easily tamed.
If a man knows how to lure them right, they come flying.
Just so, to try to win a splendid lady, a handsome knight set out.
My spirit rises when I think of that.

HEINRICH von VELDEKE

(fl. last quarter twelfth century)

The poet's name derives from the village of Veldeke, west of Maastricht in Belgian Limburg. His chief work is his romance *Eneit,* which he completed, probably between 1187 and 1189, in the court of the great patron Landgraf Hermann of Thuringia. This work was widely celebrated in its own day, and in its manner of exemplifying courtly values it was a determining influence on the courtly romance in German-speaking areas.

His lyrics are very clearly influenced by French poetry (the *Eneit* is based on the Old French *Roman d'Eneas* as well as on Vergil). From this source come, for example, the tripartite structure of the strophe, the precise rhymes and regular meter, and such themes as the imperious rule of the beloved lady and the ennobling effect of Minne—metrical and thematic innovations that would have a tremendous vogue in the later Minnesang. In both the romance and the lyric Heinrich von Veldeke was thus a pioneer for courtly poetry.

Heinrich wrote in Limburg dialect, but in the manuscripts nearly all of his poetry has been transposed into High German. In 1947 Theodor Frings published his reconstruction of the original texts, and it is Frings's edition that MF follows.

Text: *Des Minnesangs Frühling.*

9

Tristrant mûste âne sînen danc
stâde sîn der koninginnen,
want poisûn heme dâr tû dwanc
mêre dan dî cracht der minnen.
5   des sal mich dî gûde danc
weten dat ich nîne gedranc
sulic pîment ende ich sî minne
bat dan hê, ende mach dat sîn.
wale gedâne, valsches âne,
10   lât mich wesen dîn
ende wis dû mîn.[1]

10

Dî minne bidde ich ende mane,
dî mich hevet verwunnen al,
dat sî dî scône dâr tû spane
dat sî mêre mîn geval.
5   want geschît mich alse den swanen
dê singet alser sterven sal,
sî verlûset te vele dâr ane.

[1] Compare the following strophe from the lyric *D'Amors ke m'ait tolut a moy,* ascribed to Chrétien de Troyes:

> Onques del bevraje ne bui
> don Tristans fut anpoisonez,
> mes plus me fet amer que lui
> fins cuers et bone volentez.
> Bien an doit estre miens li grez,
> qu'ains de rien esforciez n'an fui
> fors de tant, que mes iauz an crui,
> par cui sui an la voie antrez,
> don ja n'istrai, n'ains n'i recrui.
> (Bartsch, *Chrestomathie de l'ancien français*)

9

Tristan had no choice
but to be faithful to the Queen,
for poison drove him to it
more than the power of love.
5   Therefore, let The Good One be grateful
to me, for I never drank
such spiced wine and I love her
more than he loved, if that might be.
O beautiful and faultless,
10   let me be yours,
and you be mine.[1]

10

I beg Minne, who has won everything
from me, and warn her:
move that beautiful lady
to increase my pleasure.
5   For if it goes with me as with the swan
that sings about to die,
she will lose too much when I am gone.

I never drank of the potion
that poisoned Tristan,
but my pure heart and my entire will
made me love more than he loved.
Therefore, mine should be the thanks for this,
for nothing forced me to love
except that I trusted my eyes,
through which I set out on the path
I shall never stray from and have never renounced.

11

Ich levede êre te ungemake
seven jâr êre ich ît sprâke
weder heren wille einech wort.
dat hevet sî vele wale gehôrt
ende wele doch dat ich clage mêre:
noch is dî minne alse sî was wîlen êre.

12

Wê mich scade ane mîner vrouwen,
deme wunsche ich des dorres rîses
dâ dî dîve ane nemen ende.
wê mîn scône ane here bit trouwen,
5   deme wunsche ich des paradîses
ende valde heme mîne hende.   I
vrâge îman wê sî sî,
dê kenne sî dâ bî:
het is dî wale gedâne,
10   genâde, vrouwe, mich.
der sunnen an ich dich,
sô schîne mich der mâne.

Wî min nôt gevûger wâre,
sô gewunne ich lîf nâ leide
15   ende blîtscap manechfalde,
want ich weit vele lîve mâre:
blûmen springen an der heiden,
vogele singen in den walde.   II
dâ wîlen lach der snê,
20   dâ steit nû grûne clê,
bedouwet ane den morgen.

11

I would rather seven years
of misery than speak
one word against her will.
She has understood this very well
yet wants me to complain some more.
Love is the same as it was before.

12

Whoever hurts my favor with my lady,
I wish him the dead branch
on which thieves snatch death.
Whoever helps me with her faithfully,
5 I wish him paradise
and fold my hands to him.   I
If anyone asks who she is,
let him know her this way:
it is The Beautiful One.
10 Lady, pity me.
To you I yield the sun:
then let the moon have light for me.

Were my misery more bearable,
I could reach to pleasure after pain,
15 to joys and joys,
for I hear lovely news:
the flowers are springing on the heath, tra la,
the birds are singing in the woods; II
where snow once lay
20 green clover grows,
covered with dew in the mor-ning.

wê wele dê vrouwe sich.
nîman ne nôde's mich.
ich bin unledech sorgen.

13

In den aprillen   sô dî blûmen springen,
sô louven dî linden   ende grûnen dî bûken,
5 sô heven bit willen   dî vogele here singen,   I
sint sî minne vinden   al dâ sî sî sûken
9 ane heren genôt,   want here blîtscap is grôt
der mich nîne verdrôt,   want sî swegen al den winter
     stille.

Dû si ane den rîsen   dî blûmen gesâgen
15 bî den bladen springen,   dû wâren sî rîke
here manechfalder wîsen   der sî wîlen plâgen.   II
19 sî hûven here singen   lûde ende vrôlîke,
nedere ende hô.   mîn mût steit ouch alsô
dat ich wille wesen vrô.   recht is dat ich mîn gelucke
     prîse.

25 Mochte ich erwerven   mîner vrouwen hulde!
kunde ich dî gesûken   alse here wale getâme!
29 ich sal noch verderven   al dore mîne sculde,   III
sî ne wolde gerûken   dat sî van mich nâme
bûte âne dôt   up genâde ende dore nôt,
35 want et got nîne gebôt   dat negein man gerne solde
     sterven.

14

Men seget vorwâr   nû manech jâr,
dî wît dî haten grâwe hâr.

So, whoever wants to, let him rejoice—
but let him not press me.
I am unfree of sorrows.

13

    In April when the flowers spring,
the lindens leaf out, the beeches turn green,
5 with a will the birds begin to sing,   I
for they all find love where they seek it,
9 in their mates, so their joy is great—
which I never minded, for all winter long they keep still.

    When they saw on the branches the blossoms
15 springing among the leaves, then they were rich
in the varied songs they always sang.   II
19 They started to sing, joyfully and loud,
low and high. My mind, too, is such
that I want to know joy. I ought to praise my luck.

25 If I could win my lady's grace,
could seek it as becomes her!
29 I shall die, and it will be my fault   III
unless she consents to accept
a penance other than death for her grace; and so it must
               be,
35 for God never commanded any man be glad to die.

14

    They have said it is true, for many a year,
that women hate gray hair.

dat is mich swâr   I
ende is here misprîs
5   dî lîver hebben heren amîs
dump dan wîs.

Des mêre noch min   dat ich grâ bin,
ich hate ane wîven cranken sin,
dî nouwe tin   II
10   nemen vore alt golt.
sî gîn sî sîn den jungen holt
dore ungedolt.

That makes it hard for me—   I
and a shame for them
5   if they prefer their lovers
clumsy rather than wise.

As much or as little as I am gray,
a feeble wit in women is what I hate—
they'd rather have   II
10   new tin than old gold.
They say they favor the young ones
because they cannot wait.[1]

[1] Literally, "from impatience."

FRIEDRICH von HAUSEN

(c. 1150–1190)

A member of a baronial family, the poet dwelt near Kreuznach in the neighborhood of Worms. He was part of the most intimate circle around Friedrich Barbarossa and his son Heinrich VI, and his presence at several important events between 1171 and 1190 is attested. He participated in the Third Crusade with Barbarossa and died in battle in Asia Minor in 1190.

He cultivated French and Provençal themes and metrical forms to a greater degree than any German poet before him. Frank publishes seven of his lyrics together with French and Provençal models. Many familiar motifs from this source are found in his poetry: the distant longing, the personification of love, the fulfilling dream and the rude awakening, the constant threat from spies and slanderers and hypocrites, "die valschen diet."

Text: *Des Minnesangs Frühling.*

15

In mînem troume ich sach
ein harte schoene wîp
die naht unz an den tach:
do erwachete mîn lîp.

5   dô wart si leider mir benomen,
daz ich enweiz wâ si sî,
von der mir fröide solte komen.
daz tâten mir diu ougen mîn:
der wolte ich âne sîn.

16

Deich von der guoten schiet
und ich zir niht ensprach
alsô mir waere liep,
des lîde ich ungemach.

5   daz liez ich durch die diet   I
von der mir nît geschach.
ich wünsche ir anders niet,
wan der die helle brach,
der füege ir wê unt ach.

10   "Si waenent hüeten mîn
die sîn doch niht bestât,
und tuont ir nîden schîn,
daz wênic si vervât;
si möhten ê den Rîn   II

15   gekêren in den Pfât,
ê ich mich iemer sîn
getrôste, swiez ergât,
der mir gedienet hât." [1]

[1] This poem is a *Wechsel,* one of the oldest and most popular lyric forms.

15

In my dream I saw
a very beautiful woman
the whole night long till day,
then I awoke.
5   Then, alas, I was bereft of her
and do not know where she might be,
from whom my joy should come.
My own eyes did this to me.
I wish I did not have eyes.

16

When I parted from my Good
and did not tell her
how she was dear to me,
I suffer for it now.
5   I left it out because of all those hypocrites   I
whose envy ruined my pleasure.
I wish them nothing else
but that the One who harried Hell
make them hurt and yell.

10   "They think they can spy on me,
though this is none of their business,
and show their envy,
but it does them little good.
They could sooner make   II
15   the Rhine flow into the Po
before I'd give him up
who served me,
no matter how things go." [1]

The first strophe is spoken by the man, the second by the lady. Compare no.
2 above.

17

Wâfenâ, wie hât mich Minne gelâzen!
diu mich betwanc daz ich lie mîn gemüete
an solhen wân der mich wol mac verwâzen,
ez ensî daz ich genieze ir güete,[1]　　　　　　　I
5　von der ich bin　alsô dicke âne sin.
mich dûhte ein gewin,　und wolte diu guote
wizzen die nôt diu wont in mînem muote.

Wâfen, waz habe ich getân sô zunêren
daz mir diu guote niht gruozes engunde?
10　sus kan si mir wol daz herze verkêren.[1]
daz ich in der werlte bezzer wîp iender funde,[1]　　II
seht dêst mîn wân,　dâ für sô wil ichz hân,
und dienen nochdan　mit triuwen der guoten,
diu mich dâ bliuwet vil sêre âne ruoten.

15　Waz mac daz sîn daz diu werlt heizet minne,
unde ez mir tuot alsô wê zaller stunde
unde ez mir nimt alsô vil mîner sinne?
in wânde nicht daz ez ieman erfunde.　　　　　　III
getorste ich es jên　daz ichz hête gesên
20　dâ von mir ist geschêhen　alsô vil herzesêre,[1]
sô wolte ich gelouben dar an iemer mêre.

Minne, got müeze mich an dir rechen![1]
wie vil du mîm herzen der fröiden wendest![1]
und möhte ich dir dîn krumbez ouge ûz gestechen,[2]
25 des het ich reht, wan du vil lützel endest　　　　IV
an mir solhe nôt　sô mir dîn lîp gebôt.
und wærest du tôt,　sô dûhte ich mich rîche.
sus muoz ich von dir leben betwungenlîche.

[1] These lines are from the 3rd edition of *Des Minnesangs Frühling*, ed.
Friedrich Vogt (Leipzig: S. Hirzel, 1920).

17

Help! How Minne has deserted me—
she made me give my soul up
to a dream that will destroy me
if I am not relieved by kindness from that one woman,[1]   I
5 the cause why I so often have no sense.
I would think I'd gotten something if she were willing
to know the distress that has settled in my mind.

Help! What dishonor have I done
that the Good does not let me have her greeting?
10 This way she can lead my heart into a trap.[1]
Behold my mad faith: that I could never find a better
                woman [1]
                                                              II
in this world. As my faith I shall uphold it
and serve her loyally,
this good woman who scourges me hard without whips.

15 What may that be which the world calls Minne,
which makes me feel continual pain
and deprives me of so much sense?
I don't think anyone can really find it out.   III
If I could claim that I had seen it,
20 the cause of so much sorrow come my way,[1]
then I would believe in it ever more.

Minne, God let me get revenge on you.[1]
How many joys have you detoured away from my heart! [1]
And if I could stick out that squinting eye of yours,[2]
25 I would be right to do it, because you make no end   IV
to the distress you commanded against me,
and if you were dead, I would think I was rich,
yes, only now I have to live beneath your power.

[2] She has looked askance at him, has withheld her favor.

18

Ich denke under wîlen,
ob ich ir nâher wære,
waz ich ir wolte sagen.
daz kürzet mir die mîlen,
swenn ich ir mîne swære   I
sô mit gedanken klage.
mich sehent mange tage
die liute in der gebære
als ich niht sorgen habe,
wan ichs alsô vertrage.

Het ich sô hôher minne
mich nie underwunden,
mîn möhte werden rât.
ich tete ez âne sinne:
des lîde ich zallen stunden   II
nôt diu nâhe gât.
mîn stæte mir nu hât
daz herze alsô gebunden
daz siz niht scheiden lât
von ir als ez nu stât.

Ez ist ein grôzez wunder:
diech aller sêrest minne,
diu was mir ie gevê.
nu müeze solhen kumber
niemer man bevinden,   III
der alsô nâhe gê.
erkennen wânde i'n ê,
nu han i'n bas befunden:
mir was dâ heime wê,
und hie wol drîstunt mê.

18

I think sometimes about
what I would tell her
if I were near enough.
It makes the miles shorter
to call my sorrow out   I
to her, with thoughts.
Often the people here
see in me the figure
of a carefree man,
for so I let it seem.

Had I not taken on
such lofty love,
I might be saved.
I did it without thinking.
And every moment now I suffer   II
pain that presses deep.
Now my own constancy
has tied down my heart
and will not let it part
from her, as things are now.

It is a great wonder:
she whom I love with greatest torment
has always acted like my enemy.
Now may no man ever get to know
what such a burden is,   III
it weighs down hard.
I thought I knew what it was before,
now I know it better.
Over there, where home is, I was sad,
and here three times more.

Swie kleine ez mich vervâhe,
sô vröuwe ich mich doch sêre
daz mir sîn niemen kan
erwern, ichn denke ir nâhe
35   swar ich landes kêre.   IV
den trôst sol si mir lân.
wil siz für guot enpfân,
daz fröut mich iemer mêre,
wan ich für alle man
ir ie was undertân.[1]

19

Mîn herze und mîn lîp diu wellent scheiden,
diu mit ein ander varnt nu mange zît.
der lîp wil gerne vehten an die heiden:
sô hât iedoch daz herze erwelt ein wîp   I
5 vor al der welt. daz müet mich iemer sît,
daz si ein ander niene volgent beide.
mir habent diu ougen vil getân ze leide.
got eine müeze scheiden noch den strît.

Ich wânde ledic sîn von solher swaere,
10 dô ich daz kriuze in gotes êre nam.
ez waere ouch reht deiz herze als ê dâ waere,
wan daz sîn staetekeit im sîn verban.   II
ich solte sîn ze rehte ein lebendic man,
ob ez den tumben willen sîn verbaere.
15 nu sihe ich wol daz im ist gar unmaere
wie ez mir an dem ende süle ergân.

Sît ich dich, herze, niht wol mac erwenden,
dun wellest mich vil trûreclîchen lân,
sô bite ich got daz er dich ruoche senden

---

[1] Compare Frank, 4b: Guiot de Provins, "Ma joie premerainne." Line 28
above from Vogt.

However little good it does me,
still I have this pleasure:
no one can stop me
from thinking close to her,
35   wherever on earth I turn.   IV
This comfort she must let me have.
If she takes it well,
that gives me joy forever,
for I, more than any other man,
40   was always hers.[1]

19

My heart and my body want to separate,
that have ridden together all my life.
The body wants to strike against the heathen,
but the heart has chosen out a woman   I
5 before all the world. It has weighed on me ever since,
that one will not go in the steps of the other.
My eyes have brought me to grief.
May God alone break up that strife.

I had hoped to be free of this great weight
10 when I took the cross for the glory of God.
It would be right if the heart were in it too,
but its own faith held it back.   II
I would truly be a living man again
if it would stop its ignorant desiring.
15 I see now, to the heart it's all one
how I shall fare at last.

Heart, since I cannot turn you back
from deserting me so sadly,
I pray God reach down to send you

20 an eine stat dâ man dich wol enpfâ.   III
   owê wie sol ez armen dir ergân!
   wie torstest eine an solhe nôt ernenden?
   wer sol dir dîne sorge helfen enden
   mit solhen triuwen als ich hân getân?[1]

20

   Mîn herze den gelouben hât,
   solt iemer man beliben sîn
   durch liebe od durch der Minnen rât,
   sô wære ich noch alumbe den Rîn;
5   wan mir daz scheiden nâhe gât,   I
   deich tet von lieben friunden mîn.
   swiez doch dar umbe mir ergât,
   got hêrre, ûf die genâde dîn
   sô wil ich dir bevelhen die
10   die ich durch dînen willen lie.

   Ich gunde es guoten frouwen niet
   daz iemer mêre quæme der tac
   dazs ir deheinen heten liep
   der gotes verte alsô erschrac.
15   wie kunde in der gedienen iet?   II
   wan ez wære ir êren slac!
   dar zuo send ich in disiu liet,
   und warnes als ich beste mac.
   gesæs si mîn ouge niemer mê,
20   mir tæte iedoch ir laster wê.

[1] Cf. Frank, 6b: Canon de Béthune, *Ahi, Amors, com dure departie.*

20 where they will welcome you in.   III
　　Alas, poor Heart, how will it go with you?
　　How could you dare to go boldly into this danger all
　　　　alone?
　　Who will help you end your cares
　　with such loyalty as I have shown? [1]

20

　　My heart believes:
　　if any man could rightly stay behind
　　for pleasure or for Minne's sake,
　　then I would still be on the Rhine.
5　　For the parting I had from dear friends   I
　　moves me deeply.
　　But whatever happens to me,
　　Lord God, let me commend
　　to your grace the one
10　I left for You.

　　I do not allow of good women
　　that the day could ever come
　　when they would love a man
　　who shrank from the way of God.
15　How could he ever serve them?   II
　　It would be a blow to their honor.
　　Therefore I send them this song,
　　and I warn them as best I can.
　　If my eye were never more to see them,
20　their dishonor still would cause me pain.

HEINRICH von MORUNGEN

(d. 1222)

Heinrich von Morungen came from a family that was settled near Sangerhausen in Thuringia. He was in the service of Landgraf Hermann's son-in-law, Dietrich von Meissen. Nothing else is known for sure about him, except that in 1217 he made over his possessions to the Thomaskloster in Leipzig, where he finished out his days. He died in 1222. It is generally assumed that his literary activity flourished in the 1190s.

Heinrich's language has the same apparent simplicity that generally characterizes the classic Minnesang; but his lyrics are distinguished by the sharp contrast between this surface clarity and the resonating complexity of the scenes he depicts. That moment (in no. 26) when the lady leads him in his solitude high over the battlements, consoling him in his grief; and the complementary moment when he stands on the ground beneath her window gazing up at her radiance and she withdraws, awakening his grief, are often cited, among many other examples, as evidence of the poet's dramatic effect and the sense of inexhaustible meaning that he evokes. His continual elaboration of the imagery of light across the whole body of his work is an example of the way he rethinks conventional themes. The power of his imagination is made all the more effective by his mastery of a great variety of metrical forms.

Heinrich's songs adopt the metrical techniques and the courtly themes that originated with the troubadours and came to German-speaking areas both directly from the troubadours and through the courtly poets of northern France, the trouvères. From these sources comes the basic idea that the courtly man is distinguished from ordinary men by the way he loves. Ordinary men cannot love unless they get something in return—something they can get hold of, not just a smile. If they do not get it, they soon stop loving, or, if the girl is from one of the lower orders, they take it by force. But usually, since ordinary men love ordinary women, they get what they want; and then, their mutual lust expended, they go their separate ways, or else, if they are restrained by some vulgar decency, they mate and settle down. In this wilderness of carnality and domesticity, nobility declines: there is no reason, and no chance, for the longing, exaltation, and self-discipline of true courtliness. This is one of the basic creeds of courtly love, and we shall see how it was re-examined and verified by two of the greatest Minnesänger, Walther and Neidhart.

The truly courtly man is superior to these ordinary people because he chooses to avoid the vulgarizing effect of their happiness. He loves a woman who cannot be possessed or truly known; she is distant, and her personality is indiscernible. The only physical and ethical qualities she has are those that correspond to the audience's notion of beauty and courtliness: she is white-skinned and bright-eyed, elegant, gentle, and virtuous. She has no personal presence in these songs, she never appears on any common ground: on the rare occasions when the singer's eyes behold her directly and he tells us what he sees, her appearance reveals nothing that might individualize her, but only expresses the singer's adoration: she is always isolated in splendor, withdrawn, framed in a high window. Most of the time, however, the singer sees nothing of her but the image in his heart, and his song recounts his responses to that image rather than any experience he has shared with her. She thus appears as an emblematic figure, a mirror of all the virtues that distinguish the courtly class. And because she is perfect and all her qualities are exemplary, his longing for her can never be satisfied by physically possessing her in the manner of ordinary people, though of course he is as lustful as they are and feels their desires even as he adores her.

The man who can love such an exemplary figure and remain steadfast in his love, though his body grieves, is a courtly man. He loves the joy he feels in the very thought of loving her more than any moment of pleasure his body can win. The singer has a constant message: his love for this lady proves his essential nobility, for no other man could renounce all natural pleasure for the privilege of longing for her. It makes him suffer that he has to forgo the satisfactions of an ordinary man, and his song is full of complaint. But his ability to withstand such suffering is the source of his pride, and his complaints are really boasts: his worth is proven, his longing for virtue means more to him than all those deadly comforts. He is a better man for loving her in sorrow than he would be if he followed the track of common men, with their little lightning of lust and their ensuing night in domesticity.

The ennobling effect of unfulfilled love and the courtly man's capacity for longing was the obligatory theme of the *liet,* a song in which the only voice heard is that of the lover, or rather of the singer enacting the rôle of a lover before his audience. There were other forms of lyric poetry, less common than the *liet,* in which other kinds of love and other voices are represented: in the *tageliet* or dawn song (no. 27), for example, it was possible to celebrate the joys of reciprocal love, and often the woman was represented as speaking in her own person in some of the strophes. But the *liet* had to be a song of exaltation and complaint, based on the theme of courtly love. This term "courtly love," incidentally, though it is in widespread use today as a scholarly term, was hardly ever used by the medieval poets, for whom the "courtly" element was too obvious to need mentioning. The German poets used the word *Minne* to designate this refined love that exists nowhere but in the circle of true nobility.

This theme already begins to appear in Heinrich von Veldeke, as we have seen. But Heinrich von Morungen seems to be one of the first poets who deal with it in a way that is characteristic of the high Minnesang: he treats the theme of courtly love in terms of the technical problems it creates for the performer. His songs are not directly about courtly love but about the position of the singer as he stands before his audience and performs a song based on this theme.

This audience, as he represents it in his song, is largely his own creation, for he characterizes it in his own terms. In the words of Wolfgang Mohr, the listeners, as they appear to the singer, "are individualized into friend and enemy, helpers, consolers, mockers, those who misunderstand, faultfinders . . ." In other words, the members of the audience are divided according to their attitudes toward the song, or toward the love he sings about. The "friends" are those who deeply sympathize with the singer's love and cherish its nobility. He and they are bound to each other. They need his song and they demand it: they regard his service and devotion to that perfect lady as a beautiful representation of the courtly man's dedication and high-mindedness, an anthem of their own ideal, a vindication of their privileged life. And the object of the singer's performance is to win their acceptance, for only as they recognize him as one of their own is his nobility revealed: the beloved lady remains forever silent, withholding her judgment of his worth, but the friends are close around him, a circle of courtliness that he enters through his song.

These friends want the singer to tell a familiar story of love and longing that ends in joy—the joy that only they can know, that arises from a noble man's sense of his own worth. The lover may sing of his grief for a while, for he can never be close to his beloved; but if he stays fixed in that grief, if he does not rise above it in joy, then he is only ordinary after all, no different from all those ignoble ones who cannot love unless they get some physical return. In the judgment of the friends, the singer who sings only of grief does not perform well. Their demands are quite exacting: the lover may decorously grieve, for his love cannot have much value unless he makes sacrifices for it, the sacrifice in this case being his own desire for ordinary pleasure; but that grief must be the prelude to a rare and transcendent joy, the joy of proven worth, of the triumph over lust, of being recognized. This joy expresses itself in the lover's appearance, in the distinctive elegance and gaiety of his manner; and this entire state of inward exaltation and social grace is what the Minnesänger mean by a term that appears in their songs almost as frequently as "Minne" itself: *hoher muot*. Thus it is a standard maneuver for the singer to raise himself out of his sorrow by remembering his friends and their expectations of joy. *Sorge ist*

unwert da diu liute sint fro, he says, "Sorrow is ignoble where
people rejoice" (no. 22) .

Now the friends, in their naïve and uncompromising high-
mindedness, have a certain perspective on the singer which ex-
cludes many things that he can see from his position before the
audience. He can see his friends, as they see him, but he can also
see the rest of the audience, including the hostile parts. There
are plenty of people there who gag whenever he sings for his
friends. "Look at him singing," they say; "if he were really
suffering, he wouldn't be doing that" (no. 22) . He is continually plagued by the accusations of these people, whom Heinrich and Reinmar in fact refer to simply as "the people," *diu
liute,* by which they mean "the rabble." These regard the singer
as a liar and a hypocrite, if not the worst fool they have ever
seen. They do not believe that any normal man can love a blank
space, which is all that the beloved seems to be; and it annoys
them, or makes them laugh, when they hear the singer con-
gratulating himself for suffering well. Ordinary lust they can
understand, as well as the need to conceal it; but they know
that this lifelong devotion to a woman who is never present is
not humanly possible. These "people" are ordinary men who
know nothing but the facts of life. But they know these facts
very well, and so they know that "courtly love" does not exist,
and that no man can sacrifice all the pleasures of the world for
the spiritual benefits of grief and privation. And so they continually search the singer's own words for proof of his hypocrisy;
and the very fact that he sings before an audience proves that
his "suffering" is just a pretense, an act.

No courtly love poet can ignore their voice, for the doubts
they raise are such as would occur to anyone listening to his
song. Ordinary men and extraordinary men share a common
world, and all are full of lust. And it is true that in the world we
all inhabit the singer's love is impossible, for no person is
capable of offering such surrender and adoration to another, and
no other person is worthy of receiving it. Somehow the singer
has to find a way to answer "the people" and silence them; for
otherwise, when he sings to rejoice his friends, the mockery and
insults of his enemies will drown out his song.

Now the way that Heinrich, as well as the other Minnesänger, deals with this predicament is first of all to acknowledge that "the people" are right: it is true that courtly love does not exist as other desires exist; and no woman can be so exalted, including his own beloved lady who is, in truth, quite ordinary, quite like other women. And they are right about him, too: he is really one of them, and his vow of service and renunciation is a pretense. The way the singer corroborates that hostile point of view is to adopt it for a time. There is always a moment in his song—usually there are several such moments—when the singer shows how ridiculous the figure of the courtly lover, which he impersonates, appears to the members of the audience whom his friends do not see or care about, and whom he now seems to serve.

This is the singer's predicament as he confronts his audience: everyone in it has his own view of him, and everyone's view is equally valid. And so, owing to the nature of his audience, the singer has to keep on switching sides. To the friends he is the ideal courtly man, and for them he praises his beloved in the highest, sometimes even in terms borrowed from the Marian hymns (as in nos. 22, line 17; 25, lines 13f and 25f), and sings of his joy in her service. To "the people" he is an ordinary man full of ordinary desires, and for them he says he wants the power to make her stay with him "three full days, and some nights" (no. 24). The multiple perspectives of the audience obviously give the singer some wonderful comic opportunities, which he exploits. As we have just seen, he can begin in the exalted tones of the courtly lover so much admired by the friends, and then say something plain and crude to show the people that he makes no pretenses after all.

But the audience gives him the opportunity for many other effects as well. Sometimes, in his rôle as the courtly lover, when he beholds the lady from the viewpoint of the people, when he sees her as they see all women, he can be incredibly moving rather than comic, as in the mirror lyric (no. 25), in which the lover is overwhelmed by his discovery of the real, unexaltable carnality of his beloved and grieves for the loss of that radiant lady who seemed to redeem his life from its ordinary emptiness. The

friends can never see her in this perspective: in the compre-
hensiveness of his vision the singer stands alone. The lyric
audience constantly forces the singer to consider his rôle and
to represent the courtly lover in a variety of modes. In this
respect, no one surpasses Heinrich von Morungen. The "I" of
his songs casts a dark cloud of doubt upon the lady's radiance
(no. 22). He has to wonder, when he considers her from the
perspective of ordinary men, whether all those glorious virtues
he worships in her are really hers; or whether, erring like Narcissus, he is in love with an image of beauty and perfection that
originates in himself and is accidentally reflected by the lady,
as by a mirror, while she herself is completely unconcerned and
altogether irrelevant to his gift of adoration. Indeed, the distance
and unattainability of the lady in the songs of courtly love are a
testimony to her essential commonness: only when she is vaguely
glimpsed and hardly known can she be glorified; when she is
seen up close, as everyone else is seen, she is only like everyone
else.

Thus the singer keeps on changing the context of his words
as he moves his eyes back and forth between those who insist on
a song of courtly love with a joyous ending, and those who insist
that nothing on earth exists beyond the reach of lust and common
sense. Though he wants to vindicate the perspective of his
friends, and though he acknowledges the "people's" claim on
him, the singer stands completely alone as he confronts the
whole audience, and he cannot give his allegiance finally to any
group, for none of them shares his perspective: they are all
arranged around him, watching him, but he alone sees them all
as they watch him. Heinrich's song, *Ich wêne nieman lebe*
(no. 26), is, among other things, about the singer's solitude as he
performs, when he must feel somewhat at odds with the audience
he serves, even with those friends whose recognition he strives
to achieve through the celebration of their privileged and ethical
life in his song.

Once the singer grants "the people" a voice in his song, he
silences them. They cannot accuse him of hypocrisy, for he does
not deny their point of view—in fact, he shares it. Now he is free
to sing for his friends again and reaffirm his devotion. In a

wonderful way, these vulgar people, in their very hostility to his courtly song, help to save it and intensify its effect. For once he has stood with them and seen the beloved lady in their vulgar and knowing way, he has won the chance to be courtly. Only now does he have the freedom to choose a nobler way. And so, when he returns to the friends' perspective and sees the lady once more in a glorious light, that return is the proof of his noble disposition. The glories he attributes to the lady may be irrelevant to her real nature, but they reveal much about his: he is as knowing a man as the most cynical of "the people"; but when he sings, he chooses to see in a way that exalts the object he desires. It is only through the presence of these people and the demands of their vulgarity that he has the great chance to make this choice: this act of choosing is the essential act of his nobility. He shares a common ground with all men and can go as low as the lowest, but in moments of song he can rise up to a vision that "the people" cannot see or imagine.

The singer's problems are not yet solved, for the fact still remains that this love of which he boasts is completely incredible, and he has to do more than just acknowledge that. The final strategy of the courtly singer is to confine his meaning to the boundaries of play, the boundaries defined by the courtly circle itself. Just how this ludic strategy saves the song we can best see in the songs of Reinmar von Hagenau. For now we can take note of the basic and definitive technique of the courtly love song: the singer constructs his song from the situation in which he performs; he articulates the different viewpoints of his audience regarding his own performing figure and the love he celebrates.

Text: *Des Minnesangs Frühling.*

21

Ich hôrt ûf der heide
lûte stimme und süezen klanc.
dâ von wart ich beide
fröiden rîch und trûrens kranc.   I
5 nâch der mîn gedanc sêre ranc unde swanc,
die vant ich ze tanze dâ si sanc.
âne leide ich dô spranc.

Ich vant si verborgen
eine und ir wengel naz,
10 dâ si an dem morgen
mînes tôdes sich vermaz.   II
der vil lieben haz tuot mir baz danne daz
dô ich vor ir kniete dâ si saz
und ir sorgen gar vergaz.

15 Ich vants an der zinnen,
eine, und ich was zir gesant.
dâ moht ichs ir minnen
wol mit fuoge hân gepfant.   III
dô wând ich diu lant hân verbrant sâ zehant,
20 wan daz mich ir süezen minne bant
an den sinnen hât erblant.[1]

22

Leitlîche blicke und grôzliche riuwe
hân mir daz herze und den lîp nâch verlorn.
mîn alte nôt die klagte ich für niuwe.

[1] Literally, "I thought I burnt up the land straightaway (that is, with the fire of my love), but the bond of her sweet love blinded my senses," in other words, the tryst and the promise of her love were only a fantasy. The order

I heard on the meadow
bright voices and sweet tones
and was at once
rich in joys, in sorrows poor.   I

5 The one toward whom my thoughts have struggled and
           soared—
I found her in the dance, singing.
Free of sorrow, I danced too.

I found her withdrawn,
by herself, and her cheeks wet,
10 in the morning where
she fathomed my death.   II
I would rather the hate of my beloved than how it felt
kneeling before her where she sat
and let go of all her pain.

15 I found her on the battlement, alone,
and I had been sent for—
and could have taken, quite without uncourtliness,
the proof of her love from her hand.   III
I thought I had burnt up the land,
20 it was only that love with its gentle bind
had darkened my mind.[1]

22

Glances that hurt and overwhelming grief
have nearly destroyed my heart and body.
I would raise a new lament for ancient suffering

of the strophes, as well as their exact meaning and the connections between
them, has never been clearly determined. Line 17, literally: "I could have
properly taken a pledge of her love." Line 10: *dá* instead of MF *dô*.

wan daz ich fürhte der schimpfere zorn.   I
5 singe ab ich durch die diu mich freute hie bevorn,
sô velsche durch got nieman mîne triuwe,
wan ich durch sanc bin zer werlde geborn.

Manger der sprichet 'nu sêt wie der singet!
wêre im iht leit, er têt anders dan sô.'
10 der mac niht wizzen maz mich sanges twinget:
nu tuon ab ich reht als ich tet aldô.   II
do ich in leide stuont, dô huop ich si gar unhô.
diz ist ein nôt diu mich leides verdringet:
sorge ist unwêrt dâ diu liute sint frô.

15 Diu mînes herzen ein wunne und ein krôn ist
vor allen frouwen diech noch hân gesên,
schône unde schôner und schône aller schônist,
ist si, mîn frouwe: des muoz ich ir jên.   III
al diu werlt sol si durch ir schône gerne flên.
20 'noch wêre zît daz du, frouwe, im lônist:
er kan mit lobe anders tôrheit begên.'

Stên ich vor ir unde schouwe daz wunder
daz got mit schône an ir lîp hât getân,
sost des sô vil daz ich sî dâ besunder,
25 daz ich vil gerne wolt iemer dâ stân.   IV
ôwê sô muoz ich harte trûrig scheiden dan:
sô kumt ein wolken sô trüebez dar under
daz ich des schînen von ir niht enhân.

23

Owê, war umbe volge ich tumbem wâne,
der mich sô sêre leitet in die nôt?
ich schiet von ir gar aller frôiden âne,
daz si mir trôst noch helfe nie gebôt.   I

if I did not fear the rage of those who mock me.   I
5 But if I sing for her who once rejoiced me,
let no man then, by God, defame my loyalty,
for I was born into the world to sing.

Many a one of them says, "Aha! look at him singing!
If he suffered, he wouldn't do that."
10 A man like that cannot know what drives me to sing.
But now, as in former days, I shall raise my voice.   II
When I stood mute in sorrow, I was worth nothing to her.
That is the anguish that oppresses me:
sorrow is despised where men rejoice.

15 She is my heart's one joy, the crown
above all women I have seen,
beautiful, more beautiful, beautiful above the most
beautiful
is she: that I must affirm.   III
Now let the whole world beg her, by her beauty:
20 "It is time now, lady, for you to requite him,
or else he speaks foolishness with his praise."

When I stand before her and look upon the wonder
God created in her beauty,
I see something so extraordinary,
25 I want to stand forever in her sight.   IV
Ah, but then I have to go away, cast down:
a dark cloud comes between us
and I have nothing of her light.

23

Alas, why do I follow that childish dream
that leads me so sorely into misery?
I parted from her barren of all joy,
because she sent no sign of comfort or help.   I

5 doch wart ir varwe liljen wîz und rôsen rôt,
and that beloved and beautiful lady sat before me
in flowering radiance like the full moon.
That was joy to my eyes, death to my heart.
und saz vor mir diu liebe wolgetâne
geblüejet rehte alsam ein voller mâne.
daz was der ougen wunne, des herzen tôt.

Mîn stêter muot gelîchet niht dem winde:
10 ich bin noch alse si mich hât verlân,
vil stête her von einem kleinen kinde,
swie wê si mir nu lange hât getân   II
alswîgend ie genôte ûf den verholnen wân,
swie dicke ich mich der tôrheit underwinde,
15 swâ ich vor ir stân, und sprüche ein wunder vinde,
und muoz doch von ir ungesprochen gân.

Ich hân sô vil gesprochen und gesungen
daz ich bin müede und heis von mîner klage.
ich bin umb niht wan umb den wân betwungen,
20 sît si mir niht geloubet daz ich sage,   III
wie ich si minne, und ich sô holdez herze ir trage.
dêswâr mirn ist nâch werde niht gelungen.
hêt ich nâch gote ie halb sô vil gerungen,
er nême mich hin zim ê mîner tage.

24

Von den elben wirt entsên vil manic man:
sô bin ich von grôzer minne entsên
von der besten die ie man ze friunt gewan.
wil si aber mich dar umbe vên,   I
5 mir zunstaten stên, mac si dan rechen sich,
tuo des ich si bite: si fröit sô sêre mich,
daz mîn lîp vor liebe muoz zergên.

5 Yet the color on her was the white of lilies, the red of
         roses,
   and that beloved and beautiful lady sat before me
   in flowering radiance like the full moon.
   That was joy to my eyes, death to my heart.

   My mind is firm, it is not like the wind:
10 I am still as I was when she left me—
   loyal to this moment since my childhood
   with all the grief she has given me so long,   II
   forced to be silent about the hidden dream,
   no matter how many times I take on this foolishness:
15 standing before her full of glorious utterance,
   and going away without a word.

   I have said so much in melody and verse,
   I am hoarse from lamenting, and out of breath.
   I am driven by nothing but the dream,
20 for she will not believe what I speak: III
   how I love her, and bear a heart that she commands.
   I have not been rewarded as I have deserved.
   Had I struggled toward God with half so great a will,
   He would take me to Him before my death.

24

   Many a man gets bewitched by the elves.
   I have been bewitched with love
   by the best a man ever won as friend.
   If she wants to be my enemy for that   I
5 and destroy me, let her get her vengeance
   by doing what I ask: then she delights me so sorely
   I pass away with pleasure.

Sie gebiutet unde ist in dem herzen mîn
frouwe und hêrer danne ich selbe sî:
10 hei wan müeste ich ir alsô gewaltic sîn
daz si mir mit triuwen wêre bî   II
ganzer tage drî und eteslîche naht!
sô verlüre ich niht den lîp und al die maht.
nust si leider vor mir alze frî.

15 Mich enzündet ir vil liehter ougen schîn
same daz fiur den dürren zunder tuot,
und ir fremden krenket mir daz herze mîn
same daz wazzer die vil heize gluot: III
und ir hôher muot, ir schône, ir werdecheit,
20 und daz wunder daz man von ir tugenden seit,
deist mir übel und wirt noch lîhte guot.

Swenne ir liehten ougen sô verkêren sich
daz si mir aldurch mîn herze sên,
swer dâ 'nzwischen danne stêt und irret mich,
25 dem müez al sîn wunne gar zergên,   IV
wan ich danne stên und warte der frouwen mîn
rehte alsô des tages diu kleinen vogellîn:
wenne sol mir iemer liep geschên?

25

Mirst geschên als eime kindelîne,
daz sîn schônez bilde in eime glase ersach
unde greif dar nâch sîn selbes schîne
sô vil biz daz ez den spiegel gar zerbrach.   I
5 dô wart al sîn wünne ein leitlich ungemach.
alsô dâhte ich iemer frô ze sîne,
dô'ch gesach die lieben frouwen mîne,
von der mir bî liebe leides vil geschach.

She commands and in my heart
is Lady, her rule is mightier than mine.
10 O if I could get the power over her somehow
and she stayed with me obediently   II
three full days, and some nights.
My body's strength would not be ebbing away.
But now she is all too free of me.

15 The light of her eyes burns me up
like fire on dry tinder.
Her distance damps my heart
like water on a rising flame.   III
And her rejoicing spirit, her beauty, and her worth,
20 and the miraculous virtues that have won her fame—
it's my sickness now, but maybe it will be my health.

When her glowing eyes turn
and she looks through my heart,
the fool that steps between us then and gets in my way,
25 may all his pleasures evaporate,   IV
because I am standing there looking out for her,
like the little bird that waits for day.
I wait for joy—how long must I wait?

25

It has gone with me as with a child
that saw its beautiful image in a mirror
and reached for its own reflection so
often till it broke the mirror to pieces;   I
5 then its contentment turned into a great unrest.
So I, once, thought I would live in continual joy
when I set my eyes on my beloved lady,
through whom, beside some pleasure, I have felt much
        pain.

Minne, diu der werlde ir fröide mêret,
10 sêt, diu brâhte in troumes wîs die frouwen mîn
dâ mîn lîp an slâfen was gekêret
und ersach sich an der besten wünne sîn.   II
dô sach ich ir werden tugende, ir liehten schîn,
schône und für alle wîp gehêret;
15 niwan daz ein lützel was versêret
ir vil fröiden rîchez rôtez mündelîn.

Grôze angest hân ich des gewunnen,
daz verblîchen süle ir mündelîn sô rôt.
des hân ich nu niuwer klage begunnen,
20 sît mîn herze sich ze solcher swêre bôt,   III
daz ich durch mîn ouge schouwe solche nôt,
sam ein kint daz wîsheit unversunnen
sînen schaten ersach in einem brunnen
und den minnen muose unze an sînen tôt.

25 Hôer wîp von tugenden und von sinne,
die enkan der himel niender ummevân,
sô die guoten diech vor ungewinne
fremden muoz und immer doch an ir bestân.   IV
ôwê leider, jô wând ichs ein ende hân,
30 ir vil wünneclîchen werden minne:
nu bin ich vil kûme an dem beginne.
des ist hin mîn wünne und ouch mîn gerender wân.[1]

26

Ich wêne nieman lebe der mînen kumber weine,
den ich eine trage,
ez entuo diu guote, diech mit triuwen meine,
vernimt si mîne klage.   I
5 wê wie tuon ich sô, daz ich sô herzeclîche

---

[1] See Frank, 17b, for a Provençal parallel.

Minne, who increases men's joy—look,
10 there, she brought me my lady by way of a dream,
where my body was turned toward sleep,
lost in the vision of its great contentment.   II
Then I gazed on all her nobleness, her shining image,
beautiful, exalted among women.   Only,
15 it was just that there was some damage
to her small red mouth, that always laughed.

It frightened me
to see her small mouth pale, that was so red.
Now for this I have raised up new laments:
20 my heart stood ready for the grief it knew,   III
and I found this terror with my eyes—
like that child without experience
who found his own reflection in a spring
and had to love it till he died.

25 Heaven itself cannot contain
women higher in virtue and mind
than this good lady. I have been brought down,
I must stay far away and cleave to her forever.   IV
O sorrow, how for a moment it could seem
30 I had reached and won her joyful, noble love.
Now here I stand, just starting out,
my contentment is gone, and my soaring dream.[1]

26

I believe there is no one alive who weeps for my sorrow,
which I bear alone,
unless the Good, whom I love loyally, should weep
            for me,
if she hears my cry.   I
5 O lord, what do I do, that I so lose

bin an si verdâht, daz ich ein künicrîche
für ir minne niht ennemen wolde,
obe ich teilen unde welen solde?

Dô si mir alrêrst ein hôhgemüete sande
10 in daz herze mîn,
des was bote ir güete, die ich wol erkande,
und ir liehter schîn.   II
si sach mich güetlîch ane mit ir spilnden ougen;
lachen si began ûz rôtem munde tougen.
15 sâ zehant enzunte sich mîn wunne,
daz mîn muot stuont hô alsam diu sunne.

Swer mir des erban, ob ich si minne tougen,
sêt der sündet sich.
swenne ich eine bin, si schînt mir vor den ougen.
20 sô bedunket mich   III
wie si gê dort her ze mir aldur die mûren.

ir red und ir trôst enlâzent mich niet trûren.
swenn si wil, sô füeret si mich hinnen
mit ir wîzen hant hô über die zinnen.

25 Ich wêne, si ist ein Vênus hêre, diech dâ minne:
wan si kan sô vil.
si benimt mir leide, fröide und al die sinne.
swenne sô si wil,   IV
sô gêt si dort her zuo einem vensterlîne,
30 unde siht mich an reht als der sunnen schîne:
swanne ich si dan gerne wolde schouwen,
ach sô gêt si dort zuo andern frouwen.

Wê waz rede ich? jâ ist mîn geloube bœse
und ist wider got.
35 wan bit ich in des daz er mich hinnen lœse?
ich was ie ir spot.   V
ich tuon sam der swan, der singet swenne er stirbet.
waz ob mir mîn sanc daz lîhte noch erwirbet,

myself in thought of her, I would not take
a kingdom for her love,
were I to set them apart and choose?

The first time she sent a jubilation
10 into my heart,
   it was her gentleness that brought the message, as I
        could recognize,
and her brilliant light.   II
She looked on me with kindness in her playing eyes,
and on her red mouth a secret smile.
15 Right then my joy lit up
and my mind stood as high as the sun.

Whoever grumbles at my loving her in secret,
behold: that man does wrong:
when I am alone, she gleams before my eyes.
20 Then I think I see: III
there, she comes this way, to me, through the castle walls.

Her greeting and her comfort do not let me grieve.
If she wills, she leads me out away from here,
with her white hand, high up, over the battlements.

25 I think it is there the noble Venus that I love,
for she has great power.
   She takes away my sadness, and my joy, and all my
        senses.
If she wills,   IV
she comes this way to a little window there
30 and looks down on me like the light of the sun.
Then when I would like to look at her,
ach, she goes to the other women, she goes back in.

Woe, what have I said? What I believe is evil
and strikes against God.
35 Why do I not pray Him set me free from here?
To her I was always a thing to ridicule.   V
I am like the swan, that sings when it is dying.
What if my song should yet gain me this one thing,

swâ man mînen kumber sagt ze mêre,
40 daz man mir erbunne mîner swêre?

27

Owê, sol aber mir iemer mê
geliuhten dur die naht
noch wîzer danne ein snê
ir lîp vil wol geslaht?   I
5   der trouc diu ougen mîn:
ich wânde, ez solde sîn
des liehten mânen schîn,
dô taget ez.

'Owê, sol aber er immer mê
10   den morgen hie betagen?
als uns diu naht engê,
daz wir niht durfen klagen: II
"owê, nu ist ez tac,"
als er mit klage pflac
15   do'r jungest bî mir lac.
dô taget ez.'

Owê, si kuste âne zal
in deme slâfe mich.
dô vielen hin ze tal
20   ir trêne nidersich,   III
iedoch getrôste ich sî,
daz si ir weinen lî
und mich alummevî.
dô taget ez.

25   'Owê, daz er sô dicke sich
bî mir ersêen hât!
als er endahte mich,
sô wolte er sunder wât   IV

wherever they tell about my sorrow:
40 that they envy me my suffering?

27

Alas, shall I not see again,
glimmering in the dark
of night, whiter than snow,
her beautiful body?   I
5   It fooled my eyes,
I thought it must be
the bright light of the moon.
Then it dawned.

"Alas, will he not again
10   stay here till the light?
May the night so pass between us
we've no reason to lament   II
'Alas, now it is day,'
as he lamented then
15   when he last lay by me.
Then it dawned."

Alas, she did not stop,
as I was sleeping, kissing me.
Then her tears came
20   falling.   III
But I gave her comfort,
and she left her weeping
and held me all around again.
Then it dawned.

25   "Alas, how many times he lost
himself looking at me,
as he took the cover off,
he wanted to see   IV

mich armen schouwen blôz.
30   ez was ein wunder grôz
daz in des nie verdrôz.
dô taget ez.'[1]

28

Vil süeziu senftiu tôterinne,   2
war umbe welt ir tôten mir den lîp,
und i'uch sô herzeclîchen minne,
zewâre, frouwe, gar für elliu wîp?
5   wênet ir ob ir mich tôtet,
daz ich iuch danne niemer mê beschouwe?
nein, iuwer minne hât mich des ernôtet
daz iuwer sêle ist mîner sêle frouwe.
sol mir hie niht guot geschên
10   von iuwerm werden lîbe,
sô muoz mîn sêle iu des verjên
dazs iuwerr sêle dienet dort[1]   als einem reinen wîbe.

[1] This lyric is both a *Tagelied* and a *Wechsel*.

poor me naked without clothes.
30   It was wonderful,
he never got tired of that.
Then it dawned." [1]

28

You sweet soft murderess,
why do you want to kill me,
when I have loved you with an honest heart,
in truth, above all women?
5 Do you really think if you kill me
I shall never look on you again?
No! Love of you has driven me
to make your soul the lady of my soul.
If nothing good shall come my way down here
10   from your noble self,
my soul must swear this oath to you:
it will serve your soul as its perfect lady   there.[1]

[1] That is, in the next world.

HARTMANN von AUE

(*b. 1160–1170; d. after 1210*)

Nothing is known about Hartmann's life. His native region can be inferred from his Alemannic dialect. In one strophe he laments the death of his patron, who has not been identified. The reference to Saladin in no. 32 may apply to the Crusade of 1197 or, more probably, that of 1189 with Barbarossa. He wrote two great romances, *Erec* and *Iwein;* a debate between *herz* and *lîp* called the *Büchlein,* which Friedrich von Hausen may have known (cf. no 19) ; a legend, *Gregorius;* and a popular moral tale, *Der arme Heinrich.* He was highly esteemed in his own day; Gottfried praises him in *Tristan.*

His lyrics show the same concern with the ethical basis of courtly behavior that distinguishes his romances. In no. 29, for example, he announces his decision to abandon the service of his lady; for the next sixty lines he dwells upon the themes that pervade all his work: loyalty, honor, decorum, and restraint; then, resuming the posture of a courtly lover, he seeks the reasons for the lady's neglect in his own failings, and ends by reaffirming his dedication to her.

His crusade song (no. 32) is one of the most splendid examples of this genre. As the lyric unfolds, so does the meaning and extent of Minne, till at the end every conceivable instance of love is fulfilled in the love of God. The sudden and surprising address to the minnesingers in the third strophe is a rejection of unfulfilled and unconsecrated love. The *wân,* the illusion, that holds the other singers in its trap is the belief that love for an image of perfect courtliness and service to a secular class can satisfy the calling of a knight. But no love, and no class, can justify themselves: they can only be justified by their aspiration. Love and service must transcend the conditions and privileges of courtly

life and be bound to a higher faith, must find favor in the eyes
of God as well as in the eyes of the audience. Only this love is in
harmony with a far greater world than the world of the court;
and though it is full of longing, it always has an answer from the
beloved. "Courtly love is, or should always be, mutual love. Its
goal is always union with the beloved, but union in its absolute
sense as the highest earthly 'salvation,' as the *summum bonum*
on earth, even as something intended by God." (Hugo Kuhn)

It is because courtly love was usually bound to the vision of a
social class anxious to safeguard its privilege and was therefore
limited in its aspiration, that poets as disparate as Gottfried, Wolfram, Jean de Meun, Dante, and Chaucer sought to represent a
better and truer love, a love that did not need to settle its longing
on a public ideal. Thus, as Hartmann's crusade song suggests,
courtly love inspired some of the greatest literature in the Middle
Ages—through revulsion.

Text: *Des Minnesangs Frühling.*

Ich sprach, ich wolte ir iemer leben: 5
daz liez ich wîte mære komen.
mîn herze hete ich ir gegeben:
daz hân ich nu von ir genomen.
5 swer tumben antheiz trage,
der lâze in ê der tage   I
ê in der strît
beroube sîner jâre gar.
alsô hân ich getân.
10 der kriec sî ir verlân;
für dise zît
sô wil ich dienen anderswar.

Ich was untriuwen ie gehaz:
und wolte ich ungetriuwe sîn,
15 mir tæte untriuwe verre baz
dan daz daz mich diu triuwe mîn
von ir niht scheiden liez
diu mich ir dienen hiez.   II
nu tuot mir wê,
20 sî wil mir ungelônet lân.
ich spriche ir niuwan guot:
ê ich beswære ir muot,
sô wil ich ê
die schulde zuo dem schaden hân.

25 Waz solte ich arges von ir sagen
der ich ie wol gesprochen hân?
ich mac wol mînen kumber klagen
und sî drumb ungevelschet lân.
sî nimt von mir für wâr
30 mîn dienest manic jâr.   III
ich hân gegert
ir minne unde vinde ir haz.

29

I said I would always live for her
and had the word spread far and wide:
I had given her my heart.
And now I have taken it back.
5   Whoever carries a foolish oath,
let him set it down   I
before the struggle
robs him of his days and years.
That is what I have done.
10 Let the battlefield be hers,
from this time forth
I shall serve elsewhere.

I always hated disloyalty—
and if I ever wanted to be disloyal,
15 disloyalty would do me much more good
than the way my loyalty stops
me from ever leaving her
who called me to her service.   II
Now it makes me grieve
20 that she will let me go unrequited.
I shall say nothing but good of her:
before I weigh her spirit down
I would rather
take on myself the guilt for all the harm.

25 What ill thing should I say about this lady
whom I have always spoken well of?
I would rather just cry out in pain
and leave her unaccused.
It is true, she took
30 my long years' service.   III
I longed
for her love and came upon her hate.

daz mir dâ nie gelanc,
des habe ich selbe undanc:
35   dûht ich sis wert,
sî hete mir gelônet baz.

Sît ich ir lônes muoz enbern,
der ich manc jâr gedienet hân,
so geruoche mich got eines wern,
40   daz ez der schœnen müeze ergân
nâch êren unde wol.
sît ich mich rechen sol,   IV
dêswâr daz sî,
und doch niht anders wan alsô
45   daz ich ir heiles gan
baz danne ein ander man,
und bin dâ bî
ir leides gram, ir liebes frô.

Mir sint diu jâr vil unverlorn
50   diu ich an sî gewendet hân:
hât mich ir minne lôn verborn,
doch trœstet mich ein lieber wân.
ichn gerte nihtes mê,
wan müese ich ir als ê   V
55   ze vrowen jehen.
manc man der nimt sîn ende alsô
daz im niemer liep geschiht,
wan daz er sich versiht
deiz sül geschehen,
60   und tuot in der gedinge frô.

Der ich dâ her gedienet hân,
dur die wil ich mit fröiden sîn,
doch ez mich wênic hât vervân.
ich weiz wol daz diu frowe mîn
65   niwan nâch êren lebt.
swer von der sîner strebt,   VI
der habe im daz.

Well, if I've never found anything better,
it is my fault:
35   if she had thought me worthy,
she'd have given me something better.

Since I have to get along without her gift
after I have served these many years,
then God let me have this one wish,
40   that all things good and honorable
fall to this beautiful lady.
And since I am bound to seek revenge,   IV
then let it be
nothing but this,
45   that I wish her well
with a better wish than any other man,
and may I be
sad for her pain, joyful for her pleasure.

To me the years are never lost
50   that I bestowed on her:
if courting her has brought no gift,
one beloved dream still comforts me.
I would desire nothing more
but to be able, as before,   V
55   to proclaim her my lady.
Many men reach the end
and have never known pleasure,
but they had faith
that it would come,
60   and the hope made them rejoice.

She whom I have served to this day—
through her I shall be with joy,
though I come away with little to hold.
I know that my lady
65   lives in honor.
Whoever seeks to leave his lady: VI
my curse.

     in betrâget sîner jâre vil.
     swer alsô minnen kan,
70   der ist ein valscher man.
     mîn muot stât baz:
     von ir ich niemer komen wil.

30

Mîn dienest der ist alze lanc
bî ungewissem wâne:
wan nâch der ie mîn herze ranc,
diu lât mich trôstes âne.
5 ich möhte ir klagen und wunder sagen   I
von maniger swæren zît.
sît ich erkande ir strît,
sît ist mir gewesen vür wâr
ein stunde ein tac, ein tac ein woche, ein woche ein ganzez
        jâr.

10 Owê waz tætes einem man
dem sî doch vîent wære,
sît sî sô wol verderben kan
ir friunt mit manger swære?
mir tæte baz des rîches haz: II
15 joch möhte ich eteswar
entwîchen sîner schar: [1]
diz leit wont mir alles bî
und nimt von mînen fröiden zins als ich sîn eigen sî.

31

Manger grüezet mich alsô
(der gruoz tuot mich ze mâze frô),

---

[1] *Schar* could also mean punishment, which in this case would be expulsion
from the realm.

His years will lie on him like a weight.
Whoever can love like that
70   is a counterfeit man.
My mind is set on something better:
I shall never come away from her.

30

I have served too long
with uncertain hope.
The lady my heart has struggled toward
lets me stand without a word.
5 I could complain to her and tell her legends   I
of pain and waiting.
Since I caught sight of her hostility,
I have felt
an hour stretch into a day, a day into a week, a week into
        one whole year.

10 Oh, what would she do
to a man who was an enemy,
when she can kill a friend
so lightly with all this grief?
I would be better off with the kaiser's hate,   II
15 yes, I could flee
somewhere from his pursuing horde.[1]
But this pain always goes with me
and takes its portion of my joys as if it were my lord.

31

Often a friend will greet me thus
(his greeting doesn't make me very glad):

'Hartman, gên wir schouwen
ritterlîche frouwen.'   I
5 mac er mich mit gemache lân
und île er zuo den frowen gân!
bî frowen triuwe ich niht vervân,
wan daz ich müede vor in stân.

Ze frowen habe ich einen sin:
10 als sî mir sint als bin ich in;
wand ich mac baz vertrîben
die zît mit armen wîben.   II
swar ich kum dâ ist ir vil,
dâ vinde ich die diu mich dâ wil;
15 diu ist ouch mînes herzen spil:
waz touc mir ein ze hôhez zil?

In mîner tôrheit mir geschach
daz ich zuo zeiner frowen sprach
'frow, ich hân mîne sinne
20 gewant an iuwer minne.'   III
dô wart ich twerhes an gesehen.
des wil ich, des sî iu bejehen,
mir wîp in solher mâze spehen
diu mir des niht enlânt geschehen.

32

Ich var mit iuwern hulden, herren und mâge:
liut unde lant diu müezen sælic sîn.
es ist unnôt daz iemen mîner verte vrâge:
ich sage wol für wâr die reise mîn.   I
5 mich vienc diu Minne und lie mich vrî ûf mîne sicherheit.
nu hât sî mir enboten bî ir liebe daz ich var.

"Hartmann, let us visit
courtly ladies."   I
5   Let him leave me in peace
and rush himself to his ladies.
From these ladies I expect no pleasure
but waiting till I'm weary.

I have one mind with ladies:
10   as they treat me, I treat them;
because I get more for my time
with just plain women.   II
Wherever I come, there they are in droves,
and there I find one that wants me,
15   and she is my heart's delight.
A lofty goal beyond my reach—frankly, who needs it?

In my inexperience it happened once,
I said to one of these ladies:
"Lady, I have set my mind
20   to loving you."   III
She looked at me down her nose.[1]
So I tell you I want
to find the kind of women
who will save me from such woes.

32

I go, with your good grace, lords and kinsmen:
bless this people and this land.
No man need ask about my voyage:
I shall tell you all truly why I go.   I
5   Love took me captive and on my sworn word set me free.
Now by the love I owe her she has commanded me to go.

---

[1] Literally, "Then I was looked at askance."

ez ist unwendic: ich muoz endelîchen dar:
wie kûme ich bræche mîne triuwe und mînen eit!

Sich rüemet manger waz er dur die Minne tæte:
10 wâ sint diu werc?   die rede hœre ich wol.
doch sæhe ich gerne dazs ir eteslîchen bæte
daz er ir diente als ich ir dienen sol.   II
ez ist geminnet, der sich dur die Minne ellenden muoz.
nû seht wies mich ûz mîner zungen ziuhet über mer.
15 und lebte mîn herre Salatîn und al sîn her
dienbræhten mich von Vranken niemer einen fuoz.

Ir minnesinger, iu muoz ofte misselingen:
daz iu den schaden tuot daz ist der wân.
ich wil mich rüemen, ich mac wol von minne singen,
20 sît mich diu minne hât und ich sî hân.   III
daz ich dâ wil, seht daz wil alse gerne haben mich:
sô müezt aber ir verliesen under wîlen wânes vil:
ir ringent umbe liep daz iuwer niht enwil:
wan mügt ir armen minnen solhe minne als ich?

---

[1] Lines 15–16 can be interpreted in two ways, neither of which is very clear.
The more probable one is given here; the other would read: "If my lord
Saladin and all his army were alive, etc." thus referring to the crusade of
1197. Hugo Kuhn proposes the following emendation in l. 15: *und lieze si
mich, her Saladin,* etc. and translates as follows: "And if she, that Mistress
Minne (the crusade *minne* which compels me as her captive to keep the
pledge I offered, upon having been granted quarter), would leave me free,
if she were to release me from this promise of mutual obligation . . . then
Sir Saladin and all his army . . . could not bring me one foot out of
Franconia" ("*Minnesang* and the Form of Performance," in *Formal Aspects
of Medieval German Poetry,* ed. Stanley N. Werbow, University of Texas
Press, 1969).

It is unalterable: I must surely go:
how unwillingly I would forswear my loyalty and vow.

Many men boast about what they would do for Love:
10 where are their works? I hear their speeches well enough,
but I would like to see her ask a single one of them
to serve her as I am setting out to serve.   II
A man who must go into exile for love—there is a man
     who loves.
Now behold how she draws me across the sea away from
     my native tongue.
15 And if my lord were living, Saladin and all his army
could not move me one foot away from home.[1]

You minnesingers, you have to fail again and again:
it is foolish hope that damages your song.
I boast that I know how to sing of Love,
20 for Love has me, and I have her,   III
that which I desire—see!—desires me as much:
but you must often lose your hopeless hope:
you struggle for a love that wants none of you:
when will you poor fellows love such Love as I?

REINMAR

(b. 1150–1160; d. before 1210)

No moment of Reinmar's life is attested in any contemporary documents. He is assumed to be the "Nightingale of Hagenau," the supreme lyric poet whose death Gottfried laments in *Tristan*. This reference plus Reinmar's elegy for Leopold V of Austria (no. 35), who died on December 31, 1194, suggest the approximate date of the poet's birth. It is also believed that a rivalry developed between Reinmar and Walther, his supposed pupil, in the court of Vienna. It is indeed probable that the two poets knew each other in the Viennese court; and Walther's lament for Reinmar (no. 48), though it expresses great admiration for Reinmar's poetry, makes it clear that no love was ever lost between them.

Reinmar is often cited as the perfect example of a courtly love poet. Those who make this judgment point to the decorum of his language, his timidity, his reflective and melancholy disposition, the absence of all concrete experience in his songs. It may be possible to verify the details of these observations in Reinmar's songs, but even so they are not very useful, because they make the fatal mistake of identifying Reinmar the poet and composer with the figure of "the courtly lover" that he creates, and that the singer impersonates before the audience.

Reinmar composed his songs with a specific performance situation in mind: this created character, the courtly lover, is stationed before those who hear his song in order to be the object of their reactions. That is why much scholarly criticism of Reinmar has erred through its representational bias: it is not Reinmar who is "melancholy," but "the lover," a character impersonated by a performer; and when the singer says that everyone is sick and tired of his complaints (no. 34), it would be a misunderstanding to think that Reinmar is reporting on his poetic career. Instead, he is following a performer's strategy: he is characterizing the audience through its reaction to the figure of the lover.

We can follow this performer's technique in the lyric we have already referred to (no. 34) : "No one needs to ask/what's the latest news with me: I am not happy./My friends are sick and tired of my complaints." These opening lines already assume an audience that has known the singer for a long time, at least long enough to expect a song of complaint as soon as they see him rise, and long enough to have gotten sick and tired of that theme. Don't expect anything different now, he tells them, I'm going to sing the same old song.

We know why these friends complain, for they are no different from their counterparts in the songs of Heinrich von Morungen: they want a pure courtly song of joy. The singer's main purpose is to satisfy their demand; but before he can do so he must take care of the other part of his audience, the ones who vex him with "insults and mockery" because they are sure his song is full of lies. These are "the people," as he often calls them, or "the happy ones," as he calls them here, the ones who are puzzled and outraged by the singer's pride in his grief and joy in his longing.

Thus the singer establishes his audience: the friends complain because he has stayed too long in grief, the enemies because the love he sings about cannot possibly exist. With the audience set up this way, he now has the program for his performance. The love that the enemies do not believe in causes the grief that the friends complain about, and so he can reply to both of them at once and get started: his grief is too real for him to sing the joyous song his friends demand. This gives him the chance now to tell "the people" that when he speaks about his suffering he doesn't mean anything that they can't understand: he wants to lie with his dearly beloved lady, and once he does that everyone will have the benefit of his "joy." Now this is something that they can go along with: a man who is unhappy because he can't get the woman he wants into bed is a man they can believe in. The singer, it seems, completely repudiates the lofty attitude of the friends, who, when they call for a song of "joy," mean the exact opposite of what he offers here, in the last two lines of the first strophe. And so we see that the courtly singer steps out of his rôle at certain strategic moments and speaks, for a time, not as a courtly lover, but as one of those who mock that lamenting figure. We can also see how necessary it is to think of the "I" as a performer. He has to save his song from the hecklers in his audience, and if he doesn't say something to make them happy or at least to shut them up, he can't go on.

Now this first strophe—especially the last two lines—makes it possible for him to go on singing and to please everyone in his audience, both the spiritualizing friends and the vulgarizing "people." For each part of the audience now can believe that the song is really meant for them. Reinmar has made sure of that, especially in the last two lines of each succeeding strophe, which always give a new turn to the thought and can have either a high or a low meaning, depending on the point of view.

These "happy ones," the ones who can't understand what this "courtly lover" wants, accuse the singer of lying when he speaks in this rôle. It's so easy to get a woman into bed, and it's what all men want; so why does he have to say all these things about staying faithful to a virtuous woman who does not requite him—as if there could be such a woman—and sound so proud and superior about it? Or they say, as they said of Heinrich: if he's so sad, why does he sing? From the friends' point of view these "happy ones" are damned in their happiness: it is the proof of their vulgarity, their inability to endure longing, their incapacity to be civilized by desire. To these friends the singer says: they dishonor themselves because they do not believe in the possibility of steadfastness and selfless love. But these "happy ones" will hear this strophe in their own way. They have to believe that the singer is being ironic when he plays "courtly lover," since they know that he is one of them. It is because of the physical presence of the singer, who continually indicates his physicality, that everyone can claim to understand the true meaning of the song, though they all have different meanings in mind.

As we saw in Heinrich and as we see here, the beloved lady is an ambiguous figure: in the perspective of the friends she is a perfect being who inspires longing in a noble man and whose greatness can never be equaled, or even adequately praised, by the

lover she redeems—redeems, as another poet (Bernart de Ventadorn) puts it, from the "nothing" that he was. But to "the
people," she is an ordinary woman, easily won, like all women.
For the friends he offers the beautiful hymn to Woman, its language reminiscent of hymns in praise of God, in the third strophe. For their sake he praises the idea of Woman rather than any
woman in particular: it is only in the last two lines that the
singer turns this general praise to his own lady. From the way this
strophe is set out, we can get a good idea of the singer's service
to the friends and the victory he hopes to win by his song. The
real object of his general praise is not any woman but the noble
way in which the friends see all women: it is their exalted, and
exalting, point of view that inspires his words. In the final two
lines, where the *du* now seems to signify his own beloved, he takes
his stand with these friends, shows them that he sees things the
way they do, that he is one of them.

But he can also see things the other way, and his adoring praise
is not unqualified. Woman is worthy of praise, she is the source
of man's happiness—provided that she is turned toward true
goodness, and provided that she stays faithful: conditions that
suggest possibilities in women that the perspective of the friends
cannot encompass. Furthermore, in the last two lines the singer
has a great opportunity to wink to the people and subvert all
his lofty praise: "You give everyone a noble disposition (*hôhen
muot*) :/when will there be a little joy for me too?" Now when
we hear the first of these two lines, we assume that he is continuing with his general praise of the name of Woman; we have no
way of knowing, as we listen, that he addresses a particular
woman when he says "You," especially since he says that the very
disposition to courtliness comes from her. With our expectations
aroused in this way, the next line is a calculated let-down. She
gives all the world *hôhen muot,* the supreme reward in the eyes
of the friends; but that is not enough for him, he wants something special just for himself, a little *fröide,* which means, as he
has already made clear, the "joy" that he will have if he ever gets
to lie beside her. You (meaning Woman) exalt the whole world's
spirit, he says (giving praise for the sake of the friends) ; now
exalt mine a little with your body, he continues (suddenly

addressing one ordinary woman and giving delight to "the people").

This continual and deliberate ambiguousness of his language represents a conflict, which the singer explains in the wonderful strophe (iv) that follows. There he considers the consequences of each point of view. If he idealizes the beloved woman, if he depicts her as she appears to the courtly friends, then she must remain forever distant, "free" of him and of every other man, for as the arbiter of every man's worth, she must be beyond every man's reach. But if he "diminishes her great worth," then she is no longer *saelic,* a blessed lady whose inspiring image always guides the lover; then she is an ordinary woman, no longer "free" of any man and incapable of avoiding "dishonor."

This is all clear enough, it is a conflict inherent in the nature of courtly love. But we have seen more than once by now that the meaning of these songs is never truly known unless they are heard in the context of the performance. This becomes clear as soon as we try to answer a question that almost seems too obvious to ask: Whose conflict is this? Who speaks in this strophe?

For a modern reader, the first answer that automatically comes to mind is "the lover." But that answer won't work. "The lover" is a rôle that the singer plays, and it is the excessive spirituality of this strange character that provokes the mockery of "the people": the lover does not have this conflict, he is a figure created to please the friends and sworn to distance and renunciation.

It is a conflict between two opposed perspectives that this strophe sets forth, the perspectives of the friends and the people, the noble and the vulgar elements of a complicated audience. And the only person whose view is large enough to embrace both perspectives is the singer—the performer who proves his skill by continually stepping out of one rôle and into another in the course of his song, who can even make the disparate parts of his audience believe that he is impersonating the character they each demand. The conflict is in the singer. It is the conflict of a performer who is a courtly man. In his performance he plays out the meaning of courtliness before an audience that includes many people who are creatures of their appetites but noble by birth, and therefore entitled to hear his song. And so, confronting this entire audience, the singer has to ask: What kind of song do I want to compose? What part of my audience do I want to please? What point of view do I want to share? What kind of love do I want to praise?

And he gives voice to this conflict only in order to prove his freedom. For his performer's pride is that he can sing both kinds of song: he has a great capacity for the nobility of his friends and for the vulgarity of the ordinary man. He can play two rôles, and more than two, this performer who impersonates his audience. And once he has tried out every attitude, he is free to make his choice.

In the final strophe he sings the song that he has so far been preparing to sing. He will remain steadfast in her service and strive continually for her favor, even though she is not, and can never be, aware of him. He takes this stand fully aware of its consequences and, when judged by ordinary experience, its absurdity. Just one word, *darunder,* is enough to reveal all the foolishness of courtly love: he does everything to make her notice him, and "meanwhile," as he does these things, she forgets all about him. Here at the end, as he takes this vow, we have our final glimpse of that glorious and insensate lady, who, in her indefinability, reveals the nobility of her lover and the meaning of courtly love.

But the very last words of all are not about the lady, or even primarily about love, but about the singer and his song. He has been called a liar, and he has been at some pains to prove that he has told the truth, and to explain how. He has proved it by showing his mastery of "the people's" song. If now he turns from it and chooses the other, the courtly song, it is no pretense but the free act of his will; for he need not sing of this sustained devotion, he is free to sing, and able to sing well, of the ordinary life of desire.

When the singer swears his lifelong devotion, the people are sure he lies. And insofar as the singer is an ordinary man whom they are well acquainted with, whom they see continually at other times than performance time, their point of view has some merit. But in the narrow perspective of their physicality, they cannot distinguish between the man they know and the rôle he impersonates, and so they cannot imagine that this lifelong vow may yet be truthful. The lover's devotion does indeed last the whole length of the lover's life, the length of the singer's commitment to a rôle, the length of the song—for "the lover" has no other life. When the singer steps into the performing circle, for a brief time he ceases to be that ordinary, mortal, lustful, changeful man whom everyone knows, and he becomes a man inspired by distance, enthralled by an image that lets him see human experience—ordinarily a welter of accidents—as an enterprise of great significance, and that bestows on him the ethical privileges of true nobility. Courtly love is play, and in its ludic context completely valid.

Only the singer and his friends can enter this play world. These friends are fully aware of the meaning of the singer's love and are impatient with every mortal detail: they want nothing but the pure ludic representation of the glory of their class. But the singer, in his embracing perspective, sees the ignoble ones, the ones who are noble only by birth, attending his song, and impatient with every ideal representation. And unlike his friends, he cannot ignore these others. And so he has to step out of his rôle during his performance and reassure these people that he is, after all, the man they know.

The wonderful thing is that because he addresses them and tries to please them, he makes his song better. The lover's precious diction extolling his servility would be hard for anyone to take straight. Furthermore, since the courtly love lyric was composed primarily of formulas, not to say clichés, any hypocrite could say such things and not sound any different from the singer whose song is his service. This is, in fact, represented as a great problem by all the early poets. The singer names these hypocrites his worst enemies, calling them *die valschen, die ungetriuwen,* "the false ones, the faithless ones": they are the false lovers, and therefore the false singers who praise the lady in exactly the same terms as the one man who really means what he says.

Every courtly poet has to face the problem that these false poets represent: how can a singer who must use these conventional formulas manage to sound like a true lover? How can he redeem these required meters and fixed phrases and standard images so that they express his dedication, the love of courtliness and the devotion to his class that he really feels?

The singer cannot distinguish himself from these "false ones" by the beauty of his language, since he is required to say expected things; or by the technical excellence of his versification and music, since his rivals are as adept in this respect as he is, or at least good enough to counterfeit his song. We can see how great a problem this is for the singer in one of Reinmar's songs (no. 34, str. v) , where he reveals that he is himself accused of the same hypocrisy that he can detect so clearly in his rivals.

It is, strangely enough, "the people" who help him out of this predicament by forcing an alternative idiom upon him, the plain language of carnality. As a master of two different languages now, he is free to choose the one that best expresses what is in his heart: he redeems these formulas of praise by freely choosing to say them. This is how he is different from "the false ones," who are committed to their hypocrisy and speak nothing but chaste platitudes: he speaks plainly of his lust. But then, in speaking of it, he makes it the proof of his love: for her, he will let his lust go wanting. The renunciation of ordinary pleasures, which, as an ordinary man, he desires, is his homage to the greatness of his lady and his testimony to the supreme joy of loving her. Thus, to prove his worth, the singer depends less on his words and music than on the situation in which he performs.

"The people" are therefore absolutely necessary in the audience, for they force the singer to reclaim his formulary language. They make him speak in terms that they can understand, they make him identify himself as an ordinary man. They ensure the full effect of his performance: a man full of common lust, a creature of change, speaks, in a formal and elevated language, an oath of unconditional fidelity and celebrates a love that transcends all change. Because of "the people" the performer's figure has an immediate human presence: he is one of us, separated from us in space only by the circle in which he stands, and in time only during those moments of his song when he is transfigured by his language.

The friends give the singer his theme, but "the people" give him his performing technique. It is they, finally, who protect his song with the very strength of their attack. Their hostility and incomprehension, as they judge the song according to the facts of ordinary experience, mark out the boundaries of the lover's relevance. Because they doubt him and misunderstand him, they make it clear that his words have nothing to do with their experience or with their whole world. Their mockery is a sign that the lover belongs to a different world, a world of play, which, carefully marked out, is the ground of a transcendent experience to dedicated men.

As the singer responds to the different parts of his audience, he has to coordinate this movement of his attention with the metrical pattern of the song. The lyric we have been discussing, *Waz ich nu niuwer maere sage* (no. 34), shows Reinmar's skill in articulating the meter of the verses with the performer's sounding of the audience.

Each strophe begins with a unit of two lines which contain four and six beats respectively and end in different sounds (*-age, -ô,* in the first strophe). This two-line unit, which is intended to fit a certain passage of music, is called a *Stolle*. Thus the Stolle has the following pattern: 4a 6b, the letters standing for the final sounds.

Next, this same pattern is repeated, to form a second Stolle. These two Stollen make up the first part of the strophe: 4a 6b 4a 6b.

The second part of the strophe follows a much freer pattern: 6c 7c 3d 5x 5d. The next-to-the-last line, the x line, does not rhyme with any other line in its own or in any other strophe.

The first part of the strophe, consisting of the two Stollen, is called the *Aufgesang*. The second part is called the *Abgesang*. Thus the strophe can be called either bipartite or tripartite. At any rate, no matter how one divides it, this structure, which comes from the troubadours, is the one most commonly followed by the Minnesänger. Its effect lies in the inherent contrast between the rigidity of the Aufgesang, with its obligatory repetitions, and the flexibility of the Abgesang, which can take off in any pattern whatever.

Now to get some idea of how the singer could use this strophic pattern for the timing of his performance, we can start with that x line, considering its place in the Abgesang: 6c 7c 3d 5x 5d. Even in this abstract scheme, we can see that it introduces a certain tension. It is separate from the other lines because it does not rhyme with any of them; at the same time, however, it is closely bound to the final line because they both have exactly the same length: they are the only two lines in the Abgesang, and the only two successive lines in the entire strophe, that match in this way, and the only two lines that have five beats.

Now every pattern of stresses and rhymes will inevitably have rhetorical consequences. We have already seen that throughout Reinmar's song the final two lines stand out from each strophe and introduce, sometimes with epigrammatic brilliance, a new turn in the thought. In every case, these lines have the same effect. They differ from the rest of the strophe, whatever its theme might be, because they express the singer's feelings at this very moment, as he performs. In the course of the strophe the singer might look to the past—to the earlier songs he has sung for this audience, to the long unrewarded service he has devoted to the lady; or praise the name of Woman, or describe the consequences of two conflicting desires. But always, when he comes to the last two lines, he neither reminisces nor reflects nor makes any claim: he tells what he desires, what he feels now; and the immediacy of his desire is in marked contrast to the expository nature of the rest of the strophe. In each strophe he talks about the past history and the consequences of his desire; in the last two lines he stands desiring before us.

This continual reference to his own performing figure reaches a climax in the final strophe. In that part of the strophe (and of the music) when we know he speaks directly from the heart, we hear him now defend his song. In this way the performance itself becomes the proof and definition of the song's truthfulness: as real as I am as I stand before you, he says in effect, so real is the desire my song expresses. Again we are led to ask about the identity of this "I" who asks us to look into his heart: he is at once an ordinary man, a courtly man, a performer, and a fictional character ("the lover"). In whatever identity he speaks, he tells the truth; but it is the truth demanded by whatever part of the audience happens to be exerting its influence as he speaks. That is why it is the performance that engenders the song's significance. The rôle in which the performer speaks governs the meaning of his words.

This final strophe, incidentally, seems to contain a significant variation. For it seems from the two imperatives *(laze, merke,* let him listen to my music and verse, let him take note) that the turn takes place not in the final two lines but in the entire Abgesang, which also seems to consist of one single sentence. We can't be sure of this, of course, because there is a line missing —a typical, tantalizing difficulty arising from the relative lateness of the manuscripts. Still, it would be fitting that the singer should break the pattern at the very end and devote the entire Abgesang to this climactic address to the audience.

It is often remarked about Reinmar's poetry that it contains practically no references to contemporary historic events (with the obvious exception of the elegy) ; this is one of the reasons why it is impossible to draw any inferences about his life from his poetry. There are numerous references to the life of the court, to the chambers and vistas of a small indoor society, to rivalries and subterfuges in close quarters, to the conventions and the common memories of a privileged in-group; but no mention of anything that can be placed geographically and dated. Even the court for which he composed is not identifiable, for the audience to which he refers is essentially his own creation, related to the actual audience as the figure of "the lover" was related to the poet or performer. Both the poet and the historic audience lent their names and faces to the fictional characters in the song, but, in this mutual and deliberate play, they revealed nothing of their historic reality. This exclusion of everything documentable reveals the play character of his songs and keeps courtly love from being confused with ordinary love. Courtly love can be cherished only within a noble enclosure: outside the walls it is madness. The court in which the singer performed became, in the words of Johan Huizinga, a "playground," which defined the whole context of the song.

The poet orients every line to a live audience, through a singer who refers continually to his various listeners. They, in the very opposition of their perspectives, represent the possibilities of courtly life. They are in disorder, their perspectives clash—until the singer steps forth, to become the one object of every gaze and to make all their energies and points of view harmonious. The singer performs in order to arrange the constituents of the audience into a significant pattern, as a composer arranges the notes of a scale. The song that is performed before these courtly people is meant to reveal the secret harmony of their assembly. This is the most definitive characteristic of the high Minnesang: the meaning intended by the song lies in the situation in which it is performed. ". . . The forms and word sequences of the *minne* songs reveal their full meaning and life only in the living situation of the minnesong as it is performed by the singer" (Hugo Kuhn).

The courtly ideal of moral earnestness, perpetual striving, discipline, and steadfastness is represented before this audience in the ludic figure of "the courtly lover." This is the representation that "the friends" demand, completely unaffected by ordinary circumstances, and completely irrelevant to them. Immediately the dignity of this figure is threatened by those who, though they belong to the courtly class, are the enemies of its ideal: "the people," who ridicule the lover's impossible high-mindedness; "the false ones," who make a mockery of his praise.

But the singer is such a great performer that he can turn these enemies, as they pursue their destructive intentions, into his allies in protecting the dignity of courtly love. By the presence of "the people," who cannot imagine that man has any other life but physical existence, he marks out the playground of his song, the ground that "the people" cannot enter. And so he uses their uncomprehending laughter as a sign that the courtly lover's praise was never meant to be spoken in ordinary life. And through his need to distinguish himself from "the false ones," who imitate the lover's language without any idea of its meaning, he reinvests the conventions of courtly life, which are always in danger of becoming empty forms, with human feeling, with the force of human will, with love.

Now this *situation,* in which the singer praises the ideal and controls the forces that try to discredit it, and even makes them participate in his praise, is a representation of courtly life, of its harmony and human dignity. Through his performance he sets all of the perspectives in the situation into a hierarchical order: the ideal view is supreme, the vision of "the people" confirms its supremacy. This is the basic conviction, the essential experience of courtliness.

As the singer takes a stand with each perspective and voices the truth that each beholds, he creates one single personality out of the disparate elements of the audience, one "heart" full of lust and adoration. This integration of the audience is a re-creation of the courtly man's character, in which many conflicting tendencies unite in subservience to an ethical ideal. Through the medium of the singer, the audience creates one encompassing song of courtly life, its music enriched, not drowned out, by the voice of carnality.

This was a noble game, an exalted play, and even after historical events and aesthetic shifts separated the lyric from the conditions of its performance, this early courtly love poetry has remained one of the major sources of the language of passionate devotion down to our own time.

Text: *Des Minnesangs Frühling.*

Niemen seneder suoche an mich deheinen rât:
ich mac mîn selbes leit erwenden niht.
nun wæn iemen grœzer ungelücke hât,
und man mich doch sô frô dar under siht.   I
5   dâ merkent doch ein wunder an.
ich solte iu klagen die meisten nôt,
niwan daz ich von wîben übel niht reden kan.

Spræche ich nu des ich si selten hân gewent,
dar an begienge ich grôze unstætekeit.
10 ich hân lange wîle unsanfte mich gesent
und bin doch in der selben arebeit.   II
bezzer ist ein herzesêr
dann ich von wîben misserede.
ich tuon sîn niht: si sint von allem rehte hêr.

15 In ist liep daz man si stæteclîchen bite,
und tuot in doch sô wol daz si versagent.
hei wie mangen muot und wunderlîche site
si tougenlîche in ir herzen tragent!   III
swer ir hulde welle hân,
20 der wese in bî und spreche in wol.
daz tete ich ie: nu kan michz leider niht vervân.

Dâ ist doch mîn schulde entriuwen niht sô grôz
als rehte unsælic ich ze lône bin.
ich stân aller vröiden rehte hendeblôz
25 und gât mîn dienest wunderlîche hin.   IV
daz geschach nie manne mê.
volende ich einest sende nôt,
si tuot mir mê, mag ichz behüeten, wol noch wê.

Ich bin tump daz ich sô grôzen kumber klage
30 und ir des wil deheine schulde geben.

33

Let no suffering lover come to me for any help—
I can't even get rid of my own disease.
I don't think it has ever gone worse for anyone,
and yet, with all that, everyone sees me looking happy—   I
5 this is a marvelous thing, take note of it.
I could lament before you about this greatest peril,
only I cannot speak ill of women.

To say things now I have forborne to say of them
would be a great disloyalty.
10 I have loved for so long in great unrest,
and here I am now, in the same toils.   II
Still, to suffer like this is better
than to speak ill of women.
I do not do that. They are too high for that by every right.

15 They love to be endlessly entreated,
and it makes them feel so good to refuse.
Say, how many moods and unfathomable acts
they carry concealed in their hearts.   III
Whoever wants their favor,
20 let him always be around them, full of praise.
That's what I do all the time. Too bad it doesn't help.

The truth is, my guilt is not so great
as my unsuccess.
I am as bare of joy as my naked hand,
25 and all my service goes bewilderingly into the past.   IV
Nothing like this ever happened to a man.
If I ever see this distress of longing to the end,
she'll never do me ill again, or good, if I can help it.

I am foolish to raise such a loud lament
30 and to want to make her guilty of my grief.

sît ichs âne ir danc in mînem herzen trage,
waz mac si des, wil ich unsanfte leben?　　　　　　　V
daz wirt ir doch lîhte leit.
nu muoz ichz doch sô lâzen sîn.
35　　mir machet niemen schaden wan mîn stætekeit.

34

Waz ich nu niuwer mære sage
desn darf mich nieman frâgen: ich enbin niht vrô.
die friunt verdriuzet mîner klage.
des man ze vil gehœret, dem ist allem sô.
5　nu hân ich es beidiu schaden unde spot.　　　　　I
waz mir doch leides unverdienet, daz erkenne got,
und âne schult geshiht!
ichn gelige herzeliebe bî,
son hât an mîner vröide nieman niht.[1]

10　Die hôhgemuoten zîhent mich,
ich minne niht sô sêre als ich gebâre ein wîp.
si liegent unde unêrent sich:
si was mir ie gelîcher mâze sô der lîp.
nie getrôste si dar under mir den muot.　　　　　II
15　der ungenâden muoz ich, und des si mir noch getuot,
erbeiten als ich mac.
mir ist eteswenne wol gewesen:
gewinne ab ich nu niemer guoten tac?

Sô wol dir, wîp, wie reine ein nam![2]
20　wie sanfte er doch z'erkennen und ze nennen ist!
ez wart nie niht sô lobesam,
swâ duz an rehte güete kêrest, sô du bist.

---

[1] "Till then, not one happy word": added. The same for "I'm impressing her" in line 40; literally, "meanwhile."
[2] Compare Walther's elegy for Reinmar, below, no. 48.

If I bear her in my heart without her consent,
what can she do, if I want to live a life of unease?   v
Perhaps it even causes her distress.
Anyway, I must leave it as it is.
35 There is no one who hurts me, only my steadfastness.

34

No one needs to ask
what's the latest news with me: I am not happy.
My friends are sick and tired of my complaints—
which always happens when something is too often heard.
5 Now I must put up with insults and mockery as well.   I
And yet, God be my witness, what I have suffered
unjustly, quite without fault.
If I do not lie with my beloved,
no one will gain from my joy—till then, not one happy
word.[1]

10 Those who *are* happy bring me accusations:
I couldn't love a woman as much as I pretend to, they
say.
They lie, and dishonor themselves.
She was always as dear to me as my own self,
and never, for all that, gave me any comfort for my love.   II
15 This unkindness and whatever else she may yet do to me
I have to abide as well as I can.
I used to have some pleasure, sometimes.
Will I ever have one good day again?

Bless you, *woman*—how pure a name,[2]
20 how pleasant to come upon it and say it!
There never was anything so worthy of praise—
when you have a mind to goodness—as you.

dîn lop mit rede nieman volenden kan.   III
swes du mit triuwen phligest, wol im, derst ein sælic man
25 und mac vil gerne leben.
du gîst al der werlde hôhen muot:
wan maht och mir ein lützel fröiden geben?

Zwei dinc hân ich mir für geleit,
diu strîtent mit gedanken in dem herzen mîn:
30 ob ich ir hôhen werdekeit
mit mînen willen wolte lâzen minre sîn,
ode ob ich daz welle daz si grœzer sî   IV
und si vil sælic wîp stê mîn und aller manne vrî.
diu tuont mir beidiu wê:
35 ich enwirde ir lasters niemer vrô;
vergât si mich, daz klage ich iemer mê.

Ob ich nu tuon und hân getân
daz ich von rehte in ir hulden solte sîn,
und si vor aller werlde hân,
40 waz mac ich des, vergizzet si dar under mîn?
swer nu giht daz ich ze spotte künne klagen,   V
der lâze im mîne rede beide singen unde sagen

. . . .

unde merke wâ ich ie spræche ein wort,
45 ezn læge ê i'z gespræche herzen bî.

35

'Si jêhent, der sumer der sî hie,[1]
diu wunne diu sî komen,
und daz ich mich wol gehabe als ê.
nû râtent unde sprechent wie.
5 der tôt hât mir benomen
daz ich niemer überwinde mê.   I

[1] This is a lament for the death of Duke Leopold V of Austria on December 31, 1194. It is Leopold's widow who speaks.

No one can fulfill your praise with words.   III
The man you care for loyally, he is blessed, a happy man
25 and can gladly live.
You exalt the whole world's spirit:
when will you give me a few joys too?

I have set myself two questions
that argue with each other in my thoughts:
30 would I really want
her towering virtue down somewhat,
or would I want it higher still   IV
and have her—blessed woman—free of me and every
          other man?
For me, either way means pain:
35 I could never rejoice in her dishonor,
but if she passes over me, I will forever complain.

If there is in everything I do, or ever did,
no other thought but to make me worthy of her grace,
and I cherish her above the whole world,
40 what can I do, if she forgets me while I'm impressing her?
Whoever says I only pretend to complain, as a joke,   V
let him have my answer in music and verse

. . . .

and take note whether I ever spoke one word
45 that did not lie in my heart before I spoke.

35

They say the summer is here,[1]
rejoicing has come again,
and I should go about as I did before.
Now let them tell me how I can.
5 Death has taken away
a thing I can never get over.   I

waz bedarf ich wunneclîcher zît,
sît aller fröiden herre Liutpolt in der erde lît,
den ich nie tac getrûren sach?
10 ez hât diu werlt an ime verlorn
daz ir an manne nie
sô jæmerlîcher schade geschach.

Mir armen wîbe was ze wol
dô ich gedâhte an in
15 wie mîn heil an sîme lîbe lac.
daz ich des nu niht haben sol,
des gât mit sorgen hin
swaz ich iemer mê geleben mac.   II
mîner wunnen spiegel derst verlorn.
20 den ich mir hete ze sumerlîcher ougenweide erkorn,
des muoz ich leider ænic sîn.
dô man mir seite er wære tôt,
zehant wiel mir daz bluot
von herzen ûf die sêle mîn.

25 Die fröide mir verboten hât
mîns lieben herren tôt
alsô deich ir mêr enberen sol.
sît des nu niht mac werden rât,
in ringe mit der nôt
30 daz mîn klagendez herze ist jâmers vol,   III
diu in iemer weinet daz bin ich,
wan er vil sælic man jâ trôste er wol ze lebenne mich.
der ist nu hin. waz töhte ich hie?
wis ime genædic, herre got:
35 wan tugenthafter gast
kam in dîn ingesinde nie.'

What shall I do in a time of rejoicing,
since the lord of joy lies in the earth, Leopold,
whom I never saw one single day in grief?
10 The world has been damaged by the loss of him
as never before by the death
of any other man.

To me poor woman it was always good
to think of him,
15 how my bliss dwelt in him.
Now because I cannot have that any more,
whatever is left of my life
passes away in sorrow.   II
The mirror of my joys is lost.
20 The man I would have wanted for my eyes' summer feast
I cannot, o misfortune, have.
When they told me he was dead,
the blood surged from my heart
beyond my soul.

25 These joys the death
of my dear lord denies me,
I must go on without him.
Since there is no other way
but to struggle with the need
30 of a heart full of grief,   III
I am she who will weep for him without rest,
for he alone, a man in bliss, would have given me com-
        fort to live.
He is gone now. What good am I here?
Lord God, be merciful to him,
35. for your house never knew
a nobler guest.

36

Der lange süeze kumber mîn [1]
an mîner herzelieben vrowen derst erniuwet.
wie möhte ein wunder grœzer sîn,
daz mîn verlorner dienest mich sô selten riuwet,
5 wan ich noch nieden boten gesach   I
der mir ie bræhte trôst von ir,　wan leit und ungemach.
wie sol ich iemer dise unsælde erwenden?
unmære ich ir, daz ist mir leit,
so enwart mir nie sô liep, kund i'z verenden.

10. Wâ nu getriuwer friunde rât?
waz tuon ich, daz mir liebet daz mir leiden solte?
mîn dienest spot erworben hât
und anders niht: ob ichz noch niht gelouben wolte,
joch wæne i'z nu gelouben muoz.   II
15 des wirt och niemer leides mir　unz an mîn ende buoz,
sît si mich hazzet diech von herzen minne.
mirn kunde ez nieman gesagen:
nu bin ichs vil unsanfte worden inne.

Daz si mich alse unwerden habe
20 als si mir vor gebâret, daz beloube ich niemer;
nu lâze ein teil ir zornes abe,
wan endeclîchen ir genâden beite ich iemer.

von ir enmac ich noch ensol.   III
sô sich genuoge ir liebes fröunt,　sost mir mit leide wol.
25 und kan ich anders niht an ir gewinnen,
ê daz ich âne ir hulde sî,
ich wil ir güete und ir gebærden minnen.

[1] Strophic order of MS. C. *Des Minnesangs Frühling* has: I, IV, II, V, III, VI.

36

My long sweet suffering [1]
for my beloved lady is renewed.
How could there be a greater wonder:
my fruitless service gives me no regrets,
5 when I never yet have seen the messenger   I
  that brought me comfort from her, but only pain and
                unrest?
  How shall I ever escape this curse?
  If I mean nothing to her, that makes me grieve;
  and nothing could be better than if I could end it.

10 Where now is the counsel of loyal friends?
  What am I doing, getting pleasure from what ought to
                grieve me?
  My service has won mockery
  and nothing else: if I refused to believe that before,
  it seems I must believe it now.   II
15 I shall not be free of suffering till I die,
  since the one I love hates me.
  There's no one who could tell me what to do.
  I have grown uneasy within.

  That she really considers me so worthless
20 as she pretends—I shall never believe that.
  Now let her anger abate a little,
  for I wait always on her grace at last.

  I cannot and should not go from her.   III
  If many others rejoice in her love, that makes me happy,
                though it hurts,
25 and if I can win nothing from her in any other way,
  rather than go without her favor
  I shall love her for her goodness and her grace.

Owê daz alle die nu lebent
wol hânt erfunden wie mir ist nâch einem wîbe
30 und si mir niht den rât engebent
daz ich getrœstet würde noch bî lebwendem lîbe.
jô klage ich niht mîn ungemach,   IV
wan daz den ungetriuwen ie   baz danne mir geschach,
die nie gewunnen leit von sender swære.
35 got wolde, erkanden guotiu wîp
ir sumelîcher werben, wie dem wære!

Ein rede der liute tuot mir wê:
dâ enkan ich niht gedulteclîchen zuo gebâren.
nu tuont siz alle deste mê:
40 si frâgent mich ze vil von mîner frouwen jâren,
und sprechent, welher tage si sî,   V
dur daz ich ir sô lange bin   gewesen mit triuwen bî;
si sprechent daz es möhte mich verdriezen.
nu lâ daz aller beste wîp
45 ir zühtelôser vrâge mich geniezen.

Mac si mich doch lâzen sehen,
ob ich ir wære liep, wie si mich haben wolte.
sît mir niht anders mac geschehen,
sô tuo gelîche deme als ez doch wesen solte,
50 und lege mich ir nâhe bî   VI
und bietez eine wîle mir   als ez von herzen sî:
gevalle ez danne uns beiden, sô sî stæte:
verliese ab ich ir hulde dâ,
sô sî verborn als obe siz nie getæte.

It's a shame: so many alive
know well how I am about a woman
30 and do not give me counsel,
that I may have some comfort while I still have some life.
But it's not really my distress I complain about,   IV
it's that faithless lovers always have so much better luck
        than I,
those who never felt the pain of longing.
35 Would God that noble women understand
the courting of those fellows, what it really is.

One thing the people say cuts me to the core
and sends me into a rage,[2]
which makes them say it all the more.
40 They keep on asking me about my lady's age
and talk of how old she must be,   V
since I have served her faithfully all this time—
they say that it must make me weary.
Now may this lady, who is still the best of all,
45 let me profit from their vulgar query.

May she yet let me see
what, if I *were* dear to her, she would do with me.
Since nothing, otherwise, will come my way,
let her act as though things were how they ought to be
50 and lay me by her side   VI
and offer it to me a while, as though from the heart.
Then let it go on forever, if it makes us both glad.
But if I lose her favor there,
let it be undone, as if she never had.

[2] More literally, "I cannot react to it with patience."

WALTHER von der VOGELWEIDE

(c. 1170–c. 1230)

Although he is mentioned in only one extant contemporary document—an item in the accounts of Bishop Wolfger of Passau, dated November 12, 1203, recording an amount given to buy a fur coat for the singer Walther von der Vogelweide—the important periods in Walther's life can be inferred from his poetry. He writes that he learned to be a poet in Austria—*Ze Osterrîche lernte ich singen unde sagen;* at the Babenberger court in Vienna he became the rival of Reinmar von Hagenau. His stay in Vienna ended in 1198 with the death of his patron, the elder son of Leopold V (see Reinmar's elegy, no. 35). He then began a life of wandering from court to court.

He was rewarded with patronage by Philip of Swabia for his support in Philip's struggle against the Papist candidate for Emperor, Otto of Brunswick (see 37 and notes). Afterwards, he was in the court of Landgrave Hermann of Thuringia, where he knew Wolfram von Eschenbach. There were several other patrons. He revisited the Viennese court—in 1203, with Bishop Wolfger—hoping, in vain, to find a place there again.

Walther continued to side with his patrons in the political disputes that arose in German-speaking areas at this time. After the death of Philip, Otto was crowned Emperor and was soon in a struggle against the Pope over land holdings in Italy. Walther supported Otto at first but later rebuked him for his stinginess and switched his support to Friedrich II, who was now also supported for Emperor by Pope Innocent III. Friedrich defeated Otto in 1214; in 1220 he gave Walther the fief which the poet asks for so piteously in 39a and exults in so deliriously in 39b. In October 1227, Friedrich was excommunicated by the Pope for failing to carry through the crusade he had begun. Walther refers to the *unsenfte brieve* from Rome—the Bull of Excommunication—in 50, which is his last datable poem.

His earliest lyrics presumably were written under the influence or tutelage of Reinmar. These vary in quality, but almost always when he wrote in the mode of Reinmar he was inferior to his master and rival. In the wonderful elegy for Reinmar (42) he gives the old man his due: "You never got tired of praising noble ladies." After his initial efforts, however, Walther apparently rebelled against the poetic tradition of which Reinmar was the paragon. He attacked every telling quality of Reinmar's poetry: the fruitless devotion, the willing pain, the self-mocking timidity. All this Walther found foolish and unnatural. It was foolish because, as Walther saw it, the poet felt unworthy of a lady whose glorious virtue was really his invention: it was he who had conceived of it and chosen her to grace with it; she would be nothing without him. It was in fact the lady who needed the poet, for his song alone distinguished her: it endowed her with a beautiful life that the whole courtly world had to venerate. So Walther turns Reinmar's Minne completely around. Where Reinmar declares, *stirbet si, sô bin ich tôt,* if she perishes, I am dead, Walther responds with a boldness that shows how far he departed from Reinmar's style: *ir leben hât mînes lebennes êre: stirbe ab ich, sô ist si tôt,* her life receives glory from my life: and if I should perish, she is dead.

Hôhe Minne, one-sided love celebrated by a boasting poet within a small circle of friends, was also unnatural to Walther. Love is supposed to be simple, effortless, mutual—*zweier herzen wünne,* one pleasure of two hearts; it bears no resemblance to that wake of self-praise and self-mortification that the poets held in court. Therefore, Walther repudiated that overwrought conscience of theirs; he stepped out of their circle, out of that enclosure with its secrets and intrigues, and into the free and open air of nature—or what he called nature. The lyrics that depict what he at this time regards as true love are set in outdoor scenes full of birds and trees and dancing troupes. The woman he discovers there is a carefully created alternative to Reinmar's imperious lady: a sweet and artless girl, grateful for love, undemanding, altogether present, all involved in pleasure; she might be of

noble birth, but she has no tutelary power, and not one wrinkle
of moral concern. The lover just leads her gently to a bed of
roses. It is all very easy and uncomplicated, like love in the
pastourelle (see for example, pt. II, no. 33), from which
Walther's girl is descended. The veil of distances that surrounds
the courtly lady is completely removed; the young woman that
appears is not ringed with silences or made attractive by ob-
stacles, she is right there: anyone passing the spot can tell by the
broken flowers just where she lay with her lover, who, she
proudly recalls, was gentle and respectful.

The difference between the *lady*—a personage of lofty station,
unapproachable, cruelly virtuous—and the woman—unenhanced,
immediate, shining with human qualities like passion, innocence, and trust—underlies a famous strophe by Walther, written
in the full swing of his revolt against the familiar courtly style:

> Wîp muoz iemer sîn der wîbe hôhste name
> und tiuret baz danne frowe, als ichz erkenne.
> swâ nû deheiniu sî diu sich ir wîpheit schame,
> diu merke disen sanc und kiese denne.
> under frowen sint unwîp,
> under wîben sint si tiure.
> wîbes name und wîbes lîp
> die sint beide vil gehiure.
> swiez umb alle frowen var,
> wîp sint alle frowen gar.
> zwîvellop daz hœnet,
> als under wîlen frowe:
> wîp daz ist ein name der si alle krœnet.

> "Woman" will always be the highest name of women,
> and is higher praise than "lady," to my mind.
> If there is one ashamed of her womanhood,
> let her listen to this song and then decide.
> Among ladies are those who are unwomanly,
> among women they are rare.
> The name of woman and the figure of woman
> are both full of grace.

However it may be with all these ladies,
all true women are ladies.
Equivocal praise is mockery—
like "lady," for instance, at times.
"Woman" is a name that sets on them all a crown.

It does seem, at first, that Walther finds a perfect escape from
hôhe Minne, a serene and mutual love that thrives in fields with
birds and flowers. But there are lots of snags in this green world
of his. He has to wonder about the moral substance of this lovely
girl, who is unspoiled but also undefined by all those indoor
virtues that made the courtly lady so distant and yet so ad-
mirable, and the struggle to reach her so ennobling. *Hast du
triuwe unde staetekeit:* an earlier poet, speaking in the rôle of
courtly lover, never had to wonder whether his lady possessed
these noble qualities, for the simple reason that he himself had
given them to her. But Walther's future is uncertain, because
the staying power of a plain woman is unknown. Gradually it
comes to him that Reinmar's lady cannot be replaced by the
vrowelîn, for this serene and easy loving will never come true:
every man may dream of it, but it lacks the one crucial thing
that made a courtier's love for the unattainable lady, with all
its anguish, an expression of his nobility: the dignity of ob-
stacles. Noble men and women cannot love like birds without
becoming less than noble; they will always long for a love that is
rare and difficult, and fosters worthiness. As things turn out, it
was nowhere but in his sleep that Walther found this willing
and perfect girl, and when he wakes he has to go round and
round looking for her. He does not have much chance of finding
her. His green girl is a wonderful dream: pure pleasure un-
adulterated by conscience; but she must remain a dream forever,
the goal of an unfulfillable longing, like the brilliant lady of the
minnesingers. The love of her is no escape from uncertainty.

So Walther wakes from one dream only to fall into another.
The exalted lady who sends down nothing but demands, and the
sweet girl of the open meadows—the *vrowe* and the *vrowelîn*—
both vanish in the daily light. Each is the center of a different
play circle, for Walther's nature is really a man-made enclosure,

like the court. The object in the game of *hôhe Minne* is to act out courtliness, and the player has to endure the strain of endless reformation; in *nidere Minne* the lover impersonates "natural man" and has to withstand great moral hunger. For Walther it is a choice of one game or the other: no. 41 makes this clear. A man encounters a woman on plain ground—and steps immediately into this circle or that. In the end, Walther returns to *hôhe Minne*, and this return after a long rebellion is the greatest confirmation of the values of courtly love.[1]

Thus Walther's apparent "revolt" against Reinmar and the courtly style in fact corroborates the old values. That is what it was meant to do. Walther's great achievement was not to discover a "natural" love, but to find in nature a new way to confirm the nobility of courtly love, which Reinmar had extolled, and to reveal its unreality and impossible demands, which Reinmar had laughed at. Whatever they may have felt about each other, and however great the difference between their styles, they took the same stand.

Walther does seem to have come upon one innovation, as a result of the setting of *nidere Minne*. In his songs on this theme, nature is really endowed with the dimensions of a realm and becomes a ground of experience: it is not, as in the *Natureingang*, simply a mirror of the speaker's feelings.

Walther gave the tradition of courtly love poetry a new turn, but in his political and moral poetry he created something that had never existed before among German poets. Before Walther there had been a kind of proverbial poetry called *Spruchdichtung*, consisting of sentences of folk wisdom in short single strophes. Walther took this over, introduced the tripartite structure from Romance poetry and the Minnesang, and the telling references to contemporary events such as he found in the *sirventes* and in Latin satiric poetry. He also introduced a very sure dramatic touch, as for example the Pope's laughter and mocking boast (38).

Walther wrote a good number of single strophes in this man-

[1] Much of the foregoing discussion is based on a study by Renata Karlin, "The Challenge to Courtly Love," to be published in the forthcoming volume, *In Pursuit of Perfection*, ed. George Economou and Joan Ferrante.

ner. However, his greatest poems go far beyond this: they are long, dignified, oracular utterances, conveying a tone of great moral elevation but full of specific details vividly dramatized. From the earliest ones to the latest there are prophetic, elegiac, tragic tones that had never before been possible in German poetry.

Walther's pre-eminence was recognized from the very beginning. Gottfried praises him lavishly in *Tristan*. For five hundred years after Walther's death—until Goethe—no German lyric poet was his equal.

Text: Friedrich Maurer, ed. *Die Lieder Walthers von der Vogelweide unter Beifügung erhaltener und erschlossener Melodien*. 3d ed. 2 vols. Altdeutsche Textbibliothek, 43 & 47. Tübingen: Max Niemeyer, 1967/69. Marks indicating vowel length added.

Ich saz ûf eime steine,[1]
und dahte bein mit beine:
dar ûf satzt ich den ellenbogen:
ich hete in mîne hant gesmogen
5 daz kinne und ein mîn wange.
dô dâhte ich mir vil ange,
wie man zer welte solte leben.
deheinen rât kond ich gegeben,
wie man driu dinc erwurbe,
10 der keines niht verdurbe.
diu zwei sint êre und varnde guot,
daz dicke ein ander schaden tuot:
daz dritte ist gotes hulde,
der zweier übergulde.
15 die wolte ich gerne in einen schrîn.
jâ leider desn mac niht gesîn,
daz guot und weltlich êre
und gotes hulde mêre
zesamene in ein herze komen.
20 stîge unde wege sint in benomen:
untriuwe ist in der sâze,
gewalt vert ûf der strâze,
fride unde reht sint sêre wunt.
diu driu enhabent geleites niht, diu zwei enwerden ê
gesunt.
25. Ich hôrte ein wazzer diezen
und sach die vische fliezen,
ich sach swaz in der welte was,
velt, walt, loup, rôr unde gras.
swaz kriuchet unde fliuget

1

---

[1] This is the earliest and most famous of Walther's *Sprüche*. In 1197 the Emperor Heinrich VI died, leaving an infant son, Friedrich, who had earlier been elected as successor. Friedrich's uncle, Philip of Swabia, and Otto of Brunswick contended for the throne, and each was crowned by his

I sat down on a rock,[1]
crossed one leg over the other leg,
set my elbow on top,
nestled my chin and one
5 cheek in my hand.
Then I thought very hard
about how a man should live in the world.
I could not find a way
for a man to gain three things at once
10 and not one of them be ruined.
Two are the honor and the goods of this life,
which often damage one another;   1
the third is God's grace,
more precious than the other two.
15 I'd like all three in one chest,
yes, but in these times it cannot be
that wealth and honor in the world
and God's grace ever
come into one heart in one accord.
20 The paths and ways are blocked before them,
treachery lies in ambush,
violence rides in the streets,
peace and justice are badly hurt.
The three shall not have safe conduct till the two are
            first restored.

25 I heard a stream rushing
and saw the fishes swimming;
I saw whatever there was in the world,
field woods leaf reed grass.
Whatever crawls and flies

supporters in 1198. The result was the disorder and violence that the poet
here decries. In the opening lines the poet assumes the ancient symbolic
posture of the prophet and thinker. In the last line, "the two" are peace
and justice.

30 und bein zer unde biuget,
daz sach ich, unde sage iu daz:
der keinez lebet âne haz.

daz wilt und daz gewürme
die strîtent starke stürme;
35 sam tuont die vogel under in,
wan daz si habent einen sin: II
si dûhten sich ze nihte,
si enschüefen starc gerihte.
si kiesent künege unde reht,
40 si setzent hêrren unde kneht.
sô wê dir, tiuschiu zunge,
wie stêt dîn ordenunge!
daz nû diu mugge ir künec hât,
und daz dîn êre alsô zergât!

45 bekêrâ dich, bekêre,
die cirkel sint ze hêre,[2]
die armen künege dringent dich.[3]
Philippe setze den weisen ûf,[4] und heiz si treten hinder
          sich!

Ich sach mit mînen ougen [5]
50 manne unde wîbe tougen,
daz ich gehôrte und gesach
swaz iemen tet, swaz iemen sprach.
ze Rôme hôrte ich liegen
und zwêne künege triegen.
55 dâ von huop sich der meiste strît
der ê was oder iemer sît,
dô sich begunden zweien
die pfaffen unde leien.
daz was ein nôt vor aller nôt,
60 lîp unde sêle lac dâ tôt.   III
die pfaffen striten sêre,

[2] The lesser nobility supporting Otto.
[3] The foreign kings, especially Richard Lion-Heart and Philip Augustus of France, who supported Otto.
[4] A precious stone in the imperial crown.
[5] In 1201 the Pope made his support of Otto clear by excommunicating Philip and his followers. The *pfaffen* and *leien* of 1. 57f are the supporters of

30 and bends its legs on the earth,
   I saw it, and I tell you this:
   not one of them lives without hate.
   Wild beasts and creeping things
   struggle in violent fights,
35 and so the birds with each other.
   And yet they have one mind: II
   they would think they are done for
   if they did not set up a strong rule.
   They decide on kings and law,
40 they install masters and servants.
   Alas for you of the German tongue,
   how does your order stand—
   flies have their king
   and your glory passes away.
45 Repent, repent!
   The coronets are too proud,[2]
   the little kings oppress you.[3]
   Put the orphan jewel [4] on Philip's head and bid them all
             get back.
   I saw with my own eyes [5]
50 the secrets of men and women,
   I saw and heard the things
   that everyone did, that everyone said.
   In Rome I heard how they lied
   and deceived two kings.
55 From that the greatest strife rose up
   that ever was or ever will be,
   for then the priests
   and laity took sides.
   It was a disaster of disasters,
60 body and soul lay there dead.   III
   The priests fought hard,

Otto and Philip respectively. The two kings deceived are Philip and his
nephew Friedrich. The stole (1. 64) is the symbol of ecclesiastical office:
Walther denounces the Church's use of spiritual power in a political conflict. At the end Walther softens his criticism of the Pope somewhat; Innocent III was thirty-seven at this time.

doch wart der leien mêre.
diu swert diu leiten si dernider,
und griffen zuo der stôle wider.
65 si bienen die si wolten
und niht den si solten.
dô stôrte man diu goteshûs.
ich hôrte verre in einer klûs
vil michel ungebære;
70 dâ weinte ein klôsenære,
er klagete gote sîniu leit:
"owê der bâbest ist ze junc: hilf, hêrre, diner kristen-
heit."

38

Ahî wie kristenlîche nû der bâbest lachet,
swenne er sînen Walhen seit 'ich hânz alsô gemachet!'
daz er dâ seit, ern sold es niemer hân gedâht.
er giht 'ich hân zwên Almân under eine krône brâht,[1]
5 daz siz rîche stœren unde brennen unde wasten.   I
ie dar under füllen wir die kasten:
ich hâns an mînen stoc gement, ir guot is allez mîn:
tiuschez silber vert in mînen welschen schrîn.
ir pfaffen, ezzent hüenr und trinkent wîn,
10 und lânt die tiutschen leien magern unde vasten.'

Sagt an, hêr Stoc, hât iuch der bâbest her gesendet,[2]
dazr in rîchet und uns tiutschen ermet unde pfendet?
swenn im diu volle mâze kumt ze laterân,
sô tuot er einen argen list, als er ê hât getân:

---

[1] Otto IV and Friedrich II (see the introduction and the notes to no. 37).
The *stoc* was an offertory container that the Pope, in 1213, ordered placed
in every church to collect money for a new crusade. Line 10, below, is defective in the MS.
[2] The *stoc* was made as a hollow stick; it thus bore some resemblance to the
shepherd's staff (see Peter Dronke, *The Medieval Lyric*, London, 1968, p.
225). "As he held his crook": added.

but the laity's number increased.
So the priests lay down their swords
and grabbed up the stole again
65 and put the ban on those they wanted out,
not on those they should have.
Then were the houses of God made desolate.
Far off, in a hermit's cell,
I heard great lamentation.
70 There a hermit wept,
he poured out his sorrows to God:
"Alas, the Pope is too young, help, O Lord, your Chris-
        tendom."

38

Ah, how like a Christian laughs the Pope at last,
as he tells his Italians, "I've finally got them finessed."
He never should have thought what he says there to their
        graces.
He says, "I've got two tedeschi under one crown,[1]
5 let them wreck their nation and burn it up and bring it
        down—
in the meantime we fill up the cases.
I've driven them like cows to my collection box—all
        their stuff is mine,
their German silver rides in my Italian chest.
Eat chicken, priests, drink wine,
10 and let the lay Germans get skinny and fast."

So tell me, Herr Collection Box, were you sent by the
        Pope, as he held his crook,[2]
to make him rich and rob us Germans of all we possess?
When in the Lateran the full measure reaches him of
        what he took,
he plays an evil trick on us, the same he's always played:

15 seit uns danne wie daz rîche stê verwarren,   II
   unz in füllent aber alle pfarren.
   ich wæn des silbers wênic kumet ze helfe in gotes lant:
   grôzen hort zerteilet selten pfaffen hant.
   hêr Stoc, ir sît ûf schaden her gesant,
   daz ir ûz tiutschen liuten suochet tœrinne unde narren.

39

a) Bittspruch.
Von Rôme voget, von Pülle künec, lât iuch erbarmen [1]
daz man mich bî rîcher kunst lât alsus armen.
gerne wolde ich, möhte ez sîn, bî eigenem fiure erwarmen.
zâhiu wiech danne sunge von den vogellînen,
5 von der heide und von den bluomen, als ich wîlent sancl
swelch schœne wîp mir danne gæbe ir habedanc,
der liez ich liljen unde rôsen ûz ir wengel schînen.
sus kume ich spâte und rîte fruo: 'gast, wê dir, wê!':
sô mac der wirt baz singen von dem grüenen klê.
10 die nôt bedenkent, milter künec, daz iuwer nôt zergê.

b) Dankspruch.
Ich hân mîn lêhen, al die werlt, ich hân mîn lêhen.
nû enfürhte ich niht den hornunc an die zêhen,
und wil alle bœse hêrren dester minre flêhen.
der edel künec, der milte künec hât mich berâten,
5 deich den sumer luft und in dem winter hitze hân.
mîn nâhgebûren dunke ich verre baz getân:
si sehent mich niht mêr an in butzen wîs als sî wilent tâten.
ich bin ze lange arm gewesen ân mînen danc.
ich was sô voller scheltens daz mîn âtem stanc:
10 daz hât der künec gemachet reine, und dar zuo mînen sanc.

[1] Addressed to King Friedrich II before his coronation as Emperor in 1220.

15 he tells us how the Holy Land must stand in great dis-
           tress   II
   till every little parish replenishes His Holiness.
   Little of the silver, I imagine, ever gets to the new cru-
           sade:
   a big take is rarely given out by priestly hands.
   Herr Collection Box, you were ordered here and made
   to seek out fools among men and women in German lands.

39

   a) Ask poem.
   Defender of Rome, King of Apulia, take pity on me,[1]
   that I, a man so rich in art, am allowed to be so poor.
   I would gladly warm myself at my fireplace, if I had a fire-
           place.
   O lord how I'd sing about those little birds again,
55 and the meadow, and the flowers, as I sang before.
   Any lovely woman who thanked me then—
   I'd let roses and lilies shine out of her face.
   As it is, I arrive late and ride out early: "Guest, alas for you."
   But the master of his own house could sing much better about
           green clover.
10 Generous king, think of this distress, and your own may soon
           be over.

   b) Thank poem.
   I've got my fief, everybody, I've got my fief!
   Now when it's cold I don't have to fear for my toes,
   I will beg a little less at stingy masters' doors—
   I have air in the summer, in winter my fire roars,
 5 and the noble king, the sweet king, is the one I have to thank.
   My neighbors find me a much more presentable man—
   they don't look at me as though I were a scarecrow any more.
   I hated being poor, and I was poor too long—
   my mouth was so full of reproaches, my breath stank.
10 Now the king has sweetened my breath—and my song.

40

Ir sult sprechen willekomen: [1]
der iu mære bringet, daz bin ich.
allez daz ir habt vernomen,
daz ist gar ein wint: nû frâget mich.   I
5   ich wil aber miete:
wirt mîn lôn iht guot,
ich gesage iu lîhte daz iu sanfte tuot.
seht waz man mir êren biete.

Ich wil tiuschen frowen sagen
10   solhiu mære daz si deste baz
al der werlte suln behagen:
âne grôze miete tuon ich daz.   II
waz wold ich ze lône?
si sint mir ze hêr,
15   sô bin ich gefüege, und bite si nihtes mêr
wan daz si mich grüezen schône.

Ich hân lande vil gesehen
unde nam der besten gerne war:
übel müeze mir geschehen
20   kunde ich ie mîn herze bringen dar   III
daz im wol gevallen
wolde fremeder site.
nû waz hulfe mich, ob ich unrehte strite?
tiuschiu zuht gât vor in allen.

25   Von der Elbe unz an den Rîn
und her wider unz an Ungerlant
mugen wol die besten sîn,

---

[1] This poem was probably addressed to the Viennese court in 1203; l. 40
conveys his request to be taken back again. It has been suggested that the
poem is a response to an attack on the Germans by Peire Vidal.

40

You should bid me welcome: [1]
I'm a man that's bringing news.
Everything you've heard before
is wind. Now just ask me.   I
5   But first I want some reward.
If the pay is any good
I may have some news you'll like.
Now let us see the honorarium.

I want to tell German women
10   such news as should make them all
more pleasing to the world.
I'll do that without asking for much—   II
what would I want as wages?
They are too high for that.
15   That's my breeding, and I ask them only
to greet me handsomely.

I have been in many lands
and looked closely at the best they had.
Damn me
20   if I can bring my heart   III
to like
foreign ways.
What good does it do me to argue some untruth?
German breeding excells all others.

25   From the Elbe to the Rhine
and from here again to Hungary
live the greatest people

die ich in der werlte hân erkant.   IV
kan ich rehte schouwen
30   guot gelâz unt lîp,
sem mir got sô swüere ich wol daz hie diu wîp
bezzer sint danne ander frouwen.

Tiusche man sint wol gezogen,
rehte als engel sint diu wîp getân.
35   swer si schildet, derst betrogen:
ich enkan sîn anders niht verstân.   V
tugent und reine minne,
swer die suochen wil,
der sol komen in unser lant: dâ ist wünne vil:
40   lange müeze ich lebe dar inne!

Der ich vil gedienet hân
und iemer mêre gerne dienen wil,
diust von mir vil unerlân:
iedoch sô tuot si leides mir sô vil.   VI
45   si kan mir versêren
herze und den muot.
nû vergebez ir got dazs an mir missetuot.
her nâch mac si sichs bekêren.

41

Aller werdekeit ein füegerinne,
daz sît ir zewâre, frowe Mâze.
er sælic man, der iuwer lêre hât!
der endarf sich iuwer niender inne
5   weder ze hove schamen noch an der strâze.   I
dur daz sô suoche ich, frowe, iuwern rât,
daz ir mich ebene werben lêret.
wirbe ich nidere, wirbe ich hôhe, ich bin versêret.
ich was vil nâch ze nidere tôt,
10   nû bin ich aber ze hôhe siech: unmâze enlât mich âne nôt.

I have ever seen on earth.   IV
If I know how to judge
30   handsome figures and handsome acts,
by God I swear plain women here
are nobler than ladies elsewhere.

German men are nobly bred
and the women made like angels.
35   Whoever reproaches them is deluded—
otherwise I can't understand him.   V
Valour, and pure love—
anyone looking for these
should come to our land: there's great joy there.
40   Long may I live in this land!

The one I have long served
and will gladly serve for ever,
she is wholly unrenounced;
yet she causes me much suffering.   VI
45   She knows how to torment
my heart and mind.
Now God forgive her for the wrongs she's done me.
Later on she may repent.

41

Author of all worth
are you, in truth, Lady Moderation:
he is a man in bliss who has your teaching.
With you he need not feel ashamed in any place,
5 neither at court, nor in the street.   I
Therefore, I seek, my Lady, your advice:
teach me how to strain every nerve by the golden mean.[1]
If I court low, if I court high, either way I am in peril.
Once, too low, I nearly died.
10 Now, too high, I am sick again, Immoderation will not
spare me her distress.

[1] Literally, "Teach me how to strive fittingly, evenly," that is, with moderation. Line 15 literally: ". . . to soar toward lofty worth." Line 17: "I wonder
why Moderation hangs back."

Nideriu minne heizet diu sô swachet
daz der lîp nâch kranker liebe ringet:
diu minne tuot unlobelîche wê.

hôhiu minne reizet unde machet
15 daz der muot nâch hôher wirde ûf swinget: II
diu winket mir nû, daz ich mit ir gê.
mich wundert wes diu mâze beitet.
kumet diu herzeliebe, ich bin iedoch verleitet:
mîn ougen hânt ein wîp ersehen,
20 swie minneclîch ir rede sî, mir mac wol schade von ir
geschehen.

42

Saget mir ieman, waz ist minne?[1]
weiz ich des ein teil, sô wist ichs gerne mê.
der sich baz denn ich versinne,
der berihte mich durch waz si tuot sô wê.   I
5 minne ist minne, tuot si wol:
tuot si wê, so enheizet si niht rehte minne.
sus enweiz ich wie si danne heizen sol.

Obe ich rehte râten künne
waz diu minne sî, sô sprechet denne jâ.
10 minne ist zweier herzen wünne:
teilent sie gelîche, sost diu minne dâ: II
sol abe ungeteilet sîn,
sô enkans ein herze alleine niht enthalten.
owê woldest dû mir helfen, frowe mîn!

15 Frowe, ich trage ein teil ze swære:
wellest dû mir helfen, sô hilf an der zît.
Low Minne unmans the lover so
his body strains to reach a sickly pleasure—

---

[1] The last two lines of each strophe are set out after the edition of Lach·
mann; Maurer publishes them as one line. Lines 20–21: after Lachmann.

it brings down wounds that bear no honor.
High Minne lures the lover up,
15 tempts his spirit to soar toward worth beyond measure—   II
she beckons to me now to go with her . . .
And Moderation hangs back, I notice with alarm.
If real love comes of it, still I am misled.
My eyes have picked a woman out.
20 Her words are full of love, and it can all work out to harm.

42

Will anyone tell me what Minne is?
Though I know a little, I gladly would know more.
Whoever understands it better,
let him tell me why it causes pain.   I
5 Minne is minne if it gives pleasure:
if it causes misery, it isn't right to call it minne—
then I don't know what it should be called.

If I guess right
what Minne is, say "Yes":
10 Minne is one joy between two hearts.
If they share alike, there is Minne: II
but if it isn't shared,
one heart alone cannot contain it.
Alas, my lady, if you would only help me.

15 Lady, I bear a little too much.
If you want to help me, help in time.

sî abe ich dir gar unmære,
daz sprich endelîche: sô lâz ich den strît,   III
unde wirde ein ledic man.
20 dû solt aber einez rehte wizzen, frouwe,
daz dich lützel ieman baz geloben kan.

Kan mîn frouwe süeze siuren?
wænet si daz ich ir liep gebe umbe leit?
sol ich si dar umbe tiuren,
25 daz siz wider kêre an mîne unwerdekeit?   IV
sô kund ich unrehte spehen.
wê waz sprich ich ôrenlôser ougen âne?
den diu minne blendet, wie mac der gesehen?

43

Lange swîgen des hât ich gedâht:
nû wil ich singen aber als ê.
dar zuo hânt mich guote liute brâht: I
die mugen mir wol gebieten mê.
5 ich sol singen unde sagen,
und swes si gern, daz sol ich tuon: sô suln si mînen
    kumber klagen.

Hœret wunder, wie mir ist geschehen
von mînes selbes arebeit.
mich enwil ein wîp niht an gesehen: II
10 die brâht ich in die werdekeit,
daz ir muot sô hôhe stât.
jon weiz si niht, wenn ich mîn singen lâze, daz ir lop
    zergât.

Hêrre, waz si flüeche lîden sol,
swenn ich nû lâze mînen sanc!
15 alle die nû lobent, daz weiz ich wol,   III
die scheltent danne ân mînen danc.

But if I do not mean a thing to you,
say so once and for all: then I'll give up the struggle,   III
and become a free man.
20 But, lady, understand one thing:
no other man can sing your praise so well.

Can my lady turn the sweet to sour?
Does she dream I'll give her pleasure in exchange for
        misery?
Should I lend her all that value
25 just to have her set it against my unworthiness?   IV
That way I must see things wrong.
O lord what am I saying, deaf and blind?
A man dazzled by Minne—how can he see?

43

To be long silent was my thought:
now I shall sing once again as before.
Gentle people brought me back to it: I
they have the right to command me.
5 I shall sing and make up words,
and do what they desire; then they must lament my grief.

Listen to this wonder, how I fared
for all my hard work:
a certain woman will not look at me—   II
10 and it was I that brought her up to that esteem
which makes her so high-minded now.
She does not know: when I leave off singing, her praise
        will die away.

Lord what curses she'd endure,
were I now to stop my song!
15 All those who praise her now, I know   III
they'll rebuke her then—against my will.

tûsent herze wurden frô
von ir genâden; dius engeltent, lât si mich verderben sô.

Dô mich dûhte daz si wære guot,
20 wer was ir bezzer dô dann ich?
    dêst ein ende: swaz si mir getuot,   IV
    des mac ouch si verwænen sich,
    nimet si mich von dirre nôt,
    ir leben hât mînes lebennes êre: stirbe ab ich, sô ist si tot.

25 Sol ich in ir dienste werden alt,
    die wîle junget si niht vil.
    sost mîn hâr vil lîhte alsô gestalt,   V
    dazs einen jungen danne wil.
    selfiu got, hêr junger man,
30 sô rechet mich und gêt ir alten hût mit sumerlaten an.

44

Herzeliebez vrowelîn,
got gebe dir hiute und iemer guot.
kund ich baz gedenken dîn,   I
des het ich willeclîchen muot.
5 waz mac ich dir sagen mê,
wan daz dir nieman holder ist? owê, dâ von ist mir vil wê.

Sie verwîzent mir daz ich
sô nidere wende mînen sanc.
daz si niht versinnent sich   II
10 waz liebe sî, des haben undanc!
sie getraf diu liebe nie,
die nâch dem guote und nâch der schœne minnent; wê
      wie minnent die?

A thousand hearts were made happy
by her kindness to me; they will suffer for it if she lets me
      perish.

When it seemed that she was gentle,
20 who was more devoted then than I?
But that's all over: whatever she does to me,   IV
she can expect the same—
if she frees me from this distress,
her life receives the glory of my life; if I perish, she is dead.

25 If I grow old in her service,
she won't get much younger in that time.
Maybe then my hair'll have such a look   V
she'll want a young man at her side.
So help you God, avenge me,
30 you young man, and have a go with switches on her
      ancient hide.

44

Dearly beloved gentle girl,
God bless you today and every day.
If I could put my thoughts of you in better words,   I
I would have a willing mind to it.
5 What is there more to say
but no one loves you more? Oh, I suffer much for that.

They censure me, saying
I set my song too low:
they do not know
10 what love is—bad luck to them,
love never touched them,
their love goes after skin and gold—lord, what kind of
      love is that?

Bî der schœne ist dicke haz: [1]
zer schœne niemen sî ze gâch.
15 liebe tuot dem herzen baz: III
der liebe gêt diu schœne nâch.
liebe machet schœne wîp:
desn mac diu schœne niht getuon, sin machet niemer
        lieben lîp.

Ich vertrage als ich vertruoc
20 und als ich iemer wil vertragen.[2]
dû bist schœne und hâst genuoc: IV
was mugen si mir dâ von gesagen?
swaz si sagen, ich bin dir holt,
und nim dîn glesîn vingerlîn für einer küneginne golt.

25 Hâst dû triuwe und stætekeit,
sô bin ich dîn âne angest gar
daz mir iemer herzeleit   V
mit dînem willen widervar.
hâst aber du der zweier niht,
30 sôn müezest dû mîn niemer werden.   owê danne, ob daz
        geschiht!

45

'Nemt, frowe, disen kranz:'
alsô sprach ich zeiner wol getânen maget:
'sô zieret ir den tanz,
mit den schœnen bluomen, als irs ûffe traget.   I
5 het ich vil edele gesteine,
daz müest ûf iur houbet,
obe ir mirs geloubet.
seht mîn triuwe, daz ichz meine.'

[1] That is, hateful qualities.
[2] That is, their reproaches.

Beauty often comes with hate: [1]
let no man rush toward beauty.
15 Love is kinder to the heart,   III
love comes first, then beauty,
love makes a woman beautiful—
but beauty does not have such power, beauty cannot
        make a woman worthy of love.

I bear it as I have borne
20 and will bear it as long as I must.[2]
You are beautiful, and you own enough—   IV
what can they say to me?
Let them talk—I love you
and would not take the gold ring of a queen for your
        ring of glass.

25 If you have loyalty and constancy,
then I need not fear the day   V
will come when you will want
the anguish of the heart to fall on me.
But if you have neither,
30 then may you never be mine, and then oh god if it works
        out that way.

45

"Lady, take this garland."
So I spoke, once, to a pretty girl.
"And when you wear it, with its pretty flowers,
you will adorn the dance.   I
5 If I had precious stones,
you would wear them on your head,
now you believe this:
See, by my good faith, I mean what I say.

'Ir sît sô wol getân,
10 daz ich iu mîn schapel gerne geben wil,
so ichz aller beste hân.
wîzer unde rôter bluomen weiz ich vil: II
die stênt sô verre in jener heide.
dâ si schône entspringent
15 und die vogele singent,
dâ suln wir si brechen beide.'

Si nam daz ich ir bôt,
einem kinde vil gelîch daz êre hât.
ir wangen wurden rôt,
20 same diu rôse, dâ si bî der liljen stât. III
des erschampten sich ir liehten ougen:
doch neic si mir schône.
daz wart mir ze lône:
wirt mirs iht mêr, daz trage ich tougen.

25 Mich dûhte daz mir nie
lieber wurde, danne mir ze muote was.
die bluomen vielen ie
von dem boume bî uns nider an daz gras IV
seht, dô muost ich von fröiden lachen.
30 do ich sô wünneclîche
was in troume rîche,
dô taget ez und muos ich wachen.

Mir ist von ir geschehen,
daz ich disen sumer allen meiden muoz
35 vast under dougen sehen:
lîhte wirt mir einiu: so ist mir sorgen buoz. V
waz obe si gêt an disem tanze?
frowe, dur iur güete
rucket ûf die hüete.
40 owê gsæhe ichs under kranze! [1]

[1] Many editors arrange the strophes as follows: I, III, II, IV, V.

"You are so beautiful,
10 I want to give you my chaplet,
   the best one I have.
I can show you many flowers—white, and red—   II
they wait, off there, in that open field.
There, where they bloom so beautifully,
15 and birds sing,
   we will go pick flowers together."

What I offered her she took
like a young girl of great nobility.
   Her cheeks grew red,
20 like a rose among lilies.   III
It made her glowing eyes bashful,
but she curtsied to me beautifully.
   That was my reward.
If I get more, I'll keep still about it.

25 It seemed to me I never
knew it better than it was then.
   Flowers fell all the time
from the tree beside us on the grass.   IV
Look now, I had to laugh for joy.
30 As I was dreaming
   in such lordly pleasure,
day broke, and I had to wake up.

The way I am now, because of her
this whole summer I have to look
35 every girl square in the eyes:
maybe one of them is the one—then I'm rid of my
        sorrows.   V
What if she's here at this dance?
Ladies, by your good grace,
   push back your hats.
40 O if underneath a garland I saw her face.[1]

46

Under der linden [1]
an der heide,
dâ unser zweier bette was,
dâ mugt ir vinden
5   schône beide   I
gebrochen bluomen unde gras.
vor dem walde in einem tal,
tandaradei,
schône sanc diu nahtegal.

10   Ich kam gegangen
zuo der ouwe:
dô was min friedel komen ê.
dâ wart ich enpfangen,
hêre frouwe,
15   daz ich bin sælic iemer mê.   II
kuster mich? wol tûsentstunt:
tandaradei,
seht wie rôt mir ist der munt.

Dô hât er gemachet
20   alsô rîche
von bluomen eine bettestat.

des wirt noch gelachet
inneclîche,   III
kumt iemen an daz selbe pfat.
25   bî den rôsen er wol mac,
tandaradei,
merken wâ mirz houbet lac.

---

[1] Maurer's edition combines the first two lines and the third and fourth lines
of each strophe.

46

Under the lime tree [1]
on the open field,
where we two had our bed,
you still can see
5   lovely broken   I
flowers and grass.
On the edge of the woods in a vale,
tandaradei,
sweetly sang the nightingale.

10   I came walking
to the meadow,
my love already was there.
And he received me,
Blessed Lady,   II
15   the joy of that will last.
Did he kiss me then? A thousand times, at least,
tandaradei,
look now, how my mouth is red.

Then he made
20   a lordly
place to lie in, all of flowers.

There's a good laugh there
even now   III
for anyone coming that way:
25   he could tell, by the roses,
tandaradei,
just where my head lay.

Daz er bî mir læge,
wessez iemen,
30   nu enwelle got, sô schamt ich mich.
wes er mit mir pflæge,
niemer niemen   IV
bevinde daz, wan er unde ich,
und ein kleinez vogellîn,
35   tandaradei,
daz mac wol getriuwe sîn.

47

Owê, hovelîchez singen,   4
daz dich ungefüege dœne
solten ie ze hove verdringen!
daz die schiere got gehœne!   I
5   owê daz dîn wirde alsô geliget!
des sint alle dîne friunde unfrô.
daz muoz alsô sîn: nû sî alsô:
frô Unfuoge, ir habt gesiget.

Der uns fröide wider bræhte,
10   diu reht und gefüege wære,
hei wie wol man des gedæhte
swâ man von im seite mære!   II
ez wær ein vil hovelîcher muot,
des ich iemer gerne wünschen sol:
15   frowen unde hêrren zæme ez wol:
owê daz ez nieman tuot!

Die daz rehte singen stœrent,
der ist ungelîche mêre
danne die ez gerne hœrent:
20   noch volg ich der alten lêre: III
ich enwil niht werben zuo der mül,
dâ der stein sô riuschent umbe gât

If anyone found out,
God forbid, he lay by me,
30 I'd be ashamed.
What he did with me there
may no one ever   IV
know, except for him and me
and one little bird,
35 tandaradei,
which will not say a word.

47

Alas, courtly singing,
that uncouth strains
should supplant you at the court.
God bring dishonor on them soon.   I
5   Alas that your dignity should be laid low.
All your friends are sad.
It must be; let it be:
Lady Vulgarity, you have won.

Should any man restore our courteous
10 and gentle joy,
O how well we'd praise him
every time we spoke of what he did.   II
That would be the soul of courtliness,
I shall always hope for it,
15 it would suit lords and ladies well.
O sorrow no one does it.

Those who drown out the good singing—
there's many more of them
than those who want to hear it.
20 But I still follow the old teaching: III
I shall not set my music to the mill,
for the stone goes round so raucously

und daz rat sô mange unwîse hât.
merket, wer dâ harpfen sül.

25   Die sô frevellîchen schallent,
der muoz ich vor zorne lachen,
dazs in selben wol gevallent
mit als ungefüegen sachen.   IV
die tuont sam die frösche in eime sê,
30   den ir schrîen alsô wol behaget,
daz diu nahtegal dâ von verzaget,
sô si gerne sunge mê.

Swer unfuoge swîgen hieze,
waz man noch von fröiden sunge!
35   und si abe den bürgen stieze,
daz si dâ die frôn niht twunge.   V
wurden ir die grôzen höve benomen,
daz wær allez nâch dem willen mîn.
bien gebûren liez ich si wol sîn:
dannen ists och her bekomen.[1]

48

Owê, daz wîsheit unde jugent,
des mannes schœne noch sîn tugent,
niht erben sol, sô ie der lîp erstirbet!
daz mac wol klagen ein wîser man,
5   der sich des schaden versinnen kan,
Reimâr, waz guoter kunst an dir verdirbet.
dû solt von schulden iemer des geniezen,   I
daz dich des tages wolte nie verdriezen
dun spræches ie den frowen wol mit . . .[1]

[1] It has been suggested, mostly on the basis of the last two lines, that this song is directed against Neidhart von Reuental. In any case, this is the first time a German poet laments the decline of courtly singing.
[1] This line is defective in the ms.

and the wheel has such awful melodies.
Notice who would harp there.

25   Those who make their shameful noise
make me laugh with anger,
they're so pleased
with such gross things.   **IV**
They're like frogs in a pond
30   who like their own croaking so much,
the nightingale loses heart,
though it gladly would sing more.

If anyone commanded vulgarity be silent,
drove it away from the castles
35   so that it oppressed these happy few no more—
what joys we'd sing about.
If it were barred from the great courts
that would all be as I wish.
I'd have it lodge with peasants;
40   that's where it came from.[1]

48

Alas, that wisdom, and youth,
and the beauty of man, and his craft
cannot be handed down when the body dies away.
A man who has lived can mourn for this,
5 who is awake to human hurt.
Reinmar, what great art dies with you.
You've the right to rejoice till the end of days   **I**
that you never lost the taste, not once,
for singing noble women's praise.[1]

10 des süln si iemer danken dîner zungen.
   hetst anders niht wan eine rede gesungen,
   'sô wol dir, wîp, wie reine ein nam!,' dû hetest alsô
           gestriten [2]
   an ir lop daz elliu wîp dir genâden solten biten.

   Dêswâr, Reimâr, dû riuwes mich
15 michels harter danne ich dich,
   ob dû lebtes und ich wær erstorben.
   ich wilz bî mînen triuwen sagen,
   dich selben wolt ich lützel klagen:
   ich klage dîn edelen kunst, daz sist verdorben.
20 dû kundest al der werlte fröide mêren,   II

   sô duz ze guoten dingen woltes kêren.
   mich riuwet dîn wol redender munt und dîn vil süezer
           sanc,
   daz die verdorben sint bî mînen zîten.
   daz dû niht eine wîle mohtest bîten!
25 sô leiste ich dir gesellschaft: mîn singen ist niht lanc.
   dîn sêle müeze wol gevarn, und habe dîn zunge danc.

49

   Ir reinen wîp, ir werden man,
   ez stêt alsô daz man mir muoz
   êr unde minneclîchen gruoz
   noch volleclîcher bieten an.
5 des habet ir von schulden græzer reht dan ê:
   welt ir vernemen, ich sage iu wes.   I
   wol vierzec jâr hab ich gesungen oder mê
   von minnen und als iemen sol.
   dô was ichs mit den andern geil:
10 nu enwirt mirs niht, ez wirt iu gar.

---

[2] See above, no. 34.

10 They ought to thank your tongue forever.
   If you had sung but the one theme—if that were all—
   "Joy to you, Woman, how pure a name," with that alone
                you would have striven [2]
   so for their praise's sake, let every woman pray for mercy
                on your soul.

   The truth is, Reinmar, I mourn for you
15 much more than you would mourn for me
   if you were living and I had died.
   I want to say this on my honor:
   you yourself I would not shed a tear for.
   I mourn the passing of your noble art.
20 You could make the joy of the whole world greater   II

   when you had a mind to something good.
   I mourn your sweet speaking mouth and tender song,
   that I have lived to see them perish,
   that you could not stay a while longer in our ranks.
25 Well, I shall be with you again, my singing is soon over.
   May your soul fare well, and your tongue have thanks.

49

   You excellent women, you valiant men,
   it is fitting now to give me
   honor and greetings of love
   in greater measure yet.
 5 You have more cause to do this now than ever before.
   If you will hear, I shall tell you why: I
   for forty years and more I have sung
   of love, and how we must live.
   In those days I had joy in it, with the others,
10 now I get nothing from it, it is all for you.

mîn minnesanc der diene iu dar,
und iuwer hulde sî mîn teil.

Lât mich an eime stabe gân
und werben umbe werdekeit
15 mit unverzageter arebeit,
als ich von kinde habe getân,
sô bin ich doch, swie nider ich sî, der werden ein,
genuoc in mîner mâze hô.   II
daz mûet die nideren. ob mich daz iht swache? nein.
20 die werden hânt mich deste baz.
diu wernde wirde diust sô guot,
daz man irz hœhste lop sol geben.
ezn wart nie lobelîcher leben,
swer sô dem ende rehte tuot.

25 Welt, ich hân dînen lôn ersehen:
swaz dû mir gîst, daz nimest dû mir.
wir scheiden alle blôz von dir.
scham dich, sol mir alsô geschehen.
ich hân lîp unde sêle (des was gar ze vil)
30 gewâget tûsentstunt dur dich: III
nû bin ich alt und hâst mit mir dîn gampelspil:
und zürn ich daz, sô lachest dû.
nû lache uns eine wîle noch:
dîn jâmertac wil schiere komen,
35 und nimet dir swazt uns hâst benomen,
und brennet dich dar umbe iedoch.

Ich hât ein schœnez bilde erkorn:
owê daz ich ez ie gesach
ald ie sô vil zuo zime gesprach!
40 ez hât schœn unde rede verlorn.
dâ wonte ein wunder inne: daz fuor ine weiz war:
dâ von gesweic daz bilde iesâ.   IV
sîn liljerôsevarwe wart sô karkelvar,
daz ez verlôs smac unde schîn.

May my courtly song go on serving you,
and let your good wishes be my pay.

Say I walked with a staff
and struggled with undaunted
15 labor for excellence and honor,
as I have from childhood to this day:
I would walk lowly, yes, but I would stand among the
          valiant,
all bent down, yet in my stature high enough.   II
This galls the truly low. Does it cast me down?   No.
20 Courtly men and women hold me all the higher.
Long merit is so precious,
let us give it our highest praise.
There never was a nobler life
if a man remembers the end as he lives out his days.

25 World, I know what your rewards are like—
whatever you give me you take away.
Naked are we all when we go from you;
it will be your shame when I, too, go that way.
I have risked my body and my soul—it was too much—
30 a thousand times for you.   III
Now I am old, and in me you have a thing to play with;
and when I am enraged over that, you laugh.
Well, laugh at us a little while more—
your day of horror is coming soon
35 and will take everything from you that you took from us
and burn you for it even so.

I made out a beautiful image,
alas that I ever saw it
and spoke with it so many times!
40 Its beauty is gone, its tongue is still.
A miracle had its dwelling there—it went
I know not where; at once the image was dumb,   IV
its color of lilies and roses became so dungeon gray
it lost its fragrance and its light.

45 mîn bilde, ob ich berkerkelt bin
in dir, sô lâ mich ûz alsô
daz wir ein ander vinden frô:
wan ich muoz aber wider in.

Mîn sêle müeze wol gevarn!
50 ich hân zer welte manegen lîp
gemachet frô, man unde wîp:
künd ich dar under mich bewarn!
lobe ich des lîbes minne, deis der sêle leit:
si giht, ez sî ein lüge, ich tobe.   v
55 der wâren minne giht si ganzer stætekeit,
wie guot si sî, wies iemer wer.
lîp, lâ die minne diu dich lât,
und habe die stæten minne wert:
mich dunket, der dû hâst gegert,
60 diu sî niht visch unz an den grât.[1]

50

Ouwê, war sint verswunden   alliu mîniu jâr![1]
ist mir mîn leben getroumet,   oder ist ez wâr?
daz ich ie wânde ez wære,   was daz allez iht?
dar nâch hân ich geslâfen,   und enweiz es niht.
5 nû bin ich erwachet,   und ist mir unbekant
daz mir hie vor was kündic   als mîn ander hant.
liut unde lant, dar innen   von kinde ich bin erzogen,
die sint mir worden frömde,   als ob ez sî gelogen.
die mîne gespilen wâren,   die sint træge und alt.
10 gebreitet ist daz velt,   verhouwen ist der walt:
wan daz daz wazzer fliuzet   als ez wîlent flôz,
für wâr mîn ungelücke   wânde ich wurde grôz.

[1] Literally, "isn't fish to the bone"; proverbial. The important thing is that
he speaks to the body in this down-to-earth peasanty way. Line 18: "all bent
down" added.
[1] The order of the lines and occasional wording from Lachmann's edition.

45 My image, if I am imprisoned
in you, let me go free, so
that we may find each other once more in joy,
for I shall enter in again one day.

May my soul fare well.
50 I have given joy to many
in this world, to many women, many men.
If only, doing that, I could have saved myself.
If I praise the body's love, it brings sorrow to my soul,
it says I lie, I rant,   V
55 and claims true love alone is constant to the end,
and tells how good love is and how it endures.
Body, leave that love that leaves you all alone
and praise the love that stays.
The thing you crave,
60 it isn't all meat right down to the bone.[1]

50

Alas, all my years, where have they disappeared! [1]
Have I dreamed my life, or is it real?
That which I thought was something, was it something?
Perhaps I have been sleeping and do not know it.
5 Now I am awake, and all seems strange
that used to be familiar, once, as my own hand.
The people and the place where I grew up
seem alien, like lies, not of my own land.   I
The children I played with now are old and slow.
10 The field is harvested, the woods are hewn.
Were it not that the water flows as it used to flow,
I would think my misery truly great.

    mich grüezet maneger trâge, der mich bekande ê wol.
    diu welt ist allenthalben ungenâden vol.
15 als ich gedenke an manigen wünneclîchen tac,
    die mir sint enpfallen sam in daz mer ein slac,
    iemer mêre ouwê.

    Ouwê wie jæmerlîche junge liute tuont,
    den ê vil unriuweclîche ir gemüete stuont!
20 die kunnen niuwan sorgen, owê wie tuont si sô?
    swar ich zer werlte kêre, dâ ist nieman vrô.   II
    tanzen, lachen, singen zergât mit sorgen gar:
    nie kristenman gesach sô jæmerlîche schar.
    nû merkent wie den frouwen ir gebende stât:
25 jâ tragent die stolzen ritter dörpellîche wât.

    uns sint unsenfte brieve her von Rôme komen,
    uns ist erloubet trûren und fröide gar benomen.
    daz müet mich inneclîchen sêre, wir lebten ie vil wol,
    daz ich nû für mîn lachen weinen kiesen sol.
30 die vogel in der wilde betrüebet unser klage:
    waz wunders ist, ob ich dâ von verzage?
    waz spriche ich tumber man durch mînen bœsen zorn?
    swer dirre wünne volget, der hât jene dort verlorn,
    iemer mêre owê.

35 Ouwê wie uns mit süezen dingen ist vergeben!
    ich sihe die bittern gallen in dem honege sweben.
    diu welt is ûzen schœne, wîz grüen unde rôt,
    und innân swarzer varwe, vinster sam der tôt.
    swen si nû habe verleitet, der schouwe sînen trôst:
40 er wirt mit swacher buoze grôzer sünde erlôst.
    dar an gedenkent, ritter: ez ist iuwer dinc.
    ir tragent die liehten helme und manegen herten rinc,   III
    dar zuo die vesten schilte und diu gewîhten swert.
    wolte got, wær ich der sigenünfte wert,
45 sô wolte ich nôtic man verdienen rîchen solt:

Many are slow to greet me that knew me well.
The world is everywhere full of the loss of grace.
15 When I think of many happy days that have fallen
away from me like a blow struck on the water, then
ever more, alas.

Alas, how miserable are the young today,
whose spirits soared in times gone by.
20 They know only sorrow—how can they live that way?
Wherever I turn on this earth no one is content,   II
dancing laughing singing have passed on into care,
no Christian man has ever seen a crowd so wretched.
Look at the women, what they wear on their heads,
25 and proud knights clothed in peasant dress.

Now cruel letters have come to us from Rome,
we are authorized to suffer, exempt from joy.
It offends me deeply—we used to live well in this land—
that I must give up my laughter and choose to weep.
30 The birds in the wilderness are cast down by our lament,
it is no wonder, then, that I despair—
But fool that I am, what does my ranting anger make me
          say?
Who runs after pleasures here has lost them *there*,
ever more, alas.

35 Alas, how the sweet things poison us.
I see the bitter gall floating in the honey.
The white green red world is beautiful outside,
and inside black, as dark as death.
Whomever it has seduced, let him look where he will
          find comfort:
40 with a soft penance he is set free from mighty sin.
Knights, think of this, it is for you, these words,
you wear the bright helms, the hard rings,   III
the strong shields, the consecrated swords.
Would God that I myself were worthy of the victory.
45 I, a needy man, would win great wages,

joch meine ich niht die huoben   noch der hêrren golt.
ich wolte selbe krône   êweclîchen tragen:
die möhte ein soldenære   mit sîme sper bejagen.
möht ich die lieben reise   gevaren über sê,
50 sô wolte ich denne singen wol,   und niemer mêr ouwê,
niemer mêr ouwê.

yet not acres of land or the gold of kings.
I myself would wear the crown of ages
that any soldier fighting for money can win with his
      spear.
If I could make that beloved voyage across the sea,
50 I would sing "Joy!" and never more "Alas,"
never more alas.

GOTTFRIED von STRASSBURG

(*fl. 1200–1210*)

Gottfried wrote one of the two greatest medieval German romances, *Tristan* (the other being Wolfram's *Parzival*). In the absence of any documentary evidence, a few things about him can be inferred from his work, particularly from one famous passage (*Tristan* 4621–4820) in which he evaluates six German poets, including Heinrich von Veldeke, Hartmann von Aue, Reinmar, Walther, and (presumably, though he does not mention his name) Wolfram. It is clear from this passage that Gottfried flourished in the first decade of the thirteenth century. Gottfried was obviously a highly educated man, well read in theology, law, rhetoric, and the classics, and in contemporary Latin, French, and German literature. The manuscripts refer to him as *meister,* rather than *hêr,* indicating that he was not a noble.

The two *Sprüche* included here are attributed to Ulrich von Lichtenstein in the one manuscript in which they have survived, but a follower of Gottfried, Rudolf von Ems, refers to the second poem, which he closely summarizes, as one that *der wîse meister Götfrit sanc.*

Text: Carl von Kraus, ed. *Deutsche Liederdichter des 13. Jahrhunderts.* 2 vols. I. Text. II. Kommentar, besorgt von Hugo Kuhn. Tübingen: Max Niemeyer, 1952/58.

51

Liut unde lant diu möhten mit genâden sîn
wan zwei vil kleiniu wortelîn 'min' unde 'din,'
diu briuwent michel wunder ûf der erde.
wie gânt si früetende unde wüetende über al
5 und trîbent al die welt umbe als einen bal:
ich wæne ir krieges iemer ende werde.   I
diu vertâne gîte
diu wahset allez umbe sich dâ her sît Êven zîte
und irret elliu herze und elliu rîche.
10 weder hant noch zunge
dien meinent noch enminnent niht wan valsch und
            anderunge;
lêre unde volge liegent offenlîche.

52

Gelücke daz gât wunderlîchen an und abe:
man vindet ez vil lîhter danne manz behabe;
ez wenket dâ man ez niht wol besorget.
swen ez beswæren wil, dem gît ez ê der zît
5 und nimt ouch ê der zîte wider swaz ez gegît.
ez tumbet den swem ez ze vil geborget.   I
fröide gît den smerzen:
ê daz wir âne swære sîn des lîbes und des herzen,
man vindet ê daz glesîne gelücke.
10 daz hât kranke veste:
swenn ez uns under ougen spilt und schînet aller beste,
sô brichet ez vil lîhte in kleiniu stücke.

51

Peoples and nations could live in grace
but for two little words, "mine" and "yours,"
which brew many astonishing things in the world.
How they bring forth rage and advantage everywhere,
5 and toss the world around like a ball:
I do not think they will ever end their wars.   I
Evil covetousness
has spread out from its center since the time of Eve
and harries every heart and every land.
10 No hand or tongue
but loves or means falsehood and inconstancy.
Moral teachings and all the things that follow are glaring
        lies.

52

Fortune goes bewilderingly up and down—
it is easier to find than to hold;
it changes as soon as you take your eye away.
Whomever it wants to burden, it gives to, too soon,
5 and too soon takes back everything it gave.
It makes a man a fool as soon as it lends him too much.   I
Joy forecasts pain:
the affliction of our hearts and bodies never ceases.
There is only fortune, which shatters like glass
10 and has no permanence:
when it is glittering under our eyes and shining like the
            best thing in the world,
that is when it breaks so lightly into pieces.

WOLFRAM von ESCHENBACH

(c. 1170–c. 1220)

Wolfram's birthplace was in Bavaria, most probably in the village now called Wolfram's Eschenbach, near Ansbach. He was of noble rank and served many patrons, including Hermann of Thuringia, in whose court he knew Walther. The approximate dates of his life can be inferred from his works: the great romance *Parzival*, completed in the first decade of the thirteenth century; the religious epic *Willehalm*, and the romance *Titurel*, the latter two written in the following decade and both incomplete.

In a famous passage in *Parzival* he declares that he was illiterate. This is a boast, rather than a confession, and certainly not true: it is Wolfram's quirky way of expressing his pride as a warrior and knight and of subordinating poetry as an avocation, in contrast to those like Hartmann and Gottfried who present themselves primarily as artists and men of learning; it also expresses his determination to treat literary conventions with a free hand. All of Wolfram's works are, in fact, strikingly original, sometimes to the point of eccentricity; Gottfried takes him to task for his "wild stories." His poetry is characterized by numerous innovations in imagery, vocabulary, syntax.

Five of Wolfram's seven extant songs are *Tageliet*, all very beautiful. The first selection here belongs to this group; it is a dialogue, with a concluding narrative strophe, between the lady and the lover's faithful friend who guards them through the night and warns them of the approach of morning. The second poem begins exactly like a *Tageliet*, but in contrast to the fearful and dangerous love one expects to hear about, the second strophe praises the honor and stability of love in marriage.

Text: von Kraus, *Deutsche Liederdichter des 13. Jahrhunderts.*

'Sîne klâwen   durh die wolken sint geslagen,
er stîget ûf mit grôzer kraft,
ich sihe in grâwen   tägelîch als er wil tagen,
den tac, der im geselleschaft
5 erwenden wil, dem werden man,
den ich mit sorgen în bî naht verliez.[1]
ich bringe in hinnen, ob ich kan.
sîn vil mangiu tugent michz leisten hiez.'

I

'Wahtær, du singest   daz mir mange fröide nimt
10 unde mêret mîne klage.
mær du bringest,   der mich leider niht gezimt,
immer morgens gein dem tage.
diu solt du mir verswîgen gar.
daz gebiute ich den triuwen dîn:
15 des lône ich dir als ich getar.
sô belîbet hie der geselle mîn.'[1]

II

'Er muoz et hinnen   balde und âne sûmen sich:
nu gib im urloup, sûezez wîp.
lâz in minnen   her nâch sô verholne dich,
20 daz er behalte êr und den lîp.
er gab sich mîner triuwe alsô
daz ich in bræhte ouch wider dan.
ez ist nu tac: naht was ez dô
mit drucke an brust dîn kus mirn an gewan.'

III

25 'Swaz dir gevalle,   wahtær, sinc, und lâ den hie,
der minne brâhte und minne enphienc.
von dînem schalle   ist er und ich erschrocken ie:
sô ninder morgensterne ûf gienc
ûf in, der her nâch minne ist komen,
30 noch ninder lûhte tages lieht,

IV

---

[1] *bî naht* (6) and *geselle* (16) —von Kraus has selle—restored from MS.

"Its claws have struck through the clouds,
it rises up with great power,
I see it turning gray, like day about to dawn,
I see day, and day will take   I
5 companionship away from him, that worthy man
whom I let in at night with danger.
I shall bring him, if I can, away.
His many virtues made me help him."

"Watchman, what you sing takes my many joys away
10 and makes my sorrows increase.
You bring news I do not welcome
every morning, alas, toward daybreak.   II
You must be still about it, all of it,
I command you on your loyalty;
15 I will make it up to you as well as I can,
just so my friend stays here."

"No, he must go, soon, without delay—
sweet woman, give him leave now.
Let him love you afterwards in secrecy,
20 and keep his life and honor.
He trusted to my loyalty
to bring him out again.
It is day now; it was night then
when you pressed him to your breast, and kissed him, and
            took him from my side."

25 "Watchman, sing what you like and leave him here,
who brought love, and received love.
He and I are always startled by your cry—
yes, when the morning star hadn't risen at all   IV
above him, who came here for love,
30 and not one bit of daylight was shining,

du hast in dicke mir benomen
von blanken armen, und ûz herzen nieht.'

Von den blicken, die der tac tet durh diu glas,
und dô der wahtær warnen sanc,
35 si muose erschricken durch den der dâ bî ir was.
ir brüstelîn an brust si dwanc.   V
der riter ellens niht vergaz
(des wolde in wenden wahters dôn):
urloup nâh und nâher baz
40 mit kusse und anders gab in minne lôn.

54

Der helden minne ir klage
du sunge ie gen dem tage,
daz sûre nâch dem süezen,
swer minne und wîplich grüezen
5   alsô enpfienc,   I
daz si sich muosen scheiden:
swaz du dô riete in beiden,
dô ûf gienc
der morgensterne, wahtær, swîc,
10   dâ von niht langer sienc.

Swer pfligt odr ie gepflac
daz er bî lieben wîbe lac [1]
den merkern unverborgen,
der darf niht durch den morgen
15   dannen streben,   II
er mac des tages erbeiten:
man darf in niht ûz leiten
ûf sîn leben.
ein offen süeze wirtes wîp
20   kan solhe minne geben.

[1] *lieben wibe*—von Kraus has *liebe*—restored.

you have often taken him from me—
out of my white arms, not out of my heart."

Because the light of day was shining through the glass,
as the watchman sang his warning,
35 she was scared, for his sake who lay by her.
She pressed her little breast against his breast.   V
The knight did not forget his prowess,
that the watchman's song wanted to make him forget.
Love's reward was given in a close
40 and closer goodbye, with many kisses, and the rest.

54

You always sang at break of day
the sorrow of hidden love—
the bitter after the sweet:
whoever took love and a woman's greeting
5   in secret   I
must now separate.
Whatever you advised the two of them
when the morning star rose up
then—Watchman, be still about that now,
10   do not sing of it again.

Whoever knows, or ever knew, what it is
to lie with a wife he loves,
with no burrowing when slanderers are near,
that man does not have to steal away
15   when it is dawn,   II
he can wait upon the day—
no need to lead him out
in peril of his life.
Such love is in the giving
20   of the master's honored wife.

NEIDHART von REUENTAL

(*fl. 1210–1237*)

There is no documentary evidence concerning Neidhart's life, but a few things can be said with some certainty. He was born between 1180 and 1190. He went on a crusade either in 1217–1219 or 1228–1229. He had a good patron in Friedrich II of Austria, who gave him a fief in the Tullnerfeld (see no. 59). He mentions Vienna and Melk and several other places in the same region. Political references in his poetry come down to the year 1237.

The problem of interpreting Neidhart has a long history. Is the butt of his satire certain peasants with courtly pretensions; or the extravagances of courtly love, which are made to appear all the more inane in the milieu of the village; or men and women of noble birth who have forsaken the courtly ideal and are therefore like village brutes in courtly costume? A great deal has been made of Neidhart's "realism," especially by those who favor the first interpretation; but, in fact, Neidhart never depicts the realities of village life: his "peasants" engage in activities that could as well characterize debased courtly people: clumsy dancing, vulgar showing-off, violent carousing, drunken brawling.

The most recent and most satisfying interpretation of Neidhart's poetry has been set forth by Renata Karlin.[1] She proposes *niedere Minne* (see above, Introduction to Walther) as the starting point. Walther had already played with the idea that a noble man could enjoy love without having to suffer from the ethical obsessions of *hohe Minne*. When it comes to their final

[1] Renata Karlin, "The Challenge to Courtly Love" (see above, p. 144). See also her unpublished Columbia dissertation, "Scenic Imagery in the Poetry of Neidhart von Reuental," 1966.

view of *niedere Minne* Walther and Neidhart stand together: no truly courtly person could love in that way and still remain courtly. Walther conveys this through the imagery of dreams and the pain of moral uncertainty, and he retreats from *niedere Minne* before he ever really tries it out. Neidhart goes further: suppose courtly people actually love in the way of *niedere Minne,* what becomes of them?

The answer, as it is graphically presented in Neidhart's poetry, is that they become degraded. They do not become more "natural" in the sense that they can love gently and spontaneously, without needing to consult an ethical code: far from becoming free, they simply exchange one morality for another—they come to be ruled by a "village morality" that fosters deception, hypocrisy, and brutality. The values of this new code are not at all unfamiliar to us today: the villagers in Neidhart's poems are very concerned with appearances, for they are all people with hidden intentions; they conceive of marriage as an economic victory, so that the girl is a commodity whose value decreases if she is not a virgin—there are many arguments between daughters eager to dance on the green and their worried mothers; there is, accordingly, a fearful distrust of the senses and of sensual experience, which is, in fact, always depicted as a brutal exploitation of the weak by the strong. In these people sexual desire cannot be distinguished from greed; when longing is not controlled by the desire for money, it leads to plain foolishness— those mothers who caution their daughters would gladly join the dance themselves, except that they are physically unfit (no. 55). Neidhart sometimes depicts the effect of this village morality on himself: his life is plagued by worries about stocking up the larder and having enough things on supply.

Thus Neidhart's "peasants" are courtly people who have betrayed the ideals of their class at every point and have become vulgar and pretentious. They are incapable of self-discipline, tenderness, or communal concern. They have no sense of real nobility and therefore do not know how to behave. They only want to show off their high station and their advantage over others, and they end by turning themselves into caricatures of true courtliness: they use courtly language, words of dignity and praise, but they mean selfish and materialistic things; their dress is loud and inappropriate—they wear arms and armor when they dance; they grab whatever they want, when they want it. There are wonderful details in Neidhart's poems—snarling conversations, vase-breaking gestures, lead-footed merriment. No other poet has so many richly set scenes.

Neidhart's songs are traditionally divided into *Sommerlieder* and *Winterlieder,* depending on the setting in the opening strophes. The *Sommerlieder,* presumably written earlier, usually do not have the tripartite strophe; they are rather closer to native dance songs. The *Winterlieder* have the full formal paraphernalia of the Minnesang, which makes it all the more striking when the unattainable lady whom the poet longs for can be had for the asking by his rivals, who are depicted as clumsy, brutal, dandified peasants.

Neidhart set before the courtly world a perfect picture of its vulgarity and degradation, and he did it all in the name of an exalted and demanding code of human behavior, to which he was deeply committed. He stands among the greatest of the medieval German poets and the most powerful defenders of the courtly ideal.

Text: Edmund Wiessner, ed. *Die Lieder Neidharts.* Altdeutsche Textbibliothek, 44. Tübingen: Max Niemeyer, 1955.

Fröut iuch, junge und alte![1]
der meie mit gewalte
den winder hât verdrungen;
die bluomen sint entsprungen.　　　　I
5　　wie schôn diu nahtegal
ûf dem rîse
in manger wîse
singet wunneclîchen schal.

Walt nu schône loubet.
10　　'mîn muoter niht geloubet,
der joch mit einem seile,'
sô sprach ein maget geile,　　　　II
'mir bunde einen fuoz,
mit den kinden
15　　zuo der linden
ûf den anger ich doch muoz.'

Daz gehôrte ir muoter:
'jâ swinge ich dir daz fuoter
mit stecken umbe den rugge.
20　　vil kleine grasemugge,　　　　III
wâ wilt du hüpfen hin
ab dem neste?
sitze und beste
mir den ermel wider in.'

25　　'Muoter, mit dem stecken
sol man die runzen recken
den alten als eim sumber.
noch hiuwer sît ir tumber　　　　IV
dan ir von sprunge vart.
30　　ir sît tôt

[1] Wiessner has the last three lines of each strophe combined into one.

Young and old, rejoice.
May with its might
has pushed winter out,
the flowers have sprung up.   I
5   How sweetly the nightingale
sings on the branch
in varied notes
its echoing song.

The woods are in beautiful leaf.
10   "My mother can't believe it,"
said a joyous maid,
"but I swear if they tied   II
one foot with a cord,
I still have to go
15   with the kids
to the lime tree on the meadow."

Her mother heard that—
"And I'll strew you your feed
with a stick on your back,
20   you little peewee,   III
where are you hopping to
out of the nest?
Sit down and sew me
my sleeve back on."

25   "Mother, they should use that stick
to beat out the wrinkles
of the old, like a drum.
This year you're an even greater fool   IV
than you were at the start.
30   It doesn't take much

vil kleiner nôt
ist iu der ermel abe gezart.'

Ûf spranc sî vil snelle.
'der tievel ûz dir belle!
35   ich wil mich dîn verzîhen;
dû wilt vil übel gedîhen.'   V
'muoter, ich lebe iedoch,
swie iu troume.
bî dem soume
40   durch den ermel gât daz loch.'

56

Ine gesach die heide
nie baz gestalt,
in liehter ougenweide
den grüenen walt: I
5 bî den beiden kiese wir den meien.
ir mägde, ir sult iuch zweien,
gein dirre liehten sumerzît in hôhem muote reien.

Lop von mangen zungen
der meie hât.
10 die bluomen sint entsprungen
an manger stat,   II
dâ man ê deheine kunde vinden,
geloubet stât diu linde:
dâ hebt sich, als ich hân vernomen, ein tanz von höf-
          schen kinden.

15 Die sint sorgen âne
und vröuden rîch.
ir mägede wolgetâne
und minneclîch,   III
zieret iuch wol, daz iu die Beier danken,

to kill you
if you die from a torn-off sleeve."

And up she sprang in a flash.
"May the Devil bark in your mouth,
35   I give up on you,
you'll come to a bad end."   V
"Yes, Mother, but I am awake,
and you can only dream.
Where there ought to be a sleeve,
40   there's just a hole along the seam."

56

I never saw the field
more beautiful,
or the green woods brighter
and more pleasing to the eyes.   I
5 In both we can pick out May.
Go two by two, you maids,
in this bright summer season, dance the round with joy.

Praise from many tongues
is May's.
10 The flowers are sprung up
in many a place   II
where you could not find one before.
The lime tree stands in leaf.
There, as I have heard, begins a dance of courtly maids.

15 They are free of cares
and rich in joys.
You maids, who are beautiful
and worthy of love,   III
adorn yourselves and let the Bavarians give you thanks,

20 die Swâbe und die Vranken!
  ir brîset iuwer hemde wîz   mit sîden wol zen lanken!

  'Gein wem solt ich mich zâfen?'
  sô redete ein maget.
  'die tumben sint entslâfen;
25 ich bin verzaget.   IV
  vreude und êre ist al der werlde unmære.
  die man sint wandelbære:
  deheiner wirbet umbe ein wîp,   der er getiuwert wære.'

  'Die rede soltû behalten,'
30 sprach ir gespil.
  'mit vröuden sul wir alten:
  der manne ist vil,   V
  die noch gerne dienent guoten wîben.
  lât solhe rede belîben!
35 ez wirbet einer umbe mich,   der trûren kan vertrîben.'

  'Den soltu mir zeigen,
  wier mir behage.
  der gürtel sî dîn eigen,
  den umbe ich trage.   VI
40 sage mir sînen namen, der dich minne
  sô tougenlîcher sinne!
  mir ist getroumet hînt von dir,   dîn muot der stê von
              hinne.'

  'Den si alle nennent
  von Riuwental
45 und sînen sanc erkennent
  wol über al,   VII
  der ist mir holt, mit guote ich im des lône:
  durch sînen willen schône
  sô wil ich brîsen mînen lîp.   wol dan, man liutet nône!'

20 and the Swabians, and the Franks.
Lace your white dresses up with silken ribbons round
your waists.

"Who should I deck myself out for?"
a young maid spoke.
"The fools are asleep.
25 I've given up hope.   IV
Honor and joy couldn't mean less to the world,
men are fickle:
not one courts a lady so she can make him better."

"That's your opinion,"
30 her girl friend said.
"We were meant to have some pleasures as we age.
There are plenty of men   V
still, who gladly serve good women.
So stop talking like that.
35 There's one, for example, courting me, can drive one's
grief away."

"Show him to me,
let's see what I think of him.
The belt I'm wearing
is yours.   VI
40 Tell me his name, the one who loves you
in such secret.
Last night I dreamt you meant to go away from here."

"It's the one they call
von Reuental,
45 whose songs they know
everywhere,   VII
who loves me, and I reward him for it with my grace.
For his sake—come they're
ringing nones—I will tie this belt of yours around my
waist."

57

Kint, bereitet iuch der sliten ûf daz îs!
da ist der leide winter kalt:
der hât uns der wünneclîchen bluomen vil benomen.
manger grüenen linden stênt ir tolden grîs;
5 unbesungen ist der walt: I
daz ist allez von des rîfen ungenâden komen.
mugt ir schouwen, wie er hât die heide erzogen?
diust von sînen schulden val.
dar zuo sint die nahtigal
10 alle ir wec gevlogen.

Wol bedörfte ich mîner wîsen vriunde rât
umbe ein dinc, als ich iu sage,
daz si rieten, wâ diu kint ir vreuden solten phlegen.
Megenwart der wîten stuben eine hât:
15 obz iu allen wol behage,   II
dar sul wir den gofenanz des vîretages legen.
ez ist sîner tohter wille, kom wir dar.
ir sultz alle ein ander sagen.
einen tanz alum die schragen
20 brüevet Engelmâr.

Wer nâch Künegunde gê, des wert enein:
der was ie nâch tanze wê;
ez wirt uns verwizzen, ist daz man ir niht enseit.
Gîsel, ginc nâch Jiuten hin und sage in zwein,
25 sprich, daz Elle mit in gê.   III
ez ist zwischen mir und in ein starkiu sicherheit.
kint, vergiz durch niemen Hädewîgen dâ,
bit si balde mit in gân.
einen site si sulen lân:
30 binden ûf die brâ.

57

Children, get your sleds out for the ice—
bitter Winter's coming on us, with its cold.
He's robbed us of so many lovely flowers.
The once green lindens stand, their tops all gray,
5 the songs have stopped in the woods—   I
all from the hoarfrost's cruelty.
Can you see how it has fallen on the heath,
which Winter's crimes have robbed of color?
And the nightingales
10 have flown away.

With one problem I badly need
my wise friends' counsel, it is this:
let them tell me where the children shall play out their
joys.
Megenwart has a big wide room—
15 Children, if that suits you   II
we'll have the dancing for the holiday right in there.
His daughter wants us to come.
Spread the word around.
Engelmar is setting up
20 a dance around the trestles.

Now, decide who will go for Künegunde,
She always had a fearful urge to dance.
She will upbraid us if we do not let her know.
Gisel, go to Jiute and tell them both,
25 and say that Elle should come along with them.   III
We all agreed on this, the four of us.
Children, don't anyone forget to rouse
Hadewige—ask her to come with them right now.
And tell them to remember not to bind
30 their headdress down over the brow.

Got gebiete den jungen wîben über al,
die der mâze wellen sîn,
daz si hôchgemuoten mannen holdez herze tragen,
ruckenz vorne hôher, hinden hin ze tal,
35 decken baz daz näckelîn.   IV
war zuo sol ein tehtier âne ein collier umbe den kragen?
wîp sint sicher um daz houbet her gewesen,
daz et in daz niemen brach.
swaz in anderswâ geschach,
40 des sints ouch genesen.

Eppe der [1] zuht Geppen Gumpen ab der hant;
des half im sîn drischelstap:
doch geschiet ez mit der riutel meister Adelber.
daz was allez umbe ein ei, daz Ruoprecht vant
45 (jâ, wæn, imz der tievel gap) :   V
dâ mit drôte er im ze werfen allez jenenther.
Eppe der was beidiu zornic unde kal;
übellîchen sprach er: 'tratz!'
Ruoprecht warf imz an den glatz,
50 daz ez ran ze tal.

Hie envor dô stuont sô schône mir mîn hâr,
umbe und umbe gie der spân.
daz vergaz ich, sît man mich ein hûs besorgen hiez:
salz und korn muoz ich koufen durch daz jâr.
55 wê, waz het ich im getân,   VI
der mich tumben ie von êrste in disen kumber stiez?
mîne schulde wâren kleine wider in.
mîne vlüeche sint niht smal,
swanne ich dâ ze Riuwental
60 unberâten bin.

[1] *der:* restored.

Now may God command young women everywhere
who want to be the sort
that bear to valiant men a heart that's kind,
to move it back in front and bring it down behind,
35 and cover the little neck a little more.   IV
What's the sense of a helmet minus a collier, and the neck
          revealed?
Women never had to fear before
that anyone would break their heads.
And if something happened to them in another place they
          have,
40 it healed.

Eppe grabbed Geppe away from Gump,
he used the handle of his threshing flail.
Adelber took a stick and broke it up.
The whole thing started with an egg that Ruoprecht
          found,
45 yes, I swear the Devil gave it to him.   V
He kept threatening to heave it.
Eppe was standing there, angry and bald,
and spiting him—"I dare you," he said.
Ruoprecht got him on his gleaming head
50 and it all ran down.

In times gone by what a head of hair I had,
the curls flowed out all around.
I've let all that go, since I have a house to care for—
the whole year through now I must buy salt and corn.
55 Alas, what did I do to harm the man   VI
who pushed me, ass that I was, into all this grief?
My debts to him were small.
My curses multiply
when I, at home in Reuental,
60 have nothing on supply.

58

Sumer, dîner süezen weter müezen wir uns ânen:
dirre kalte winder trûren unde senen gît.
ich bin ungetrœstet von der lieben wolgetânen.   I
wie sol ich vertrîben dise langen swæren zît,
5 diu die heide velwet unde mange bluomen wolgetân?
dâ von sint die vogele in dem walde des betwungen,
daz si ir singen müezen lân.

Alsô hât diu vrouwe mîn daz herze mir betwungen,
daz ich âne vröude muoz verswenden mîne tage.
ez vervæhet niht, swaz ich ir lange hân gesungen;   II
10 mir ist alsô mære, daz ich mêre stille dage.
ich geloube niht, daz si den mannen immer werde holt:
wir verliesen, swaz wir dar gesingen unde gerûnen, ich
und jener Hildebolt.

Der ist nû der tumbist under geilen getelingen,
er und einer, nennet man den jungen Willegêr:
15 den enkunde ich disen sumer nie von ir gedringen,   III
sô der tanz gein abent an der strâze gie entwer.
mangen twerhen blic den wurfen si mich mit den ougen
an,
daz ich sunder mînes guoten willen vor in beiden ie ze
sweime muose gân.

Wê, daz mich sô manger hât von lieber stat gedrungen
20 beidiu von der guoten unde ouch wîlent anderswâ.
œdelîchen wart von in ûf mînen tratz gesprungen.   IV

58

Summer, now we must live without your sweet weather:
this cold winter gives us grief and longing.
I have no comfort from my dear and beautiful.   I
How shall I pass this long, slow, heavy time
5 that has made the moorland pale, and many lovely
        flowers?
Thus the birds in the woods are driven to forsake their
        song.

My lady has my heart so in her power
I must waste my days without joy.
All that I have sung for so long now—it does no good,   II
10 I could just as well be silent from now on.
I do not think she ever will be kind to any man:
whatever I sing, whatever he whispers, we lose—I and
        that Hildebolt.

Among the merry peasants he is now the biggest fool
        there is,
he and one they call young Willeger—
15 the whole summer long I never could get him away from
        her   III
when the dance went round toward evening in the street.
They gave me many a dirty look with those eyes of
        theirs,
and I always had to take a walk, against my will, when
        they showed up.

What a pity so many have driven me from a place I
        loved,
20 both from my good one and also, before that, another
        place.
It was hateful the way they danced to spite me.   IV

ir gewaltes bin ich vor in mînem schophe grâ.
iedoch sô neic diu guote mir ein lützel über schildes rant.
gern mugt ir hœren, wie die dörper sint gekleidet:
 üppiclîch ist ir gewant.

25 Enge röcke tragent si und smale schaperûne,
rôte hüete, rinkelohte schuohe, swarze hosen.
Engelmâr getet mir nie sô leide an Vriderûne,   v
sam die zwêne tuont. ich nîde ir phellerîne phosen,
die si tragent: dâ lît inne ein wurze, heizet ingewer.
30 der gap Hildebolt der guoten eine bî dem tanze; die
 gezuhte ir Willegêr.

Sagte ich nû diu mære, wie siz mit ein ander schuofen,
des enweiz ich niht: ich schiet von danne sâ zehant.
manneglîch begunde sînen vriunden vaste ruofen;   vi
einer der schrê lûte: 'hilf gevater Weregant!'
35 er was lîhte in grôzen nœten, dô er sô nach helfe schrê.
Hildeboldes swester hôrte ich eines lûte schrîen: 'wê
 mir mînes bruoder, wê!'

Wâ bî sol man mîn geplätze hinne vür erkennen?
hie envor dô kande man iz wol bî Riuwental.
dâ von solde man mich noch von allem rehte nennen: vii
40 nust mir eigen unde lêhen dâ gemezzen smal.
kint, ir heizet iu den singen, der sîn nû gewaltic sî.
ich bin sîn verstôzen âne schulde: mîne vriunde, lâzet
 mich des namen vri!¹

Mîner vînde wille ist niht ze wol an mir ergangen:
wolde ez got, sîn mähte noch vil lîhte werden rât.
45 in dem land ze Oesterrîche wart ich wol enphangen   viii
von dem edeln vürsten, der mich nû behûset hât.²
hie ze Medelicke bin ich immer âne ir aller danc.

¹ Neidhart often mentions his name in the final strophe of his poems. Since
he no longer has any possessions in "Reuental," he would just as soon give
up the name altogether and stop singing.
² Friedrich of Austria (see headnote) .

Because of their violence there is gray in my forelock.
Still, my good one bows her head to me a little, passing
by.
You will love to hear how these villagers are dressed, how
high-class are their clothes.

25 They wear narrow tunics and small cloaks,
red hats, buckled shoes, black hose.
Engelmar never hurt me so with Vriderun   v
as these two did. I envy them the silken pouches
they wear—they have a spice in it called ginger.
30 Hildebolt gave my Good a little of it at the dance;
Willeger grabbed it away.

Now I ought to tell you all about what they created there
with one another,
except that I don't know: I got out of there fast.
They all cried out for their friends.   vi
One screamed loud, "Help, Godfather Weregant!"
35 He must have been in bad trouble, crying out for help
like that.
Once I heard Hildebolt's sister screaming, "O my poor
brother, O!"

How shall anyone recognize my foolish verses any more?
They used to know it by the "Reuental" before.
By right that's what they ought to call me still.   vii
40 What I own and what I get there comes to very little.
Children, ask the man who owns it now to sing to you.
I've been driven out, and through no fault of mine. My
friends, let me be free of that name.[1]

My enemies weren't able to do what they wanted to
against me.
God willing, there may be a way out for me yet.
45 I've been well received in Austria   viii
by the noble prince, who has housed me now.[2]
I am here in Melk, and they don't like that.

mir ist leit, daz ich von Eppen und von Gumpen ie ze
  Riuwental sô vil gesanc.

Rädelohte sporen treit mir Fridepreht ze leide,
50 niuwen vezzel hât er baz dann zweier hende breit.
  rucket er den afterreif hin wider ûf die scheide,   IX
  wizzet, mîne vriunde, daz ist mir ein herzenleit!
  zwêne niuwe hantschuoh er unz ûf den ellenbogen zôch.
  mugt ir hœren, wie der selbe gemzinc von der lieben
    hiuwer ab dem tanze vlôch?

59

Mirst von herzen leide,
daz der küele winder
verderbet schœner bluomen vil:
sô verderbet mich ein senelîchiu arebeit.
5 dise sorge beide
dringent mich hin hinder   I
ze ende an mîner vreuden zil.
owê, daz diu guote mit ir willen daz vertreit,
sît si wol geringen mac
10 alle mîne swære!
owê, gelebte ich noch den tac,
daz sî genædic wære!

Swenne ich mich vereine
unde an si gedenke,
15 wær inder wîbes güete dâ
diune hæte sich sô lange bî ir niht verholn.
sît si lônet kleine
mîner niuwen klenke,   II
wan mag ich dienen anderswâ?
20 nein, ich wil mit willen disen kumber langer doln.

I only regret I ever sang so much about **Eppe** and **Gump**
   at Reuental.

Fridepreht wore jing-a-linging spurs, much to my annoy-
   ance,
50 and he had a new sword-belt on, more than two hands
   wide.
He trailed the loop behind him round the scabbard.   IX
Friends, believe me, that pains my heart.
He drew two brand-new gloves on right up to his elbows.
Would you want to hear how this same jumping buck
   ran from my beloved this year at the dance?

59

There is pain in my heart,
the cold winter
is destroying so many beautiful flowers.
And a great travail of longing is destroying me.
5 These two cares
always thrust me   I
back from my goal of joy.
What sorrow that The Good lets this happen willingly,
for she can make
10 my sorrows small.
Oh, if I could live to see the day
she's kind.

When I go off by myself
and think of her, it seems
15 if the goodness of a woman were in her
it could never have stayed hidden all this time.
Since she gives small wages
for my foolish songs,   II
why shouldn't I serve somewhere else?
20 No! I shall endure this sorrow with a patient will.

waz ob noch ein sælic wîp
gar den muot verkêret?
vreu mîn herze und trœste den lîp!
diu zwei diu sint gesêret.

25 Zuo dem ungemache,
den ich von ir lîde,
sô twinget mich ein ander leit,
daz vor allem leide mich sô sêre nie betwanc,
swiech dar umbe lache
30 und gebâre blîde: III
mir hât ein dörper widerseit
umbe anders niht wan umbe den mînen üppeclîchen
              sanc.
derst geheizen Adeltir,
bürtic her von Ense.
35 zallen zîten drôt er mir
als einer veizten gense.

Hiwer an einem tanze
gie er umbe und umbe.
den wehsel het er al den tac:
40 glanziu schapel gap er umb ir niuwen krenzelîn.
Etzel unde Lanze,
zwêne knappen tumbe,   IV
die phlâgen ouch, des jener phlac.
Lanze der beswæret ein vil stolzez magedîn;
45 eine kleine rîsen guot
zarte er ab ir houbet,
dar zuo einen bluomenhuot:
wer het im daz erloubet?

Owê sîner hende!
50 daz si sîn verwâzen!
die vinger müezen werden vlorn,
dâ mit er gezerret hât den schedelîchen zar!
hiete er ir gebende
ungezerret lâzen,   V

Why couldn't a generous woman
change her mind some day?
May you rejoice my heart and comfort my body,
for both are in distress.

25 Add to the hardship
I suffer from her
another torment oppressing me,
that hounds me more than any other pain,
though I smile through it all
30 and act gay—   III
a peasant has declared himself my enemy
for no other reason than my lordly poetry.
His name is Adeltir,
he came here from Enns.
35 He looks at me menacingly all the time.
He would look like that at a fat goose.

This year at a dance
he went everywhere
making exchanges all day long:
40 he gave bright-colored chaplets for their little garlands.
Etzel and Lanze,
these two bungling boys,   IV
were trying to do the same.
Lanze annoyed a splendid girl.
45 He grabbed a dainty little
kerchief off her head,
and a little garland too.
Who could have stood that?

O his hands!
50 A curse on them,
may he lose the fingers
he grabbed with, doing such damage!
If he hadn't pulled
her headdress apart,   V

55 daz kränzel hiete ouch si verkorn.
   er ist ungevüeger, danne wîlen Engelmâr,
   der gewalticlîchen nam
   den spiegel Vriderûne.[1]
   des bin ich dem dörper gram,
60 dem selben Walberûne.

   Dise alten schulde
   wecket mir diu niuwe:
   ez hât jener getelinc
   hiwer an mir erwecket, swaz mir leides ie geschach.
65 ê ichz langer dulde,
   sêt des mîne triuwe,   VI
   gespringe ich zuo zim in den rinc,
   er bestât sîn buoze, daz er ir ze vrouwen jach,
   der ich lange gedienet hân
70 her mit ganzer stæte.
   wolde er si gerouwet lân,
   wie rehte er danne tæte!

   Wê, waz hât er muochen!
   si kumt im niht ze mâze.
75 zwiu sol sîn pîneclîch gebrech?
   im enmac gehelfen niht sîn hovelîch gewant.
   er sol im eine suochen,
   diu in werben lâze.   VII
   diu sînen rôten buosemblech
80 diu sint ir ungenæme gar, dar zuo sîn hiufelbant.
   enge ermel treit er lanc,
   die sint vor gebræmet,
   innen swarz und ûzen blanc.
   mit sîner rede er vlæmet.[2]

---

[1] The theft of Vriderun's mirror is a frequent theme in Neidhart's poetry. Its meaning is not fully understood, but it is clearly intended to convey the brutality and degradation of the "peasants." For an interesting interpretation, see Renata Karlin, op. cit.

[2] That is, apes the speech of the knights of Flanders, who were considered exemplary.

55 she would have given up the garland, like the others.
He's a bigger ruffian than Engelmar some time ago,
who took the mirror
from Vriderun by force.[1]
For that I am angry at that peasant,
60 that Galoot.

This new violence
makes me remember the old—
that lummox has awakened
in me this year all the wrongs I ever suffered.
65 But I shall suffer it no longer—
I swear—   VI
if I spring upon him in the ring,
he'll pay for claiming her his lady—
whom I have served
70 for so long faithfully.
If he'd leave her alone,
how right he would be acting.

Oh lord, what wild conceits he has.
He does not measure up to her.
75 What does he expect, with his rough tearing-off?
His courtly raiment cannot do him any good.
Let him find some woman
who'll let him court her.   VII
His red breastplate
80 and his hip belt must strike my lady as so many blem-
            ishes.
He wears long narrow sleeves,
trimmed in front,
black inside and white outside,
and when he talks he flemishes.[2]

ULRICH von LICHTENSTEIN

(*1198–1275 or 1276*)

The poet was born in 1198 into a wealthy and important noble
family in Steiermark. He appears in numerous documents between 1227 and 1274, having participated in many military and
political events in his native Austria, most notably the wars
against Hungary, during which Friedrich II, the last Babenberger, was killed in 1246. Ulrich was made Steward (*Truchsess*)
and then Marshall of Steiermark. He died in 1275 or 1276.

Around 1255 he began the work for which he is chiefly known
today, a long verse narrative of his own life, called *Frauendienst*.
The story tells how Ulrich was the page of a noble lady whom he
loved and served faithfully well into his young manhood. He
withdrew his service to her after some mysterious misdeed of
hers, stayed a "free man" for a while, and then dedicated his
service to another lady, with whom he experienced only joy and
smooth sailing. Many historic personages and events appear in
the work, including Friedrich II and the Battle on the Leitha in
which he perished, and also including Ulrich's wife, family and
retainers in his castle on the Frauenberg. Despite all these fac-
tual details, however, the *Frauendienst* is a work of fiction:
Ulrich simply uses details from his own life and times as material
for a romance modeled on the romances of *Parzival* and *Tristan*
and the works of many venerated poets of the classic period.

Far more striking than his adaptations of traditional lyric and
romance themes are the narratives of Ulrich's own devising. On
one occasion he travels through Austria and Italy dressed up as
Frau Venus, all decked out in white samite robes and sporting
two pinned-on golden braids, and challenges all worthy knights
to joust with him, or rather her. People flock to this parade, and
the jokes come flying, especially when Frau Venus sits among

the ladies in church. Another time, Ulrich comes to his lady's castle disguised as a leper, like Tristan, and hides in a ditch to wait for a sign from her. Then he has to endure an unexpected test of his valor, a test that he passes, though in circumstances that do not encourage rejoicing: he manfully keeps still, lying in the ditch, and avoids detection while the lady's steward, pausing on his rounds, unwittingly urinates on him. The work is full of such "adventures," and the comic possibilities are fully realized by Ulrich, who cannot honor the noble traditions of courtly love without mocking them.

These conflicting attitudes and the deliberate inclusion of actual people and events within a literary frame indicate that the "world" of the courtly lyric has changed. That world is no longer the setting of the performance, the situation that unites the singer and his audience. We need only think for a moment of the poets of the early Minnesang—of Heinrich, or Reinmar—to see what Ulrich has done. The earlier lyric was a commemoration of the audience, to whom the singer constantly referred, a notation and an arrangement of the listeners' various perspectives. When we look at Ulrich's songs, we see immediately that this performance situation no longer exists.

Take, for example, no. 61, *Wizzet, frouwe wol getân,* with its interesting rhyme scheme. The man's strophes each have one rhyme, in marked contrast to the lady's, which seem to have no rhymes at all: each line in the first of her strophes rhymes only with the corresponding line in the second strophe. The man speaks poetry, but the lady, in her rhymeless strophe, just seems to talk, and talk straight. He voices the highest ideals of courtly love, she speaks with caution and common sense. This dialogue between the poetic and the prosaic—with the latter having the last word—goes on, in one form or another, through all of Ulrich's work.

The man, like the singers of old, speaks to the glorious lady in his mind. But this time the lady speaks in her own person; she is present, and heartbreakingly ordinary. He speaks from the idealizing viewpoint of "the friends"; but now it is the lady who speaks for "the people." Once the distant beloved gets bored with her enthralling vagueness and decides to put in an actual appearance, taking sensible precautions, the old game is over, the performance has lost its meaning.

The familiar cast of characters, the audience to whom the earlier singers delivered their song, represented many different perspectives; specifically, many different ways of seeing one object, either the lady, or the singer who praised her. Since the lady had no definite character, the way she appeared depended entirely on the character of the beholder. But the moment Ulrich's lady steps into the room, that audience becomes as uncomplicated as she is. She is so definite and practical that she appears the same to everyone, to the noblest and to the most vulgar—indeed, nobility and vulgarity have no meaning in her regard. It is not possible any longer for the singer to speak in many rôles that answer to his listeners' varied demands. She repudiates his attempt to play "courtly lover." He carries on bravely in that rôle, but in the presence of the solid woman he wants to glorify, he can only sound foolish and out of date, until he is finally silenced. With this performer capable of only one rôle, this articulate loved one, and this monolithic audience, the dialectical technique of the classic Minnesang is obsolete, gone for good.

This denigration of the lover suggests that the courtly ideal of devoted service and continual striving has lost its influence. These songs are composed for a world in which comfort and good humor have become the telling marks of a high station, where nobility is felt as an advantage rather than as an ethical obligation—the world of "the people," in short. The old language of devotion has become a source of social platitudes, the great themes are adapted as ground rules for public games and pastimes. The play of courtly love has lost its joyful exclusiveness, it is no longer marked off from the ordinary world—the Venus Journey is international in its range, and everyone participates.

Once the old setting is dissolved, no setting has any meaning any more. The next step in the transformation of the lyric is illustrated, with alarming clarity, in Ulrich's song, *Guot wîp, miner fröiden lêre* (no. 62). This song begins in the old vein, but soon the high Minnesang introduction comes to an abrupt halt, and a coy pornographic fantasy takes the stage. It ends with a great pile-up of arms and legs—a rousing finale to this session of group sex for one. There is a good deal of humor and wit (of a sort) in it: he can only pray to be admitted into the paradise of her heart; but once he gets her image into *his* heart there is no limit to the mastery he exercises or the pleasures he invents.

Whether this steaming dream of erotic revenge, with its weird humor so typical of Ulrich's later songs and of the narrative verses of *Frauendienst,* appeals to anyone is a matter of taste. The important point now is that, after the introduction, the lyric is set entirely within the scaffolding of Ulrich's "heart." The only possible "audience" that can be mentioned is Ulrich himself, who observes an "activity," as he calls it, that is completely interior and impossible to locate on a secular grid.

This withdrawal from the circle of the court into the lover's "heart" still does not wholly account for the development of the later medieval lyric. Something more takes place: that inner life becomes completely objectified, ruled by laws, and its functions can be described in terms of a regular technology. We shall see how this begins when we come to Burkhard von Hohenfels. But Ulrich shows us the first crucial step: the inner life is no longer the center of the lover's responses to experience, responses called forth by the various segments of an objective audience: it is now the very locus of experience, a new setting to replace the one that is gone, the court.

The extent to which the classic Minnesang depended on the presence of an audience can be measured by the extent to which its essential terms are debased in such songs as Ulrich's. *Hôher muot,* as we have seen, was almost synonymous with courtliness itself; it signified both a distinctive form of behavior and an exultant awareness of personal worth. But it cannot have any meaning at all apart from a courtly society, a society that recognizes true adherents in its light. Once the lyric audience disappears, *hôher muot* can signify nothing, least of all a man's right to belong to an ethical community. And so here, in Ulrich's song, it is utterly debased and signifies only Ulrich's own image in a private fantasy.

With this change of setting a new kind of poetry arises, one that depends for its value and meaning on the possibilities of language itself, rather than the performance situation. When the poets used this new setting for the development of figurative language, the results were wonderful—as, for example, in northern France, and particularly (as we shall see) in Italy. But when they continued to use language that made sense only before an attending audience, the results were, as often in German-speaking areas, very bad—and sometimes even grotesque, lacking both humor and seriousness. Ulrich comes off better than most.

Text: von Kraus, *Deutsche Liederdichter des 13. Jahrhunderts.*

In dem walde süeze dœne
singent kleiniu vogelîn.
an der heide bluomen schœne
blüejent gen des meien schîn.   I
5   alsô blüet mîn hôher muot
mit gedanken gen ir güete,
diu mir rîchet mîn gemüete
sam der troum den armen tuot.

Ez ist ein vil hôch gedinge
10   den ich gen ir tugenden trage,
daz mir noch an ir gelinge,
daz ich sælde an ir bejage.   II
des gedingen bin ich frô.
got gebe daz ichz wol verende,
15   daz si mir den wân iht wende
der mich fröit sô rehte hô.

Sie vil süeze, valsches âne,
frî vor allem wandel gar,
lâze mich in liebem wâne
20   die wîl ez niht baz envar;   III
daz diu fröide langer wer,
daz ich weinens [1] iht erwache,
daz ich gen dem trôste lache
des ich von ir hulden ger.

25   Wünschen unde wol gedenken
dest diu meiste fröide mîn.
des sol mir ir trôst niht wenken,
si lâze [2] mich ir sîn   IV
mit den beiden nâhen bî,
30   sô daz si mit willen gunne

[1] *weinens* from L. Von Kraus has *wænens*.
[2] *lâze* from CL. Von Kraus has *enlâze*.

60

In the woods the little birds
sing sweet strains.
On the meadow pretty flowers
blossom in the coming of the light of May.   I
5   So my exultant spirit flowers up
with thoughts of kindness coming
from her who fills my heart with riches—
like the dream that gives wealth to the poor.

There is one high hope
10   I have in her virtues:
the day will come
when I have bliss in her.   II
In this hope I know joy.
God grant I have it to the end,
15   and she does not take away the dream
that rejoices me to the sky.

May she who is sweet, without falsehood
free of imperfection
let me stay in this beloved dream,
20   as long as nothing better comes my way.   III
That my joy lasts long,
that I do not wake in tears,
that I laugh for the comfort I shall have:
these things I look for in her grace.

25   Wishing, imagining happiness
is my greatest joy.
For that way her comfort shall not fail me,
she lets me come close,   IV
in wishes and thoughts, beside her,
30   and so she gives me willingly

mir von ir sô werder wunne
daz si sælic iemer sî.

Sælic meie, dû aleine
trœstest al die werelt gar.
35   dû und al diu werlt gemeine
fröit mich min dann umbe ein hâr.   v
wie möht ir mir fröide geben
âne die vil lieben guoten?
von der sol ich trôstes muoten;
40   wan ir trôstes muoz ich leben.

61

Wizzet, frouwe wol getân,
daz ich ûf genâde hân
herze und lîp an iuch verlân.
daz riet mir ein lieber wân: i
5   durch des rât hân ichz getân
und wil es niht abe gestân.
daz lât mir ze guote ergân.

'Sît ir dienstes mir bereit,
tuot ir daz ûf lônes reht,
10   sô lât mich erkennen daz,
wie der dienest sî gestalt,   ii
den ich mich sol nemen an,
wie der lôn geheizen sî,
der iu von mir sol geschehen.'

15   Frouwe, ich wil in mînen tagen
sô nâch iuwern hulden jagen,
daz ez iu muoz wol behagen,
den muot durch iuch hôhe tragen   iii

of her own noble joy,
that she may be blessed ever more.

Blessed May, you alone
bring comfort to the world.
35   Now you and the whole world together
don't give me a nickel's worth of joy.   v
How could you give me pleasure
without my well loved Good?
I shall go on longing for comfort from her,
40   for the hope of her comfort is my life.

61

My beautiful lady, know
I have put body and heart
in your command to win your grace.
A cherished hope would not be stilled,   I
5   it counseled me, and I obeyed
and shall not turn back.
Let this one hope be fulfilled.

"If you are offering me your service
in order to have a claim to some reward,
10   then tell me exactly
what sort of service it is   II
that I would be taking on,
and what sort of reward
you'd be getting from me."

15   Lady, to the end of my days
I shall struggle for your grace
that my service may please you and win your accord;
and I shall bear my spirit high for you   III

unde an fröiden niht verzagen,
20   iuwer lop der werlde sagen,
und des lônes noch gedagen.

'Sît ir frô, dar zuo gemeit,
mir ze dienest alse ir jeht,
ez gefrumt iuch selben baz
25   danne mich wol tûsentvalt.   IV
tuot daz schamelop hin dan:
mirst der spiegel swære bî,
dar inn ich mîn leit sol sehen.'

Iuwer lop die wirde hât,
30   daz ez wol ze hove gât,
baz dann aller künge wât
âne scham aldâ bestât.   V
'lieber herre, sælic man,
ir sît spotes alze frî.
35   dest unprîs, tar ichs gejehen.'

62

Guot wîp, mîner fröiden lêre,
tugende rîche frouwe mîn,
wizze daz mich jâmert sêre   I
in daz reine herze dîn.
5   dâ solt dû mich hûsen in:
in dem süezen paradîse ich gerne bin.

Dâ hât inne guot gemüete
mit der wîpheit fröiden vil:
dîn vil hôchgelopte güete   II
10   spilt dâ êrenbernde spil
mit den tugenden alle zît.
wol mich, wol, ob mir dîn güete hûs dâ gît.

and not despair of joy one day,
20 and sing the whole world songs in your praise,
and keep silent forever about my reward.

"If it makes you happy and overjoyed
to be in my service, as you say it does,
then it does you a thousand times
25 more good than it does me.   IV
Go away with your praise, it will shame me.
I have only to look in this mirror,
which is painfully close, to see my disgrace."

There is so much honor in the praise I sing,
30 it passes well in court
and belongs there, without shame,
more than the raiment of a king   V
"My dear happy man, my lord,
you're a little too free with your mockery,
35 which is rather nasty, if I may say so."

62

Good woman, bible of my joys,
my lady rich in virtues,
know I ache with longing   I
to enter your pure heart.
5 Give me there a dwelling place:
how gladly I would be in sweet paradise.

There a noble mind
shares many joys with Womanhood;
your goodness, highly praised,   II
10 plays among the Virtues there
in honor, every moment.
What joy, if your goodness gives me lodging there.

Tuo ûf: ich klopf an mit worten.
lâ mich in: sô bistu guot.
15   sliuz ûf schiere mir die porten.   III
bî mir hie ist hôher muot,
der ouch gerne dienet dir.
erst dir holt mit triuwen, daz geloube mir.

Er hât sîn vil wol genozzen,
20   daz er dir ist alsô holt:
ich hân in zuo dir geslozzen   IV
in mîn herze, dâ er holt
wunnebernder fröiden vil.
er tuot dir dâ, liebiu frouwe, swaz er wil.

25   Hôher muot gewan mit wîbe
nie sô mange fröide grôz.
ich hân in bî dînem lîbe   V
ofte funden decke blôz.
dâ kust er wol tûsentstunt
30   dînen kleinvelhitzerôten süezen munt.

Güetlîch triuten, küssen suoze,
drucken brust an brüstelîn,
dise liebe süeze unmuoze   VI
trîbet in dem herzen mîn
35   mit dir, reiniu frouwe guot,
dîn guot friunt, mîn minnegernder hôher muot.

Alse er im ein fröide tihtet
in dem herzen mîn mit dir,
arme und bein er danne flihtet,   VII
40   im und dir, dir unde mir,
hin und her, sus unde sô.
daz tuot herzenlîchen wol und machet frô.

Open, I knock on the gate with my words.
Let me in: that would show you are kind.
15 Quick! unlock the gates for me.   III
I come with my exultant Spirit,
he would also serve you willingly.
Believe this: he stands before you in loyal devotion.

He has known great contentment
20 for loving you so much.
I have locked him up with you   IV
inside my heart, where he gets
so many joyful pleasures.
There he does with you, dear Lady, whatever he wants
     to do.

25 No rejoicing Spirit ever got such
mighty pleasure with a woman.
I have often found him   V
beside you, without a stitch.
There he kissed a thousand times at least
30 your little soft red-hot sweet mouth.

Gentle caressing, sweet kissing,
pressing of breast on little breast,
this dear sweet occupation   VI
your good friend inside my heart,
35 chaste gentle Lady,
carries on with you, my exultant Spirit desiring love.

Thus he makes this pleasure up
inside my heart with you,
he weaves arms and legs together,   VII
40 his and yours, and yours and mine,
like this and like that, hither and hence.
That does the heart good, now that contents.

BURKHARD von HOHENFELS

(*fl. first half thirteenth century*)

The poet's ancestral home was the castle of Hohenfels on Lake Constance, near Überlingen. He was in the entourage of several patrons, beginning with Friedrich II and Heinrich VII and ending with the Bishop of Constance, as many documents dating between 1212 and 1242 testify.

His poetry is characterized by intricate versification and by an intense elaboration of metaphor, which leads inevitably into allegory. These qualities typify the later Minnesang.

In the selection included here, the traditional metaphor of the amorous hunt is considerably elaborated—to a far greater degree than would have occurred among the earlier poets, who would have found such an extended figure in conflict with the tempo of their responses to the various segments of the audience. This metaphor is the basis of the first, second, and fifth strophes. In the fourth, the poet works out a different but related image, that of bird-snaring. In the third strophe, there are two or three other traditional images, such as that of the anchor gripping in the "ground" of the lover's heart.

Altogether, quite a hodgepodge. But even as these metaphors rise up and fall away, the thing that strikes us most is the poet's attempt, in the first two strophes, to convey an illusion of painstaking technical precision. We are invited to ask ourselves the exact meaning of such common words as *herze, muot, sin, gedanke,* and to notice how they are distinguished from each other. In the earlier poetry, these terms never pretended to such precise and mutually exclusive definitions. *Muot,* for example, had a tremendous range of meanings: thought, feeling, will, sense, soul, spirit, mind, mood, disposition, intention. However, the word "heart" had pretty much the same range, as did the other terms that Burkhard uses; and no matter what word was used in any context, most of these meanings were usually relevant.

But we cannot feel this way when we begin Burkhard's song, for each word has taken on the appearance of a technical term. They are all explicitly distinguished from each other, and their relations are specified: the heart does the sending, the sense and the spirit do the hunting, thoughts go before them. And this impression of technical precision is strengthened by the parallel naming of the lady's faculties in the same strophe: "sense" is paired off with "sense," "spirit" with "spirit," "thought" with "thought." The heart seems to be the inclusive term, for it causes the other faculties to issue forth. Finally, this appearance of a complex order is intensified in the second strophe, where each faculty is given what seems to be a defining attribute: thoughts are "quick," sense is "wise," spirit is "strong." Let us not fall for the appearance and actually try to define these terms. It is enough for us to note that they seem to call for definition, they convey a sense of complicated relationships which, far from being familiar and easily understood, require study.

Burkhard gives up on this kind of thing after the first two strophes. After that, when the words *herze* and *muot* occur, they no longer seem to have technical force: in line 26, for example, there would be no semantic loss if any of the other terms were substituted for the word *muot*. Now the metaphors come like Maybugs, short-lived and in disorder. Then, as we are bedazzled by these comparisons, the singer disappears: after the third strophe, we cannot find the first personal pronoun or any personal reference whatever. From that point on, the lyric is no longer about the singer's love but about love itself, as an abstract, universal condition.

What is the effect of this allegorization of the self that Burkhard attempts? The most telling effect is the disappearance of the speaker. When the lover's faculties are turned into rôles, the "I" becomes as multifarious as a situation. It is not possible then for the singer to impersonate a man in love, for he is no longer a discrete figure. His personality is dissolved; he is no longer a man who loves: he is now the condition of love. His inner life becomes, as we saw in Ulrich, the ground of experience, his faculties the agents of experience.

In Burkhard's poem the heart causes sense, spirit, and thought to issue forth to hunt. They go out searching, but their quarry is hard, in fact, impossible, to imagine, for the lady, too, has been analyzed into nonpersonality: the objects sought are her sense, her spirit, her thought. Where does this hunt take place? Not in any secular space, not in any "world"; and no audience can be assumed into this lyric, as in the early period the courtly audience was assumed into each song and became the lyric audience, the friends and enemies of the lover.

Once the performance situation ceases to be the locus of meaning, and the technique of impersonation is no longer appropriate, it becomes necessary to find a new way of ordering the lyric. The poet can no longer use the perspectives of the assembled audience as the unifying principle of his song. He has to compose a lyric that has its own internal coherence, a unity based on its language and no longer dependent on the conditions in which it is performed. And then it follows that the song has to have a different subject matter; it has to express something other than the performer's relation to his audience.

The elaboration of a metaphor into a conceit or an allegory across several strophes is one way of achieving a coherence that is completely verbal. But a metaphor has no secular existence. When it is activated—when "the hunting heart" is equipped with weapons and dogs and pursuers and moves out in search of the quarry—then it needs a setting. For an action must "take place": where there is an action, there must be an encompassing space. Now there is only one possible space for the elaboration of a metaphor, or of any figure of speech, since it exists only in the imagination: its field of action has to be the inner life. And so we can see here, in Burkhard's song, an early example of one of the most characteristic maneuvers of the later medieval and the Renaissance lyric: the elaboration of metaphor to describe the processes of the inner life. Burkhard does it badly here, because he is still using terms that have no meaning apart from an attending audience. But he is responding to a need that all of the later poets felt.

This same need led, around this time, to the appearance of books setting forth the rules of composition for these new songs—books in which the problem of coherence is a prime concern, and which can therefore be very misleading today if they are applied without judgment to the songs of the earlier poets. One of the earliest of these vernacular poetics dealt with the Provençal lyric, the *Razos de Trobar* of Raimon Vidal (before 1240), in which, characteristically enough, the author criticizes a song of one of the greatest of the earlier troubadours, Bernart de Ventadorn, on the grounds that it contained *razons mal continuadas,* themes lacking in continuity.

The need to develop an internal principle of coherence, in the absence of the lyric audience and the old techniques, spurred the creation of wonderful poetry in Italy. To create a language that would be adequate to express the laws of inner experience, the stilnovisti went into new fields, into medicine and science and philosophy, to find their imagery. Cavalcanti really could "demonstrate" the phenomenon of love as a technical and scientific process that took hold in the inner life under celestial influence, apart from any social context whatever.

In general, the later lyric did not do too well in German-speaking areas, where the old courtly language was still considered obligatory. And so the later German poets became masters of a language that had nothing to express.

Text: Carl von Kraus, ed. *Deutsche Liederdichter des 13. Jahrhunderts.*

Mîn herze hât mînen sin
wilt ze jagen ûz gesant.
der vert nâch mit mînem muote.
vil gedanke vert vor in.
5 den ist daz vil wol bekant,   I
daz daz wilt stêt in der huote
bî der, der ich dienstes bin bereit.
ir sin ir muot ir gedenken
kan vor in mit kunste wenken:
10 wol bedorfte ich fuhses kündekeit.

Wie wirt mir daz stolze wilt?
daz ist snel, wîs unde starc.
snel gedenken vert vor winde,
wîser sin bî minschen spilt,
15 sterke in leuwen sich ie barc: II
der gelîch ir muot ich vinde.
ir snelheit mir wenket hôhe enbor,
ir wîsheit mich überwindet,
mit ir sterke sî mich bindet.
20 sus ir schœne tôrte mich hie vor.

Trûren mit gewalte hât
gankert in mîns herzen grunt:
dâ von hôher muot mir wildet.
fröiden segel von mir gât,
25 werder trôst ist mir niht kunt.   III

sist mir in dem muot gebildet,
wol versigelt und beslozzen dâ,
sam der schîn ist in der sunnen.
diu bant hânt die kraft gewunnen,
30 daz siu bræche niht des grîfen klâ.

63

My heart sent my out sense
to hunt a quarry.
It goes, with my spirit, in pursuit.
Many thoughts lead the way.
5   They know quite well   I
the wild quarry lies in the covert
where *she* dwells, whom I stand ready to serve.
Her senses, her spirit, her thoughts
can zigzag past them craftily.
10   I would need the cunning of a fox.

How shall I make the proud quarry mine?
It is quick, wise, and strong.
Swift thoughts fly faster than the wind,
wisdom is at play in the human mind,
15   and the strength of her spirit   II
is like the strength that lies couched in the lion.
Her swiftness eludes me in the air,
her wisdom masters me,
she binds me with her strength.
20   Her beauty has made a fool of me this way before.

Grief lies anchored
gripping in the bottom of my heart,
and the exultant spirit is strange to me,
the sails of joy go far away from me,
25   good comfort is unknown to me.   III

She is imaged in my spirit,
sealed fast, enclosed
like the sun's splendor in the sun.
The bonds have grown stronger,
30   the griffin's claw could not break them apart.

Ir vil liehten ougen blic
wirfet hôher fröiden vil,
ir gruoz der gît sælde und êre.
ir schœne diu leit den stric
35   der gedanke vâhen wil;   IV
des gît sî gedanken lêre
mit zuht, daz irz nieman wîzen sol.
swes gedenken gen ir swinget,
minne den sô gar betwinget,
40   daz er gît gevangen fröiden zol.

Minne vert vil wilden strich
unde suochet triuwen spor:
zuo dem wirte ¹ wil si pflihten.
wunderlîch si liebet sich:
45   si spilt im mit fröiden vor,   V
wunsches wils in gar berihten,
mit gedanken sîm entwerfen kan
wünneclîch in sîme sinne
herzeliep: von dem gewinne
50   scheiden muoz, swer triuwe nie gewan.

¹ *wirte* restored from MS. Von Kraus has *wildrer*.

The look of her brilliant eyes
casts joy before me like a lure,
her greeting brings bliss and honor.
Her beauty lays the trap
35   that is set to catch my thoughts—   IV
but then she teaches them the ways
of courtly breeding, so that no one can reproach her.
The man whose thought soars toward her
is so held fast by Minne
40   that he, a captive, pays the toll of all his joys.

Minne follows a strange track
searching for the trace of Loyalty—
she comes in friendship to the one who fosters it.
She becomes wonderfully pleasant,
45   she plays out his joys before him—   V
she wants to bring forth what he desires,
she can draw with thoughts the image of
his joy upon his senses:
it is a prize no man can win
50   who has not first won Loyalty.

DER WILDE ALEXANDER

(*late thirteenth century*)

The poet did not belong to the noble class, as the title *meister* in one manuscript makes clear. The adjective *wilde* means "wandering," "vagabond": the poet traveled from place to place. His dialect is Alemannic.

He wrote a number of religious lyrics, of which the following is the best and most famous—this is no fond recollection of the simple joys of childhood. The other meaning of the forest, the children, the snake, the warden, etc., can be easily inferred. The conclusion refers to the parable of the five foolish virgins and to the bride's search for the bridegroom in the Song of Songs (5, 6–7).

Text: Carl von Kraus, ed. *Deutsche Liederdichter des 13. Jahrhunderts,* with parts of the following lines restored from J: 1, 4, 9, 15, 21, 23, 39, 42, 46, 47.

Hie bevorn dô wir kinder wâren
und diu zît was in den jâren
daz wir liefen ûf die wisen
von jenen her wider ze disen,   I
5   dâ wir under stunden
vîol vunden,
dâ siht man nu rinder bisen.

Ich gedenke wol daz wir sâzen
in den bluomen unde mâzen
10   welch diu schœnest möhte sîn.
dô schein unser kintlich schîn   II
mit dem niuwen kranze
zuo dem tanze.
alsus gêt diu zît von hin.

15   Seht, dô lief wir ertberen suochen
von der tannen zuo der buochen
über stoc und über stein
der wîle daz diu sunne schein.   III
dô rief ein waltwîser
20   durch diu rîser
'wol dan, kinder, unde gêt hein!'

Wir enpfiengen alle mâsen
gestern, dô wir ertberen lâsen;
daz was uns ein kintlich spil.
25   dô erhôrten wir so vil   IV
unsern hirten ruofen
unde wuofen
'kinder, hie gêt slangen vil.'

Ez gienc ein kint in dem krûte,
30   daz erschrac und rief vil lûte

64

Years ago when we were children
and at an age
where we'd run across the meadows,
from one to another and back,   I
where sometimes
5   we'd find violets—
you see cattle plagued by flies there today.

I remember how we sat
among flowers and compared
10   which one was fairest.
Our childhood shone   II
with the garlands we wore
at the dance.
So the time passes on.

15   See how we ran then looking for strawberries
from the fir to the beech,
over fences and stones,
as long as the sun would shine.   III
Then a man who watched in the woods
20   called through the branches,
"Now, children, go home now."

We all got covered with red spots
yesterday, when we picked strawberries.
To us it was all great fun for children.
25   Then we heard our shepherd   IV
calling loud,
and grieving,
"Children, there are many snakes in there!"

One child went into the high grass
30   and started, and screamed,

'kinder, hie lief ein slang în,
der beiz unser gfeterlîn;　　　　　　　　　　v
daz enheilet nimmer,
ez muoz immer
35　　　sûren unde unsælic sîn.'

Wol dan, gêt hin ûz dem walde!
unde enîlet ir niht balde,
iu geschiht als ich iu sage:
erwerbet ir niht bî dem tage　　　　　　vi
40　　　daz ir den walt rûmet,
ir versûmet
iuch und wirt iuwer vröuden klage.

Wizzet ir daz vünf juncvrouwen
sich versûmten in den ouwen
45　　　unz der künic den sal beslôz?
ir klage unde ir schade was grôz;　　　vii
wante die stocwarten
von in zarten
daz si stuonden kleider blôz.

"Children, a snake's rushed in here
and bit our comrade,   V
and he can't be saved,
he'll be black
35   and sick forever!"

Well then, get out of the woods!
And if you don't hurry soon,
I'll tell you what will happen:
if you don't take care   VI
40   to leave the woods by day,
your joy will turn
to grief, for you will stay too long.

Do you know five virgins
tarried in the meadows,
45   and the king went in to his betrothed
and locked the hall? They were horrified.   VII
The watchman tore
their garments from them,
and they had to stand unclothed.

PART II

Italian Lyrics

Contents

GIACOMO DA LENTINO

(fl. first half thirteenth century)

The poet was a notary in the imperial court of Frederick II in Sicily and is attested in documents between 1233 and 1240; he undoubtedly died before 1250. Dante cites one of his *canzone* for praise in *DVE*, I, 12, but without mentioning him by name and mistakenly considering him an Apulian. Il Notaro, as he is frequently called, is mentioned in a famous passage in *Purgatorio*, XXIV, as the leader of one of the poetic schools surpassed by the *dolce stil novo*.

The court situation under Frederick II was clearly favorable for the continuation of the courtly lyric as it developed among the troubadours. Giacomo was among the first, if not the very first, to write such lyrics in Italian; and his achievement made him esteemed in his own time and continually thereafter. In the following selections the poet's close fidelity to the strophic forms, the themes, and even the vocabulary (*sbaldimento, gabbando,* etc.) of the Provençal lyric is easy to see. In his poetry are found many of the rhythms and rhetorical figures that will characterize Italian poetry throughout the Middle Ages and the Renaissance. No sonnets earlier than his have ever been found, and it has become customary to regard him as the inventor of that form. About forty of his poems are extant.

Text: Bruno Panvini, ed. *Le Rime della scuola siciliana*, vol. I. Biblioteca dell' "Archivum Romanicum," 65. Florence: Leo S. Olschki, 1962; with some minor changes in spelling and punctuation in this and the following selections.

1

Maravigliosamente
un amor mi distringe
e sovenmi ad ogn'ura;
com'om che tene mente
5   in altra parte e pinge   I
la simile pintura,
così, bella, facc'eo:
dentra lo core meo
porto la tua figura.

10   In cor par ch'eo vi porti
pinta como parete,
e non pare di fore.
Anzi m'assembra morti
che non so se sapete   II
15   com io v'amo a bon core;
ca son sì vergognoso
ch'eo pur vi guardo ascoso
e non vi mostro amore.

Avendo gran disio
20   dipinsi una pintura,
bella, a voi simigliante;
e quando voi non vio,
guardo in quella figura,   III
e par ch'eo v'aggia avante;

25   sì com'om che si crede
salvare per sua fede,
ancor non via inante.[1]

Così m'arde una doglia
com'om che ten lo foco

---

[1] That is, he cannot see the object of his faith.

1

Wonderfully
a love holds me bound
and stays now in my thoughts continually;
like a man who keeps his mind
on a distant thing and paints   I
the likeness of his thought:
O Beautiful, I do the same:
inside my heart
I bear your image.

I feel I bear you in my heart
in your painted likeness,
nothing shows outside;
but it is like dying
not to know whether *you* can tell   II
how I love you with an honest heart;
because I am so full of shame
I even look at you from under cover
and do not let you see my love.

Filled with great desire
I painted a picture,
O Beautiful, it was your likeness;
and when I do not see you
I look upon that image,   III
and then it seems I have you before me—

like a man who hopes
to be saved by his faith
in things he cannot see.[1]

A sorrow burns in me,
I am like a man holding fire

30 a lo suo seno ascuso,
    che quanto più lo 'nvoglia
    tando prende più loco   IV
    e non pò stare incluso;
    similmente eo ardo
35 quando passo e non guardo
    a voi, viso amoruso.

    Si 'n corpo quando passo,
    inver voi non mi giro,
    bella, per isguardare,
40 andando, ad ogni passo
    si getto uno sospiro   V
    che mi faci ancosciare.
    E certo bene ancoscio,
    ch'a pena mi conoscio,
45 tanto, bella, mi pare.

    Per zo s'io v'ò laudato,
    madonna, in molte parti
    di bellezze ch'avite,
    non so se v'è contato
50 ch'eo lo faccia per arti,   VI
    chè voi ve ne dolite.
    Sacciatelo per singa [2]
    zo' ch'eo vi dire' a linga,
    quando voi mi vedite.

55 Canzonetta novella,
    va canta nova cosa—
    levati da maitino—
    davanti a la più bella,
    fiore d'ogni amorosa,   VII
60 bionda più ch'auro fino:
    —Lo vostro amor, ch'è caro,

---

[2] That is, by my outward bearing. Panvini has v and vi in reverse order. In lines 20 and 23 he has *pintura* and *figura* in reverse order.

30   hidden in his bosom—
        the more he covers it,
        the more it spreads   IV
        and cannot be contained;
        so I burn
35   when I pass by and keep from looking
        at you, whose face is the face of love.

        If I pass you, face to face,
        I do not turn,
        O Beautiful, to look at you again.
40   Walking on, each step
        I sigh,   V
        which puts me in agony.
        And I am truly deep in agony
        and scarcely know myself,
45   suffering, O Beautiful, has left such marks on me.

        Since I have praised you in great measure,
        my lady, everywhere,
        for the beauty that is yours,
        I don't know if they've come to you
50   with stories that my praises are an artifice,   VI
        for you are aggrieved.
        By the signs on me confirm [2]
        the words I'd speak with my tongue
        when you see me.

55   Canzonetta newly made,
        go and sing this new theme—
        rise up in the morning—
        before the most beautiful,
        flower of all women worthy of love,   VII
60   fairer than purest gold:
        'Your precious love

donatelo al Notaro,
ch'è nato da Lentino.

2

Dolce cominciamento
canto per la più fina
che sia, a mio parimento,
d'Agri infino in Messina;   I
5   cioè la più avenente.
"O stella rilucente,
che levi la maitina,
quando m'apar davanti
li tuo' dolzi sembianti
10   m'incendon la corina."

"Dolce meo sir, se 'ncendi,
or io che deggio fari?
tu stesso mi riprendi
se me ve' favellari
15   ca tu m'ài 'namorata;   II
a lo cor m'ài lanzata,
sì ca di for non pari.
Rimembriti, a la fiata,
quand'io, tebi abrazata . . .
20   a! li dolzi basciari!"

Ed io basciando stava
in gran dilettamento
con quella che m'amava,
bionda, viso d'argento.
25   Presente mi contava,   III
e non mi si celava,
tutto suo convenente;
e disse: "io t'ameraggio,
e non ti falleraggio

give to the Notary,
born in Lentino.'

2

A sweet beginning
I shall sing for the gentlest one
there is, to my eyes,
down from Agri to Messina,
5   the most beautiful—   I
"O shining star
that raises up the morning,
when you rise up before me
the sweet sight of you
10   sets my heart on fire."

"My sweet lord, if you are on fire,
what must I do?
You yourself reproach me
if you see me telling others
15   you made me fall in love;   II
you put a lance through my heart
in a way that no wound shows.
Remember that time
when I, your arms around me . . .
20   ah, the sweet kisses!"

And all the while I was sharing
kisses in great delight
with her who loved me,
she was blond, her brow of silver.
25   Straight out she told me   III
everything she felt,
she kept nothing back,
and said: "I will love you
and not betray you

30   a tutto 'l mio vivente."

             "Al mio vivente, amore,
             io non ti falliraggio
             per lo lusingatore,
             che parla di fallaggio;
35   ed io sì t'ameraggio.   IV
             Per quello ch'è salvaggio,
             Dio li mandi dolore!
             Unqua non vegna a maggio! [1]
             tant'è di mal usaggio,
40   che di stat' à gelore."

                        3

        Io m'aggio posto in core a Dio servire,
        com'io potesse gire in paradiso,
        lo santo loco, ch'aggio audito dire
        si mantiene sollazo, gioco, e riso.

 5   Sanza mia donna non vi vorria gire,
        quella c'à blonda testa e claro viso,
        chè sanza lei non poteria gaudire,
        estando de la mia donna diviso.

        Ma no lo dico a tale intendimento
10   perch'io peccato ci volesse fare,
        se non veder lo suo bel portamento,

        lo bel viso e lo morbido sguardare:
        chè lo mi terria in gran consolamento,
        veggendo la mia donna in gloria stare.

[1] The time for festivals and rejoicing. The assignment of the speeches—a difficult matter—here differs from Panvini.

30   my whole life.

        "Love, my whole life
        I will not betray you,
        for all those evil tongues
        that lisp such treachery;
35   and I will love you   IV
        despite that brute.
        God send him diseases,
        let him never come in May—[1]
        that man is so unfit,
40   in summer he freezes."

3

I have set my heart to serving God
that I may go to Paradise,
the holy place, where, as I have heard,
there is always sweet conversation, play, and laughter.

5 I would not want to go without my lady,
   without my lady of the fair hair and clear brow,
   for without her I could know no joy,
   being cut off from my lady.

   But I do not say this in the sense
10 that I would want to commit a sin;
   but only to see her beautiful bearing,

   that beautiful face and soft gaze turned on me:
   for I would stay eternally content
   to behold my lady standing there in glory.

4

Lo bascilisco a lo spleco lucente
traggi a morire cum risbaldimento,
lo cesne canta plù gioiosamente
quand'egli è presso a lo so finimento,

5   lo paon turba, istando plù gaudente,
cum a soi pedi fa riguardamento,[1]
l'augel fenice s'arde veramente
per ritornare in novo nascimento.

In tai nature eo sentom'abenuto,
10   chi allegro vado a morte a le belleze,
e 'nforzo 'l canto presso a lo finire,

estando gaio torno dismarruto,
ardendo 'n foco inovo in allegreze,
per vui, plù gente, a cui spero redire.

5

Chi non avesse mai veduto foco,
no crederia che cocere potesse,
anti li sembraria sollazzo e gioco
lo so isprendore, quando lo vedesse.

5   Ma, s'ello lo toccasse in alcun loco,
ben li sembrara che forte cocesse:

---

[1] According to the bestiaries, the peacock was embarrassed about his feet, which were not, he thought, as lovely as the rest of him. The attribution of this lyric is not certain. Text: Carlo Salinari, *La Poesia lirica del Duecento*. Turin: Unione Tipografico—Editrice Torinese, 1951.

4

The basilisk before the shining mirror
dies with pleasure;
the swan sings with greatest rapture
when it is nearest death;

5 at the height of its pleasure the peacock
gets upset when it looks at its feet; [1]
the phoenix burns itself all up
to return and be reborn.

I think I have become much like these creatures,
10 I who go gladly to death before her beauty
and make my song lusty as I approach the end;

in merriment I suddenly despair,
burning in fire I am made new again in joy
because of you, whom I long to return to, gentlest one.

5

A man who had never seen fire before
would never think that it could burn;
rather, its splendor would strike him,
when he first saw it, as a delight, great fun.

5 But if he ever touched it anywhere,
then it would seem to him it burned—and bad.

quello d'amore m'à toccato un poco:
molto me coce. Deo, che s'apprendesse!

Che s'apprendesse in voi madonna mia,
10   che mi mostrate dar sollazzo amando,
e voi mi date pur pen' e tormento:

certo l'Amore fa gran villania,
che no distringe te, che vai gabbando;
a me, che servo, non dà isbaldimento.

The one that belongs to Love has touched me a little:
it burns me a lot. God, if it only took hold!

if it only took hold in you, my lady,
10 who make me think you mean to comfort me by loving me
and give me only torments and distress.

Certainly Love acts ignobly,
for he does not tie you down who come forth only with words;
I serve. Yet he gives me no happiness.

PIER DELLA VIGNA
(*1180–1249*)

Pier was born in Capua, apparently in modest or humble circumstances. He studied at Bologna and entered the court of Frederick II as a scribe. He soon became a favorite of the Emperor and one of his most trusted counselors. He became a notary in 1220, a judge in 1225, and Chancellor in 1249, by which time he was one of the most powerful statesmen in Europe. In 1249, for reasons unknown, he was accused of treason and imprisoned. It is said that in prison, overwhelmed by grief, he ended his life.

Dante had many reasons for championing his memory—his culture and eloquence, as they are evidenced not only in his poetry but in his other writings, especially his letters; and most of all his efforts in Frederick II's struggle against the Papacy. In *Inferno,* XIII, the soul of Pier della Vigna, forever imprisoned in the trunk of a tree in the circle of the suicides, utters magnificent words of loyalty and vindication. The elegance and rhetorical complexity of Pier's lyrics reflect his culture and

Text: Panvini.

Amore, in cui disio ed ò speranza,
di voi, bella, m'à dato guiderdone;
guardomi, infin che vegna, la speranza,
pur aspettando bon tempo e stagione.   I
5 Com'om ch'è in mare ed à spene di gire,
quando vede lo tempo ed ello spanna,
e giammai la speranza no lo 'nganna,
così faccio, madonna, in voi venire.

Or potess'eo venire a voi, amorusa,
10 come lo larone ascoso e non paresse:
ben lo terria in gioia aventurusa,
se l'Amor tanto bene mi facesse.   II
Sì bel parlante, donna, con voi fora,
ed ameraggio infin ch'eo vivo ancora.
e direi como v'amai lungiamente,
15 più ca Piramo Tisbia dolzemente,

Vostro amor è che mi tene in disiro,
ch'eo non curo s'io doglio od ò martiro,
e donami speranza con gran gioi,
20 membrando l'ora ched io vegno a voi.   III
Ca s'io troppo dimoro, par ch'io pera,
aulente lena, e voi mi perderete.
Adunque, bella, se ben mi volete,
guardate ch'io non mora in vostra spera.

25 In vostra spera vivo, donna mia,
e lo mio core adesso a voi dimanda,
e l'ora tardi mi pare che sia
che fino amore a vostro cor mi manda.   IV
Guardo tempo che vi sia a piacimento
30 e spanda le mie vele in ver voi, rosa,

6

Love, in whom I have my hope and desire,
has rewarded me, o beautiful, in you;
I keep watch for this hope, it is coming,
and always I await good weather and season.   I
5   As a sailor has hopes of setting out
when he sees the weather is right, and he sets his sails,
and that hope never deceives him—
so I prepare, my lady, to come to you.

If only I could come to you, o worthy of love,
10   under cover, like a thief, unseen:
I'd think, rejoicing, it was good luck
if Love did this great thing for me: II
once with you, lady, I'd be so eloquent
and tell you how I have loved you long,
15   more sweetly than Piramus his Thisbe,
and will love you all the while I live.

It is love of you that keeps me full of desire
and gives me hope, which gives me joy,
because I do not care if I am troubled and tormented
20   remembering the time when I shall come to you.   III
If I must wait too long, I think I shall perish,
o fragrant breath, and you will lose me.
Therefore, o beautiful, if you wish me well,
take care I do not die in hope of you.

25   In hope of you I live, my lady,
and give my heart into your hands forever,
and I think there is left but little time
for true love to bring me to your heart.   IV
And I watch for the moment of your pleasure,
30   when I may set my sails toward you, o rose,

225

e prenda porto là ove si riposa
lo meo core a lo vostro insegnamento.

Mia canzonetta, porta esti compianti
a quella c'à 'n ballia lo meo core,
35   e le mie pene contale davanti,
e dille com'eo moro per suo amore,   v
e mandimi per suo messaggio a dire
com'io conforti l'amor ch'in lei porto;
e s'io ver lei feci alcuno torto
40   donimi penitenza a suo volire.

and come to port where, in your gentleness
my heart finds its repose.

My Canzonetta, carry these complaints
to her who has my heart in power,
35 and speak before her of my sufferings,
and tell her how I die for love of her;
and let her send me a messenger, to tell
how I may comfort my love for her:
and if I ever did her any injury,
40 let her give me penance at her will.

V

RINALDO D'AQUINO

(first half thirteenth century)

Many attempts have been made to identify this poet, but none
have had certain success. He might have belonged to the family
of Saint Thomas, might even have been his brother; he might
also have been a page and falconer of Frederick II. Dante twice
cites one of his *canzone* (*Per fin' amore vao sì allegramente*) in
DVE (I, xii; II, v) ; but Rinaldo wrote better poems than that
one. Staying close, like the others of the Sicilian school, to the
Provençal models, he shows considerable skill in his handling
of the traditional forms and themes.

Text: Panvini.

7

Già mai non mi conforto   6
nè mi voglio rallegrare.
Le navi sono giute a porto
e vogliono colare.   I
5   Vassene lo più gente
in terra d'oltramare,
ed io, lassa, dolente,
como deggio fare?

Vassene in altra contrata
10   e no lo mi manda a diri,
ed io rimagno ingannata;
tanti sono li sospiri   II
che mi fanno gran guerra
la notte co la dia.
15   Nè 'n cielo ned in terra
non mi par ch'io sia.

Santus, Santus, Santus Deo,
che'n la Vergine venisti,
salva e guarda l'amor meo
20   poi da me lo dipartisti.   III
Oit alta potestade
temuta e dottata,
la mia dolze amistade
ti sia acomandata.

25   La croce salva la gente
e me face disviare.
La croce mi fa dolente,
e non mi val Dio pregare.   IV
Oi croce pellegrina,
30   perchè m'ài sì distrutta?
Oi me, lassa, tapina,
chi ardo e 'ncendo tutta.

7

I shall never more take comfort,
I do not want to know joy again,
the ships have reached their port,
they are gone.   I

5   The gentlest man is going away
to a land beyond the sea.
Alas, I, weary, sorrowing,
what must I do?

He is going away to another country,
10   and does not send to let me know,
and I stay on back here, deceived.
How many are the sighs   II
at war in me
night and day.
15   I don't feel in heaven, or
on earth.

Holy, Holy, Holy God,
who came to us in the Virgin,
watch over my love,
20   for you parted him from me.   III
O high, dread,
fearful Power,
my sweet love
be in your care.

25   The cross saves humanity
and makes me lose the way.
The cross fills me with grief,
I get no help praying to God.   IV
O pilgrim cross,
30   why have you destroyed me?
Alas, weary, wretched,
I burn and am all consumed.

Lo 'mperadore con pace
tutto lo mondo mantene,
35   ed a me guerra face,
chè m'à tolta la mia spene.   V
Oit alta potestate
temuta e dottata,
la mia dolze amistate
40   vi sia acomandata.

Quando la croce pigliao,
certo no lo mi pensai,
quelli che tanto m'amao;
ed illu tanto amai   VI
45   chi eo ne fui battuta,
e messa in pregionia,
e in celata tenuta
per la vita mia.

Le navi sono collate,
50   in bonor possan andare,
con elle la mia amistate
e la gente che v'à andare.   VII
Oi Padre criatore,
a porto le conduci,
55   che vanno a servidore
de la santa cruci.

Però ti priego, Duccetto,[1]
che sai la pena mia,
che me ne faci un sonetto
60   e mandilo, in Soria,   VIII
ch'io non posso abentare
la notte nè la dia.
In terra d'oltre mare
sta la vita mia.

---

[1] Panvini suggests this term of endearment derives from the poet's name:
"Rinaldo-Rinalduccio-Rinalduccetto-Duccio-Duccetto."

The Emperor keeps
the whole world in peace
35 and makes war on me,
he has taken my hope away. V
O high, dread,
fearful Power,
my sweet love
40 be in your care.

When he took the cross
I surely never expected it,
he loved me so much;
and I loved him so much VI
45 I was scourged for it
and put in a dungeon
and kept in darkness
for all my life.

The ships have vanished,
may they go with luck,
and my love with the others,
and all who are to go. VII
O Father Creator,
lead them to safe port,
55 for they go in the service
of Your holy cross.

And I beg you, my Duccetto,[1]
who know my grief,
write a song of this for me
60 and send it when you are in Syria. VIII
For I cannot rest
night or day.
My life is now
in a land beyond the sea.

8

Amorosa donna fina,
stella che levi la dia
sembran le vostre bellezze.
Sovrana fiore di Messina!
5   Non pare che donna sia
vostra para d'adornezze.   I
Or dunque non è maraviglia
si fiamma d'amor m'appiglia
guardando lo vostro viso,
10 che l'amor m'infiamma in foco.
Sol ch' i'o vi riguardo un poco,
levatemi gioco e riso.

Gioco e riso mi levate,
membrando tutta stagione
15 che d'amor vi fui servente,
nè de la vostra amistate
non eb'io anche guiderdone,
se no un bascio solamente.   II
Quello bascio m'infiammao,
20 chè dal corpo mi levao
lo core e dedilo a vui.
Deggiateci provedere:
che vita po l'omo avere,
se lo cor non è con lui?

25 Lo meo cor non è co' mico,
ched eo tutto lo v'ò dato;
e ne son rimaso in pene:
di sospiri mi notrico,
membrando da voi so errato,
30 ed io so perchè m'avene: III
per illi sguardi amorosi

8

Gentle lady bearing love,
the star that raises up the day
is like your beauty.
Sovereign flower of Messina!
5   No lady in sight can be
your equal in loveliness.   I
Therefore it is no wonder
if the fire of love takes hold in me
when I look at your face,
10   for love ignites me into flame.
If I cannot have some sight of you,
you take away my joy and laughter.

My joy and laughter you take away
from me remembering always
15   I have been your servant in love
and have as yet had no reward
from your friendship . . .
well, one kiss only.   II
That kiss inflamed me,
20   lifted the heart
out of my body and gave it to you.
You should have foreseen:
what life can a man have
if the heart is no longer with him?

25   My heart is no longer with me,
I have given it over to you
and no longer move away from pain:
I feed on sighs,
am martyred remembering you;
30   and I know why this befalls me: III
it is those looks of love

che, savete, sono ascosi
quando mi tenete mente;
chè li sguardi micidiali
35   voi facete tanti e tali,
che aucidete la gente.

Altru aucidete che meve,
chè m'avete in foco miso
che d'ogne parte m'alluma.
40   Sutto esto manto di neve,[1]
di tal foco so' racciso
che mai non me ne consuma: IV
d'uno foco che non pare,
che'n la neve fa 'llumare,
45   ed incende tra lo ghiaccio.
Quell'è lo foco d'amore,
ch'arde lo fino amadore
quando ello non à sollaccio.

Lo sollazzo non avesse,
50   se non di voi lo sembiante
con parlamento isguardare,
a gran gioi quando vollesse;
perchè pato pene tante
ch'io non le poria contare.   V
55   Ned a null'omo che sia
la mia voglia non diria,
dovesse morir penando:
se non estu Montellese,[2]
cioè lo vostro serventese,
60   a voi lo dica in cantando.

[1] That is, beneath this appearance of indifference: the lover must conceal this
feelings before the world (Santangelo, Panvini).
[2] This man from Montella; probably the poet.

which, you know well, stay under cover
when you notice me;
because you design
35   those lethal looks
to murder people.

Murder the others, not me!
for you have put me in the fire
that engulfs me.
40   Beneath this mantle of snow [1]
I am lighted with a fire
that does not yet consume me: IV
with a fire that does not show,
that lights up in the snow
45   and burns in the midst of ice.
That is the fire of love,
that burns the true lover
when he has no comfort.

I could have no comfort
50   if I could not gaze
on the image of you and speak,
with great joy, as I desired;
because I endure more pains
than I could tell about.   V
55   Nor would I tell a living
man of my desire,
I should die suffering
—unless this Montellese,[2]
this servant of yours,
60   should tell you about it in song.

9

Ormai quando flore   e mostrano verdura [1]
le prate e la rivera,
li auselli fanno isbaldore   dentro de la frondura
cantando in lor manera,   I
5 infra la primavera   che ven presente
frescamente   così frondita,
ciascuno invita   d'aver gioia intera.

Confortami d'amore   l'aulimento dei fiori
e'l canto de li auselli.
10 Quando lo giorno appare   sento li dolci amori
e li versi novelli   II
che fan sì dolci e belli   e divisati
lor trovati   a provasione;
a gran tenzone   stan per li arbuscelli.

15 Quando l'aloda intendo   e'l rusignuol vernare,
d'amor lo cor m'afina,
e magiormente intendo   ch'è legno d'altr'affare,
che d'arder no rifina.   III
Vedendo quell'ombrina   del frescho bosco,
20 ben cognosco   ca acortamente
serà gaudente   l'amor che m'inchina.

China, ch'eo sono amata   e giammai non amai;
ma 'l tempo mi 'namura
e fami star pensata   d'aver merzè ormai
25 d'un fante che m'adura,   IV
e sacio che tortura   per me sostene
e gran pene. L'un cor mi dice
che si disdice,   e l'altro m'incora. [2]

[1] The first and third lines of each strophe are each set as single lines in Panvini.

[2] Panvini amends *mincora* to *mi sicura* and translates: "On the one side my heart tells me this is not proper, on the other it reassures me."

9

Now when meadow and bank[1]
show green and flower,
the birds are merry in branches,
singing in their way   I
5 amidst the spring, which comes now
all new, so in leaf,
invites each one to perfect joy.

I am encouraged to love by the scent of the flowers
and the song of the birds.
10 At daybreak I hear their sweet loves
and the new songs   II
they make so sweet and beautiful, and their varied
lyrics in contest—
they have a great rivalry all through the bushes and
          shrubs.

15 When I hear the lark and the nightingale voicing the
          spring,
my heart is made perfect for love;
and I see more clearly it is wood of a different kind,
for it never stops burning.   III
Seeing that soft shade in the tender grove
20 I know very soon
rejoicing will come to the love that bends me.

Bends me, for I am loved and have never loved,
but the season fills me with love
and makes me think of taking pity now
25 on a young man that adores me   IV
and I know stands torture
and great pain for me. One heart tells me
to refuse, the other gives me heart.[2]

Però prego l'Amore   che m'intende e mi svoglia
30 come la foglia vento,
che no mi facia fore   quel che presio mi toglia,
e stia di me contento.   v
Quelli c'à intendimento   d'avere intera
gioia e cera   del mio amore
35 senza romore,   nonde à compimento.

So I pray Love, who fills me with desire and makes me
     shake,
30 as the wind the green leaf,
do not carry me away, which would debase me,
and be content with me.   V
The one that longs to have the perfect
pleasure and the welcome of my love
35 in secret, is not yet at the goal.

GIACOMINO PUGLIESE

(first half thirteenth century)

Various attempts to identify Giacomino have not been convincing; in fact, they have almost certainly been all wrong. He was apparently not renowned as a poet in his own time. In the themes and verse forms that he cultivated, he clearly belongs to the Sicilian school.

Text: Panvini.

10

Morte, perchè m'ài fatta sì gran guerra,
che m'ài tolta madonna, ond'io mi doglio?
La fiore de le belleze mort'ài in terra,
per che lo mondo non amo nè voglio.
5 Villana morte, che non ài pietanza,   I
disparti amore e tolgli l'allegranza
e dài cordoglio.
La mia allegranza post'ài in gran tristanza,
chè m'ài tolto la gioia e l'allegranza
10 c'avere soglio.

Sollea aver sollazo e gioco e riso
più che null'altro cavalier che sia;
or se n'è gita madonna in paradiso,
portòne la dolze speranza mia,
15 lasciòmi in pene e con sospiri e planti,   II
levòmi de sollazo, gioco e canti
e compagnia.
Or no la veggio nè le sto davanti,
e non mi mostra li dolzi sembianti
20 che solia.

Oi Deo, perchè m'ài posto in tale iranza?
Ch'io son smarruto, non so ove mi sia,
chè m'ài levata la dolze speranza,
partit'ài la più dolza compagnia,
25 che sia in nulla parte, ciò m'è aviso.   III

Madonna, chi lo tene lo tuo viso
in sua ballia?
Lo vostro insegnamento e dond'è miso?
E lo tuo franco core chi mi l'à priso,
30 madonna mia?

10

Death, why have you made so great a war against me?
For you took my lady from me, and now I grieve.
You have killed the flower of all beauty on earth,
and now I love this world no more and want no part
       of it.
5 Brutal Death, you have no pity,   I
you break love in two and remove joy
and bring sorrow to the heart.
You turned my joy to sadness,
you bore away the joy and pleasure
10 I used to have.

I used to have sweet discourse, joy, and laughter,
more than any knight alive.
Now my lady is gone to Paradise
and took away with her that sweet hope of mine
15 and left me here in griefs and sighs and tears   II
and wrested me away from joy, discourse, songs,
the company.
Now I do not see her, or stand before her,
and she does not look tenderly upon me
20 as she used to.

O Lord, why have you put me in such despair?
I am confused, do not know where I might be,
because you took away my one sweet hope
and parted the sweetest friendship
25 in the world, I know.   III

My lady, who has the sight of you
in his power?
And your gentleness, where has it been taken?
And who has deprived me of your great heart,
30 my lady?

Ov'è madonna e lo suo insegnamento,
la sua belleza e la gran canoscianza,
lo dolze riso e lo bel portamento,
gli occhi e la bocca e la bella sembianza,
35 lo adornamento e la sua cortesia?   IV
Madonna, per cui stava tuttavia
in allegranza,
or no la veggio nè notte nè dia,
e no m'abella, sì com far solia
40 in sua sembianza.

Se fosse mio lo reame d'Ungaria,
con Greza e Lamagna infino in Franza,
lo gran tesoro di Santa Sofia,
non poria ristorar sì gran perdanza,
45 come fu in quella dia che si n'andao.   V
Madonna, d'esta vita trapassao,
con gran tristanza
sospiri e pene e pianti mi lasciao,
e giammai nulla gioia mi mandao
50 per confortanza.

Se fosse al meo voler, donna, di voi,
dicesse a Dio sovran, che tutto face
che giorno e notte istessimo ambonduoi.
Or sia il voler di Dio, da c'a Lui piace.
55 Membro e ricordo quand'era co mico,   VI
sovente m'apellava dolze amico—
or no lo face,
poi Dio la prese e menolla con sico:
la sua vertute sia, bella, con tico
60 e la sua pace.

Where is my lady, her gentleness,
her beauty and great wisdom,
her sweet smile and lovely bearing,
her eyes, her mouth, her beautiful presence,
35 her grace and courtliness? IV
My lady, through her I always dwelt
with joy—
I do not see her now, not by day, not by night,
and do not, as I used to once, delight
40 in her presence.

If I got the kingdom of Hungary,
and Greece and Germany all the way to France,
the great treasure of Santa Sophia,
it could not make good the great loss
45 that happened the day my lady went V
away, passed beyond this life.
In the company of sadness,
sighs and pains and tears she left me,
and never again sent down joy
50 to comfort me.

If it were with you as I desire, my lady,
I would tell our sovereign God, who can do all,
that we must be together always, night and day.
Let it be as God wills, for so it pleases Him.
55 I remember and go over the time when she was with me, VI
she often called me Sweet Friend—
she does not do it now,
since God took her and led her away with him.
His power be, O beautiful, with you,
60 and His peace.

GUIDO DELLE COLONNE

(born c. 1210)

Guido was a judge in Messina from 1243 to 1280. He is probably the same man as the author of the *Historia Trojana,* also called *Historia Destructionis Troiae,* a Latin prose paraphrase of the *Roman de Troie* by Benoît de Sainte Maure. Guido's *Historia,* completed in 1287, was much admired by Geoffrey Chaucer, to whom it proved a useful source on many occasions. The poet Guido is praised by Dante, who cites three of his *canzone* (among them the one included here) in *DVE* (I, xii; II, v, vi). He was a master of rhetorical forms in the lofty style; and, as Contini points out, his use of scientific imagery to explain the phenomenon of love is directly echoed by Guinizelli.

Text: Panvini, who has lines 2, 5, 7, 9, 10, 11, and 12 in every strophe as two single lines, each divided where the caesura appears here.

11

Anchor che l'aigua per lo foco lassi
la sua grande freddura,   non cangeria natura
s'alcun vasello in mezzo non vi stassi;
anzi avverria senza lunga dimura
5 che lo foco astutassi   o che l'aigua seccassi,
ma per lo mezzo l'uno e l'autra dura.
Cusì, gentil criatura,   in me à mostrato Amore   I
l'ardente suo valore:
che sensa amore   era aigua fredda e ghiaccia,
10 ma amor m'à allumato   di foco che m'abbraccia,
ch'eo fora consumato,   se voi, donna sovrana,
non fustici mezzana   infra l'Amore e meve,
ca fa lo foco nascere di neve.

Imagine di neve si po diri
15 om che no ha sentore   d'amoroso calore:
ancor sia vivo non si sa sbaudiri.
Amor è uno spirito d'ardore
che non si po vediri,   ma sol per li sospiri
si fa sentire in quello ch'è amadore.
20 Cusì, donna d'aunore,   lo meo gran sospirare   II
vi poria certa fare
de l'amorosa flamma und'eo so involto.
E non so com'eo duro,   sì m'ave preso e tolto.
Ma parm'esser siguro: che molti altri amanti
25 per amor tutti quanti   funo perduti e morti,
che non amaro quant'eo, nè sì forti.

Eo v'amo tanto che mille fiate
in un'or mi s'arranca   lo spirito, che manca
pensando, donna, le vostre beltate.
30 E lo disio c'ò lo cor m'abbranca
crescemi volontate,   mettemi in tempestate
ogni penseri, che mai non si stanca.

11

Though water relinquishes through fire
its deep coldness, its nature would not change so
if some vessel did not stand between;
otherwise the fire quickly
5 would die, or the water dry;
but through the medium each one endures.
Just so, gentle lady, love has revealed in me   I
its power to burn:
without love I was cold water and ice,
10 but love lit me up with a fire that embraced me,
and I would have been consumed, if you, sovereign lady,
had not been intermediary there, between Love and me,
for Love brings forth fire out of snow.

He can be called a picture of snow
15 who does not feel the heat of love:
he may be alive but does not know what joy is.
Love is a fiery spirit
that cannot be seen, but only through sighs
makes itself felt—in one who loves.
20 Just so, lady whom I honor, my great sighing   II
should make you certain
the fire of love envelops me.
And I do not know how I endure, it has so caught hold
       in me.
But I know this: many other lovers
25 have been destroyed by love, and slain,
who did not love as long as I, or with such passion.

And I love you so much, a thousand times
an hour my spirit is pulled away, faints,
thinking, lady, of your beauty.
30 And desire in my heart lays hold of me,
makes my love grow greater, and my thoughts never
       weary
and every thought puts me in a storm.

O colorita e blanca   gioia, de lo meo bene   III
speranza mi mantene,
35 e s'eo languisco, non posso morire;
ca, mentre viva sete,   eo non poria fallire,
ancor che fame e sete   lo corpo meo tormenti;
ma sol ch'eo tegna menti   vostra gaia persona,
obbrio la morte, tal forza mi dona.

40 E non credo che sia quel ch'avia
lo spirito che porto, ched eo fora già morto,
tant'ò passato male tutta via.
Lo spirito chi aggio, und'eo mi sporto,
credo lo vostro sia,   che nel meo petto stia
45 e abiti con meco in gran gioi e diporto.
Or mi son bene accorto,   quando da voi mi venni,   IV
che quando mente tenni
vostro amoroso viso netto e chiaro,
li vostri occhi piagenti   allora m'addobraro,
50 chè mi tennero menti   e diedermi nascoso
uno spirito amoroso   ch'assai mi fa più amare
che non amò null'altro, ciò mi pare.

La calamita, contano i saccenti,
che trarre non poria   lo ferro per maestria
55 se non che l'aire in mezzo lu consenti.
Anchor che calamita petra sia,
l'altre petre neenti   non son cusì potenti
a traier, perchè non n'àno bailia.
Così, madonna mia,   l'Amor s'è apperceputo,   V
60 che non m'avria potuto
traer a sè se non fusse per vui.
E sì son donne assai,   m'àno nulla per cui
eo mi movesse mai,   se non per voi, piagente,
in cui è fermamente   la forza e la vertuti.
65 Adonque prego l'Amor che m'aiuti.

O white O rose O joy, the hope of my well-being   III
keeps me alive,
35 though I languish I cannot die;
for while you live, I cannot pass away,
though hunger and thirst torment my body:
if I keep my mind on the courtly image of you,
I forget death, it gives me such strength.

40 I do not believe the spirit within me
is the same one as before, for then I should be dead,
such sufferings have I passed through every moment.
This new spirit, which gives me motion—
I think it is your spirit, and it stays in my breast
45 and dwells with me in joy and pleasure.
Now I remember well, when I parted from you,   IV
and held my gaze
on your pure bright face reflecting love,
your beautiful eyes won twice their power over me,
50 for they looked at me and sent forth secretly
an amorous spirit that makes me love far more,
I think, than any other loved before.

The magnet, so the learned say,
could not attract iron with such force,
55 if the air between them did not permit it.
Though the magnet may be stone,
no other stones have the faculty
of attraction, because they do not have the power.
Just so, my lady, Love understood   V
60 he could not
draw me to himself except through you.
Now there are many ladies, but none by whom
I ever could be moved—only by you, O beautiful,
in whom the power and the faculty are firm and staid.
65 Therefore I pray Love give me aid.

GUITTONE D'AREZZO

(c. 1235–1294)

The certain facts of Guittone's life are few: for example, in a
letter he mentions the name and occupation of his late father,
Viva di Michele, receiver of public monies of Arezzo. Guittone, a
Guelph, was exiled by the Ghibellines in 1260. In 1266 he
entered a religious order and thereafter wrote religious, moral,
and political poetry exclusively, forsaking the love songs of his
earlier years. In his new life he dwelled at various times in
Arezzo, Bologna, and Florence, in which last city he died.

Guittone was the leader of the second great school of Italian
poetry, centered in Tuscany. As the most prominent target to
aim at, he got plenty of knocks from Dante. In *DVE* I, xiii, Dante
denounces Guittone and the other Tuscans who presumed
to lay claim to the illustrious vernacular: their language, he
says, far from being eloquent, rather was dialectal, vulgar, in-
discreet; only the ignorant extolled them.[1] Guittone's language
is in fact characterized by a far greater number of Provençal and
learned Latin terms in comparison with the poetry of the
Sicilians; it is richer in rhetorical figures and more complex
periods and in other elements drawn from the tradition of the
Latin rhetorics. Dante's own development as a lyric poet seems
to have gone opposite to the historical order: an orthodox
Guittonian at the outset, he renounced that style and at a later
stage actually cultivated the simpler and more mellifluous diction
of the Sicilians.[2] Quite apart from what Dante considered the

[1] He attacks him again in II, vi. Guittone is mentioned in *Purgatorio*, XXIV,
as the leader of one of the two poetic schools that failed to achieve "the
sweet new style" (the other leader being Giacomo da Lentino), and is finally
and totally rejected in *Purgatorio*, XXVI.
[2] See Foster and Boyde, *Dante's Lyric Poetry*, II, 1ff, 212ff.

objectionable elements of Guittone's style, his hostility also reflects the determination of a young poet struggling to find his language and therefore needing to escape from a paralyzing influence. For Guittone was the most influential and revered poet when the effect of the Sicilian school was waning and before the stilnovisti emerged.

The truth is, everyone—not only the Guittonians but also the stilnovisti, including Dante—were considerably influenced by Guittone. It was he who showed how it was possible to continue to write poetry when the day of the Sicilian school was over. The Sicilians were lodged in a great court where it made sense to continue the style, and to uphold the values, of the courtly lyric. But in Guittone's day, the court no longer served as poetry's shelter and frame of reference. The poet had to address a new audience now, the up-and-coming municipal citizen; but his poetic equipment had originally been fashioned to serve a noble audience that claimed the exclusive privilege of excellence. It was Guittone who showed how poetry, with all its traditions, could be rejuvenated outside the court, in a new world. The ideals of service and fidelity to class fade out in Guittone, remaining only as heirloom ornaments; a new ideal forms up, a new valuation of energy and self-sufficiency. Lauded now is not the man who comes into a great inheritance of land and privilege, or the man who subscribes to an ideal in the presence of his peers, but the one who goes out and gets things for himself and who upholds and guides himself in every weather. This celebration of energy and rectitude finds its expression in Guittone's style, which is at once urgent, tortuous, rhetorical, full of verbal explosions, and, quite as Dante maintained, full of "unpoetic" and unmellifluous "plebeian" terms. These same qualities persist in his religious poetry.[3]

The situation in which Guittone wrote was one that poets everywhere had to face: what is to happen to the tradition of courtly poetry once poetry moves out of court? The German poets failed completely to solve this problem. On the continent, in fact, it was only in Italy that great poetry was written in this

---

[3] These points are well made by Carlo Salinari, *La poesia lirica del Duecento;* and by Gianfranco Contini in *Giornale storico della letteratura italiana,* 1941.

predicament, poetry that surpassed the courtly limits of the tradition. This victory was finally achieved by the *dolce stil novo;* but they came to their way because Guittone was there for them to bounce off of. In rebounding they rejected his "plebeianism," for they had a doctrine of exclusiveness more severe than that of the courtly love lyric; but they imitated his recherché rhymes, his learned rhythms, his belief in poetry, his exaltation of rectitude.

In this respect Guittone and his school can be called, as they almost always are, "transitional." But Guittone has an integrity of his own that needs no justification from what came after him. He maintained the traditional forms—even his conversion and change of theme are wholly in the Provençal tradition; but he took them down from that high aristocratic redoubt, reinterpreting but not destroying their nobility, and brought them into the city for the encouragement of the citizens. The result was a poetry all of its own kind: highly rhetorical, hortatory, ultraconservative in its adherence to traditional prescriptions, and yet really new in its range of meaning.

Text: Francesco Egidi, ed. *Le Rime di Guittone d'Arezzo.* Scrittori d'Italia, 175. Bari: Gius. Laterza, 1940.

12

Dolcezza alcuna o di voce o di sono
lo meo core allegrar non può gia mai,
pensando che diviso e lontan sono
da quella ch'amo, ameraggio ed amai.

5 Nè per dolzore in cantando risono;
ma pur di doglia canteraggio omai:
come l'augel dolci canti consono,
ch'è preso in gabbia e sosten molti guai.

Tante gravose doglie e pene porto
10 e 'n viso ed in diviso com mi pare,
se di presso vi sono o di lontano.

Sempre mi trovo in tempestoso porto,
e lo dolor per mezzo il volto appare:
credendomi appressare, io m'allontano.

13

Ora che la freddore
desperde onne vil gente
e che falla e desmente
gioia, canto, ed amore,
5 ho di cantar voglienza
per mantener piacenza,
tutto che perta e danno
e travaglio ed affanno
vegname d'onne parte;
10 ma per forza sen parte.

Quand'omo ha 'n suo piacere
tempo, stagione, e loco,

12

No sweetness in voice or melody
can ever rejoice my heart again—
I remember I am severed and am far
from the one I love, will love, have loved.

5 Nor for the sweetness in singing shall I ever raise my voice,
I shall sing henceforth only from pain:
I shall sound sweet songs like a once free bird
that is trapped in a cage and suffers much regret.

I bear many heavy pains and sorrows
10 on my face and in my mind,
sorrows that come from near and far.

Always I find myself in a stormy port,
and grief shows its face by my face:
Believing I come closer, I drift further away.

13

Now that the cold
dispels the unworthy,
and joy, song, love
falter and grow weak,
5 I have a will to sing   I
to keep pleasure alive,
though loss and injury,
torment and trouble,
come at me from every corner—
10 for they withdraw before my force.

When a man has the time,
the weather, and the place in his favor,

mester faceli poco
isforzarse a valere;
15　ma mester falli allora　　　　　　　　　　II
che nel contrar dimora,
per mantenersi a bene;
e cento tanti tene
pregio nochier, ch'a torto
20　vento acquista bon porto.

S'eo per forza de core,
contra de tutta noia,
prendo e ritegno gioia,
e canto ora in favore
25　d'onne sconfortato omo,　　　　　　　　　III

che conforti! e mir' como
val meglio esser gaudente
non avendo neente,
ch'aver lo secol totto
30　dimorando a corrotto.

Piangendo e sospirando
non acquista l'om terra,
ma per forza di guerra
saggiamente pugnando.
35　E quello è da laudare,　　　　　　　　　IV
che se sa confortare
là dov'altr'om sconforti;
ma che prodezza porti
sì che 'n bon stato torni,
40　non che dorma e sogiorni.

Conforti ogn'omo e vaglia,
chè per valor convene
che di mal torni a bene
e, s'è 'n basso, che saglia;
45　che 'n dannaggio om valente　　　　　　V
non fu mai lungiamente,

he doesn't need much manliness
to force himself to be brave;
but what great manliness he needs   II
to keep his spirits up
when things go against him.
And a hundred times more valiant
is the man at the helm who reaches
port when the wind is wrong.

If I by the force of my heart
take hold of joy and keep it
against all vexation,
and sing now for the good
of every disheartened man—   III

let him take heart now and see
how it is better to be joyful
having nothing
than to own the whole world
and be broken within.

No man gets land
by weeping and sighing—
he gets it by the force of war,
fighting wisely.
And the man to praise is the one   IV
who can give himself heart
when every other loses heart;
only let him be brave
and turn it all to good,
and not sleep, and not linger.

Let every man take heart and be strong,
for by his valor he should
turn bad luck to good,
and, if he is down, leap up.
For no man worth his salt ever lived   V
with his defeat for long,

perchè non vol d'un danno
far due, ma grande affanno
metter, como quell' ono
50   torni per forza a bono.

Perfetto om valoroso
de' fuggir agio e poso;
e giorno e notte affanno   VI
seguir, cessando danno,
55   e prender pregio e prode;
e sì detto è l'om prode.

Ser Orlando da Chiuse,
in cui già mai non pose
perduta disconforto,   VII
60   se 'l tempo è stato torto,
par che dirizzi aguale;
per che parrà chi vale.

14

Amor, merzede, intende s'eo ragione   2
chero davante la tua segnoria,
che for m'hai   miso di mia possessione,
e messo in quella de la donna mia,

5   e sempre mi combatti onne stagione.
Perchè lo fai, poi sono a tua balia?
Chè non fer quella, che contra te pone
suo senno e suo talento e te guerria?

Mostri che tu non se' commun segnore,
10   se lei riguardi e me vuoi far morire,
o vero che non hai tanto valore.

Ben credo l'averesti in tuo servire.

he will not make out of one loss
two, but gives everything
he has to turn the one loss
50   into profit, by force.

A real man, a valiant man
must fly from comfort and repose
and struggle night and day   VI
to put an end to every loss
55   and take hold of profit and honor.
And then he is called a brave man.

Ser Orlando da Chiuse,
whom no loss ever
caused to lose his nerve—   VII
60   if the weather has been wrong,
it seems it's getting better now;
and so we shall see who has any worth.

14

Love, have mercy, judge whether I seek
a reasonable thing before your court,
for you have put me out of my own dominion
and set me in my lady's,

5   and you fight against me in every weather.
Why do you do this, since I'm already in your power?
Why not strike *her,* who sets her force
and wit against you, and makes war on you?

You show yourself a lord unlike the others
10   if you spare her and want to make me die.
Or else you do not have such great power.

I still believe you could have her one of yours.

Ma, se non poi di me, tuo servidore,
or non te piaccia ch'io deggia perire.

15

Gioia ed allegranza   2
tant'hai nel mio cor data, fino amore,
che pesanza non credo mai sentire;
però tanta abondanza,
5   ch'è dei fin beni, avanzala tuttore,
che de ciascun porea sovragioire.   1
E no lo porea dire,
di sì gran guisa, come in cor la sento:
però mi tegno ad essere tacente,
10   chè no lo guida fin conoscimento
chi contr'al suo forzor vo star rapente.

Rapente disianza
in me è adimorata per mant'ore,
caro amore, de te repleno gire.
15   Amor, perch'altra usanza
me non porea far degno prenditore
del gran riccore ch'aggio al meo disire?   II
Avegna ch'en albire
lo mi donasse grande fallimento,[1]
20   or l'ho preso e posseggio, al meo parvente,
standone degno, chè for zo no sento
che 'l core meo sofferissel neente.[2]

Neente s'enavanza
omo ch'acquista l'altrui con follore,
25   ma perta fa, secondo el meo parire,

---

[1] It was his own imperfection that made him fall in love with a perfect being
(*gran riccore*).
[2] That is, could not support that "great richness."

But if you cannot, for me, your servant, at least
let it not be your pleasure that I must be destroyed.

15

Such joy and liveliness
you have put in my heart, exalted Love,
I believe I shall never feel grief;
for grief is surpassed each time
5 by the great and subtle pleasures of love,
which I could enjoy more than any other.   I
I could not describe it
as wonderfully as the way it feels in my heart,
and so I keep still about it—
10 there's no fine wisdom in any man
who tries to seize something beyond his powers.

One desire seizes me
that has dwelt in me long—
precious Love, to go forth filled with you.
15 O Love, why could no other way
have made me worthy to take hold
of that great richness I desire?   II
I admit it was a great failing
that put this treasure in my power,[1] but—
20 I've got it now, I know, it is mine,
and I am worthy of it, for without love I feel
my heart could never bear it.[2]

A man gains nothing
but a loss, it seems to me,
25 when he gets something by deceit, because he steals.

    e sofferir pesanza
    per acquistare a pregio ed a valore,
    è cosa ch'a l'om dea sempre piacire.   III
    Ed eo posso ben dire
30 che, per ragion di molto valimento,
    ho preso ben, che m'è tanto piacente,
    che tutt'altra gioi ch'ho no è già 'l quento
    di quella, che per esso, el meo cor sente.

But to suffer, if he has to,
to gain by his own worth and manliness—
that is a man's way.   III
And I have a right to say
30 that by great manliness
I have won something great which so pleases me
that any other joy I have isn't worth a fifth
of that which, for this reason, my heart feels.

BONAGIUNTA ORBICCIANI
DA LUCCA

(d. between 1296 and 1300)

Bonagiunta Orbicciani da Lucca was a notary, but aside from
that no documented or certain fact about his life has been established. In *DVE*, I, xiii, he is cited as one of the Tuscans whose
language is plebeian rather than courtly. Although he is grouped
with Guittone there, his poetry is really closer to the older,
Sicilian school, and he was apparently the first mainland con-
tinuator of that tradition. His distinctness from Guittone seems
to be assumed in the famous passage in *Purgatorio*, XXIV, where
he speaks as a leader of one of three poetic movements that fell
short of the achievement of the *dolce stil novo*.

Text: Carlo Salinari, ed. *La Poesia lirica del Duecento*. Clas-
sici Italiani, 1. Turin: Unione Tipografico—Editrice Torinese,
1951.

16

A Guinizelli

Voi che avete mutata la mainera
de li piacenti ditti dell'amore,
de la forma, dell'esser, là dov'era,
per avansare ogn'altro trovatore—

5   avete fatto come la lumera
ch'a lo scuro partito dà sprendore,
ma no quine ove luce l'alta spera,
la quale avanza e passa di chiarore.

E voi passat'ogn'om di sottigliansa,
10 e non si trov'alcun che ben ispogna,
tant'è iscura vostra parlatura.

Ed è tenuta gran dissimigliansa,
anchor che 'l senno vegna da Bologna,[1]
traier canson per forsa di scrittura.

17

Un giorno aventuroso,
pensando in la mia mente
com'amor m'avea innalzato,
i'stava com'om dottoso,
5   da che meritatamente
non serve a chi l'ha onorato.
Però volsi cantare   ı

[1] Location of a great university. This sonnet is one of the earliest criticisms
of the abstruseness and recherché imagery of the *dolce stil novo*. See Guinizelli's reply, *Omo ch'è saggio non corre leggero* (no. 24, below).

16

To Guinizelli

You who have changed the manner
of the once delightful songs of love,
transmuted it in form and essence
in order to surpass every other poet,

5   you have acted like a candle
that gives a little brightness in the dark—
but is nothing when the lofty sphere of heaven shines,
which surpasses all in splendor.

And you, you surpass everyone in complexity,
10 and there's not one man who can explain you,
so obscure are your discourses.

And it is considered a strange thing,
even though the sense comes from Bologna,[1]
to drag a song out of learned sources.

One lucky day
measuring in my mind
how Love raised me high,
I stood like one afraid
5   he serves unworthily
the one who honored him.
For I wanted to tell in song   1

　　　　lo certo affinamento,
　　　　perchè l'amor più flore
10　　　e luce e sta 'n vigore
　　　　di tutto piacimento,
　　　　gioia tene in talento
　　　　e fa ogn'atro presio sormontare.

　　　　Montasi ogni stasione,
15　　　però fronde e fiore e frutta,
　　　　l'affinata gioi' d'amore.
　　　　Per questa sola rasione
　　　　a lui è data e condutta
　　　　ogne cosa c'ha sentore—
20　　　sì come par, li auselli   II
　　　　chiaman sua signoria
　　　　tra lor divisamente
　　　　tanto pietosamente,
　　　　e l'amorosa via
25　　　commenda tuttavia
　　　　perchè commune volse usar con elli.

　　　　Donqua, la commune usanza
　　　　ha l'amor così agradito,
　　　　che da tutti 'l fa laudare.
30　　　Gentil donna, pietanza
　　　　inver'me, che so ismarito
　　　　e tempesto più che mare.
　　　　Non guardate in me, fina,   III
　　　　ch'eo vi son servidore:
35　　　tragete simiglianza
　　　　da l'amorosa usanza,
　　　　che da al picciolo onore
　　　　in gran guisa [1] talore,
　　　　e 'l ben possente a la stasion dichina.

[1] Salinari has: *ingrandisce*.

how Love makes everyone better,
because Love flowers,
10   glows, has vigor
beyond every other pleasure,
yearns for joy,
makes every other virtue grow.

It grows greater in every season,
15   for this perfect joy of love
brings forth frond and flower and fruit.
Alone for this reason
all things that have feeling
are drawn and given over to Love—
20   it is clear the birds   II
proclaim his lordship,
each one in its style,
with such great piety
that always they commend
25   the path to love:
thus everyone should follow them.

Therefore this following
has pleased Love greatly,
for all things praise him.
30   Noble lady, pity me,
for I am in disorder:
more than the sea I storm.
Gentle one, seeing me, do you not know   III
I am your servant?
35   Imitate
the way of Love,
which gives the smallest homage
a great reward sometimes,
and, sometimes, brings the mighty low.

CHIARO DAVANZATI

(fl. second half thirteenth century)

It has, so far, proved impossible to determine which of two men, so named, who fought in the famous battle of Montaperti in 1260, when the Ghibellines routed the Guelphs,[1] was our poet; one died in 1280, the other in 1303. Although he was extremely prolific and, moreover, carried on a considerable poetic correspondence with other Florentine poets of his day, he seems to have had no influence and is completely unnoticed by succeeding generations.

Text: Aldo Menichetti, ed. *Chiaro Davanzati, Rime.* Collezione di opere inedite o rare publicata dalla Commissione per i Testi di Lingua, 126. Bologna: Commissione per i Testi di Lingua, 1965.

[1] See *Inferno*, X, 85; XXXII, 81.

18

Come Narcissi, in sua spera mirando,
s'inamorao, per ombra, a la fontana,
veggendo se medesimo pensando
ferissi il core e la sua mente vana,

5   gittovisi entro, per l'ombria pilgliando,
di quello amore lo prese morte strana;
ed io, vostra bieltate rimembrando,
l'ora ch'io vidi voi, donna sovrana,

    inamorato sono sì feramente,
10 che, poi ch'io volglia non poria partire,
sì m'ha l'amor compreso strettamente.

    Tormentami lo giorno e fa languire,
com'a Narcissi parami piagente,
veggendo voi, la morte sofferire.

19

D'un'amorosa voglia mi convene
cantare allegramente, rimembrando
com'io partivi da la donna mia,   I
ca dolzemente mi dicea abbrazzando:
5 "Se vai, meo sire, non agge 'n obria
tornare a l'amoroso nostro bene,

    ma rimembra lo nostro fin diporto,
a ciò che di tornare agge voglienza.
    Prendi lo core e me ne la tua baglia,   II
10 sì che mi porti avanti tua parvenza,

18

As Narcissus, gazing in his mirror,
came to love through the shadow in the fountain,
and, seeing himself in the midst of regretting—
his heart and vain mind smitten—

5   plunged in, to catch the shadow,
and then strange death embraced him with that love,
so I, remembering how beautiful you were
when I saw you, sovereign lady,

fall in love so wildly
10 I could not, though I might want to, part from you,
love holds me in its grip so tightly.

Day torments me, draws off my strength,
and, like Narcissus, to me it looks like pleasure,
as I gaze on you, to suffer death.

19

I have to sing with joy
about my love when I remember
how it was when I parted from my lady,   I
she embraced me and said in all her sweetness,
5 "If you are going, my lord, do not forget
to come back again to the great good of our love,

but remember our fine delight,
so that you desire to return.
Take my heart and me on board   II
10 so that you hold me in your sight,

pinta in core, come io sono 'n intaglia:
di simile voler faraggio porto."

Ed io, abbracciando, l'amorosa cera
basciando, dolzemente le parlai:
15 "Gentil mia gioia, in voi è la mia vita,   III
altra speranza non avraggio mai
che solamente della mia redita
a voi, che siete del mio cor lomera."

Ed ella a sè mi strinse inmantenente:
20 "Dolze meo sire, a Dio sia accomandato,
dàmi   tua fe presente di tornare."   IV
Ed io lel diè, piangendo a lo commiato,
dissile: "Amore meo, non sconfortare,
membra che la tornata sia presente."

25 Così partivi da lo mio diletto.
Canto, che mi sovvien de l'amorosa
e doglio forte de lo dipartire,   V
per tanto che lo so che m'è gravosa.
Così fosse cangiato a uno redire,
30 che fosse in sicurtà de lo dispetto.

Pertanto mi soverchia l'allegranza:
membrandomi la gioia ch'avemo insembra:
quando io verraggio a simile disio?   VI
ché di null'altra cosa più mi membra,
35 ché di tornar colà donde partio:
che di gioie torni doppio di speranza.

painted in your heart, as in this etching.
I shall harbor my answering desire."

And I embraced her and kissed
her face full of love and gently told her:
15 "My noble joy, in you is my life,   III
I shall never have any other hope
but only hope of my return
to you, the beacon of my heart."

And with that she pressed me to her,
20 "My sweet lord, God be with you,
give me your promise to return soon."   IV
And I gave it to her, weeping over the parting,
and said to her, "My love, do not be discomforted,
remember, my return is at hand."

25 Then I parted from my pleasure.
I sing, for I remember my love
and suffer much for my departure,   V
for I know how heavy it weighs on me.
May it change into a return
30 and thus be certain not to cause a grudge.

And so I am overcome with joy
thinking of the pleasure we shall have together:
when shall I see her, full of equal desire?   VI
for I think of nothing so much
35 as coming back to where I parted.
May our joys be double our hope.

GUIDO GUINIZELLI

(*fl. second half thirteenth century*)

The attempt to identify the poet has not come free of doubt, partly because there are two men documented by that name in Bologna in the latter half of the thirteenth century. The more accepted candidate was a judge and a member of a prominent family; as a Ghibelline he was exiled in 1274 and died in Padua in 1276. This identification has been questioned on the grounds that the inferred date of birth (around 1230) would make the poet an age-mate, if not the senior, of Guittone d'Arezzo: this would be hard to square with the poet's early veneration of Guittone as his model (Contini, II, 447).

Apart from whatever notice his own undoubted talent might have won for him, his name is familiar to us mostly because of his importance to Dante, who saw in him the "father" of all those Italian poets who followed him in the "modern use," that is, wrote illustrious vernacular poetry (*Purgatorio*, XXVI, 94–114). Dante cites him several times in his other writings, always as a model poet (*DVE*, I, ix, xv; II, v, vi; *Convivio*, IV, xx). Dante's sonnet *Amore e 'l cor gentil sono una cosa* (below, no. 40) simply assumes the absolute authority of Guinizelli's most famous poem.

This *canzone*, *Al cor gentil*, has come to be considered a seminal poem—an "eloquent manifesto," a "great programmatic *canzone*" (Foster and Boyde, II, 96, 105)—with regard to the development of the *dolce stil novo*. In this *canzone* the poet compares the lady to the angelic intelligences who intuit the divine will and, in loving obedience to it, turn the heavens in their orderly courses: as God "shines" upon these beings and endows them with the love by which they love to obey His will, so the lady ought to shine in the eyes of the lover and bestow upon him the desire that never ceases to obey her. In the final strophe, imagining himself accused by God for using the whole creation of the cosmos and its hierarchical heavens, not to discover the majesty of God, but just to pay a pretty compliment to a lady, the poet defends himself on the grounds that she seemed to him an angel from God's holy kingdom. Both in these two strophes and throughout the poem Guinizelli uses terms and images and structural patterns drawn from sources other than the courtly tradition and the standard rhetorical practices. For all these reasons the *canzone* has been held to be the "manifesto" of the *dolce stil*, the authorization of its characteristic imagery and the first expression of what has been regarded as its central mysterious conceit: the mortal lady who walks the earth and draws the poet's love is at the same time an angel come from heaven to redeem him, his specific Christ.

This sounds a lot like Dante, and the stilnovisti were for a long time regarded as his precursors, and often still are. Dante himself distinguished them from other poets and gave them the name by which they have collectively come to be known (*Purgatorio*, XXIV, 57). It is natural to suppose that they too had conceived of a redemptive lady who could be worshipped with utter piety because she was really an angel. If it is true that they did, then they invented something other than courtly love, something truly new. The lady of the troubadours had been redemptive in a purely secular sense: she redeemed her lover as a courtly man, defined him as a member of a social class. But once the lady is an angel, love soars beyond the walls of the court; it never stops taking on ever higher meaning till it reaches Paradise, led there continually by the lady.

The *dolce stil novo* was read for a long time in this Dantean light. But now it has become a disputed question whether they really had this idea: if Dante is left out of the picture, their poetry does not look so new any more. Alone, by itself, it strikes us not as less secular than earlier poetry, but as less courtly. As a matter of fact, it looks then as though the stilnovisti were trying to sound as many of the old themes of courtly love as they could in their circumstances, the court having vanished, and were using the novelty of their rhetoric to achieve a kind of exclusiveness, a small circle without walls. They certainly made their work impenetrable to those who were outside their circle, that is, to those who had conventional expectations about poetic language —witness Bonagiunta and his reaction to this talk of celestial intelligences and all those other university terms. Were the stilnovisti true precursors of Dante—did they originate an idea that he fulfilled—or have they only borrowed meaning from the future? One way or another, they have benefited much from his reflected glory.

If, for example, we look at Guinizelli's poetry without thinking ahead to Dante, we are impressed first of all by the wider sources of its imagery (in comparison with the earlier schools of poetry) and its learned argumentative form—and then by the familiarity of its theme. For it finally is much more conventional than its innovative rhetoric and its resolute air would lead us to expect. The abiding emotion in it is a reactionary nostalgia; nearly everything in it has a long series of precedents. The inquiry concerning the origin and moral value of love was carried out with distinction by Guido delle Colonne, for example, and before him it was a standard theme among the troubadours. The emancipation of the concept of nobility from the circumstances of birth was the great theme of Guinizelli's "father" (as Guinizelli called him), Guittone d'Arezzo. The imagined interview and self-defense in heaven occurs often in troubadour poetry, most notably in the Monk of Montaudon and Peire Cardenal, both of whom are more daring and inventive than Guinizelli when they stand up to God. The idea that love and the gentle heart imply and substantiate each other comes straight from the convention of courtly love; the same is true of the elevation of the lady to the level of an analogous divinity: the lady was the courtly lover's "lord" in a psychic and ethical as well as a feudal sense, and the lover's nobility was proved and actualized by his love for her.

As he puts forth these ancient lyric theses, Guinizelli seems to be guided by his "father's" ideal of nobility; but in truth he is recoiling from it. He rejects Guittone by looking beyond him—to the Sicilians, and perhaps even beyond them. He really longs for the old courts, the high walls, the privileged audience. But, of course, there is none of that around. The best that he can do, in his circumstances, is to set up in the air a court of "gentle hearts," which, precisely because it has no status, is far more exclusive than the former courts in castles. "Guinizelli establishes the bases for substituting for the real court of the Provençals and the Sicilians an ideal court, the cenacle of gentle hearts, the restricted and refined circle of initiates in the secrets of love" (Salinari).

Guido's analogy of God and the intelligence of heaven is a new and unexpected kind of image: poetry is no longer enclosed by a court, and so, out in the open now, it has a wider range of things to use in its comparisons—including all the lore of the heavens. But among the stilnovisti this greater vocabulary never engendered a greater meaning than that which was defined by the boundaries of the court. The terms of Guinizelli's comparison are unusual, but its meaning is not new: it lends the lady the same judicial and tutelary image she bore in the old courtly lyric. The lady looks like an angel: she is very good and very beautiful. It is a two-hundred-year-old compliment. (See the excellent discussion in Maurice Valency, *In Praise of Love,* Chapter Eight, "The New Style.")

The new thing that Guinizelli started, which Cavalcanti and the others continued after him, was the institution of a new lyrical rhetoric. These poets turned to sources little used before them—Aristotelian and Averroistic writings, scientific texts (especially in medicine), theology—to find new ways of constructing a poem and of defining love. Even the traditional imagery (for example, that drawn from the lapidaries) they endowed with a sudden freshness by incorporating it into this new framework of terms. Within the *dolce stil novo* the chief poetic effect was to give to the expression of courtly love an illusion of objectivity and a cosmic resonance, a sense that the inner experience of love can be described in scientific and universal terms. For as soon as poetry was dislodged from the court, heaven and earth were its only objective setting; and the problem the stilnovisti faced was how to universalize the court, how to maintain the old values without walls—how to express the idea that love is the integrative force, not merely of a privileged community, but of all reality. This does not mean that they had a larger (Dantean) conception of love, but only that they had a larger space to fill with their song. Their situation was unprecedented, and their response was to try to make the old methods work with some new material.

This objectification of poetic terms is just what other poets in similar circumstances tried to achieve (compare Burkard von Hohenfels) . But the *dolce stil novo* alone was successful, because the stilnovisti stopped looking for their materials in the life of an actual court. The old values of courtly love were otherwise kept intact: the lady was exalted to the same level and had the same meaning—she had even been called an angel before, both in Provençal and Italian, though her locus then was the court, not the city or the heavens above; the poet still sought to reveal the harmony between his inner experience and the life of a defined community. But the stilnovisti found a language that more precisely fit the possibilities of belief in the new conditions in which poetry was created and in the experience of the audience to which it was addressed.

This was a great achievement, and it produced some wonderful poetry—best and most truly understood when it is joined to the tradition of troubadour and early Italian poetry, and dissociated from Dante. It also produced a new poetic language, new "colors" that were not traditionally rhetorical—it happens that Dante began something with this language, but that should not mislead us into distorting this excellent poetry by overloading it. The achievements of the *dolce stil* were not more innovative than the idea the Sicilians had of expressing troubadour love themes in Italian rather than Provençal, or than Guittone's new ideal of rectitude and nobility. The *dolce stil novo* by itself would never outshine the other schools of Italian poetry were it not defined— falsely defined—by the reflexive light of Dante, who brought out the possibilities of its language and imagery beyond anything the stilnovisti would have had the courage for, not even considering the question of genius.

It is very tempting to read back into the *dolce stil* elements of the vision which is his alone, for the great gap between him and the others upsets our expectation of process and development. And of course it is always possible to insist that such a reformation of rhetoric inescapably implies a new meaning, a new world.

That is probably true, but the important thing is the poet's commitment to that new meaning, his willingness to cherish what comes forth from his own engendering imagery. It was Dante, not the stilnovisti, who made a universe out of this new language, for he alone was capable of such brave faith in the image and the word.

Text (except where noted): Gianfranco Contini, ed. *Poeti del Duecento*, vol. II. La Letteratura Italiana, Storia e Testi, 2, ii. Milan and Naples: Riccardo Ricciardi, 1960; with some changes in punctuation.

Al cor gentil rempaira sempre amore
come l'ausello in selva a la verdura;
nè fe' amore anti che gentil core,
nè gentil core anti ch'amor, natura,
5 ch'adesso con' fu 'l sole,   I
sì tosto lo splendore fu lucente,
nè fu davanti 'l sole;
e prende amore in gentilezza loco
così propïamente
10 come calore in clarità di foco.

Foco d'amore in gentil cor s'apprende
come vertute in petra prezïosa:
che de la stella valor no i discende,
anti che 'l sol la faccia gentil cosa.[1]
15 Poi che n'ha tratto fore,   II
per sua forza lo sol ciò che li è vile,
stella li dà valore.
Così lo cor, ch'è fatto da natura
asletto, pur, gentile,
20 donna, a guisa di stella, lo 'namura.

Amor per tal ragion sta 'n cor gentile
per qual lo foco in cima del doplero;
splendeli al su' diletto, clar, sottile:
non li starìa altra guisa, tant'è fero.
25 Così prava natura   III

recontra amor como fa l'aigua il foco
caldo, per la freddura.

---

[1] "The whole strophe spells out the notions of potency and act: the sun
purifies the stone and makes it capable of receiving from its specific star the
definite properties of a gem; nature corresponds to the sun, the (noble)
heart to the (precious) stone, the lady (who actualizes the potentiality for
love) to the star." (Contini)

20

Love seeks its dwelling always in the gentle heart,
like a bird in the green of the forest;
nor did nature create love before the gentle heart,
or the gentle heart before love—
5 just as when the sun came into being,   **I**
in that instant its splendor shone forth,
nor did that splendor come before the sun;
and love takes its place in the gentle heart
as naturally
10 as heat in the brightness of fire.

The fire of love takes hold in the gentle heart
like the virtue in a precious stone,
to which no power comes down from the star
before the sun has made it a noble thing;[1]
15 for after the sun with its force   **II**
draws everything vile in it away,
the star gives it power.
Just so, once nature makes the heart
capable, pure, and noble,
20 the lady, like a star, fills it with love.

Love stays in the noble heart in the same way
fire stays on the point of a torch;
it glows there freely, bright and subtle,
nor would any other way befit it, it is so proud.
25 But a vile nature   **III**

stops love, as water stops
the burning fire, through coldness.

Amor in gentil cor prende rivera
per suo consimel loco,
30 com'adamàs del ferro in la minera.[2]

Fère lo sole lo fango tutto 'l giorno,
vile reman, nè 'l sol perde calore.
Dis' omo altier: "Gentil per sclatta torno";
lui semblo al fango, al sol gentil valore.
35 Chè non de' dare om fé   IV
che gentilezza sia for di coraggio,
in dignità d'ere',
sed a vertute non ha gentil core:
com'aigua porta raggio,
40 e 'l ciel ritèn le stelle e lo splendore.[3]

Splende in la intelligenzïa del cielo
Deo crïator, più che 'n nostri occhi 'l sole;
ella intende suo fattor oltra 'l cielo,
e 'l ciel vogliando, a lui obedir tole,
45 e con' segue al primero   V
del giusto deo beato compimento:
così dar dovrìa, al vero,
la bella donna, poi che 'n gli occhi splende
del suo gentil, talento,
50 chi mai da lei obedir non si disprende.[4]

Donna, Deo mi dirà, "Che presumisti?"
siando l'alma mia a lui davante:
"Lo ciel passasti e 'nfin a me venisti,
e desti, in vano amor, me per semblanti;
55 ch'a me convèn la laude,   VI

---

[2] According to the lapidary of Marbod of Rennes, iron in the earth produces
the diamond (Contini).
[3] "The ordinary interpretation makes the water a term of comparison with
the ignoble heart (like the mud) and the sky a term of comparison with the
noble heart; it really fits the context better if the shining sky represents the
lady, the source of virtue, and the water the gentle heart, naturally disposed
to receive that virtue." (Contini)
[4] See introductory note.

Love takes its dwelling in the noble heart
as its natural place,
30 like the diamond in a vein of iron.[2]

The sun strikes the mud all day:
The mud stays vile, nor does the sun lose heat;
the haughty man says: "I am noble by descent":
I compare him to mud, true nobility to the sun.
35 For no man may believe   IV
there is nobility outside the heart,
in the condition of being an heir,
if his heart is not bent toward virtue—
just as water reflects the beams,
40 and heaven holds the stars and all their splendor.[3]

Upon the Intelligence of heaven shines
God the creator, more than the sun upon our eyes;
and she understands, beyond heaven, her creator:
turning the sky she is poised to obey him
45 and just as, in that instant, there follows   V
the fulfillment of the just God's holy will,
so should the beautiful lady
bestow, once she shines in the eyes
of the noble man, that desire
50 which never ceases to obey her.[4]

Lady, God will say to me, "What did you presume?"
when my soul stands before him;
"You passed through heaven, and you finally came to
        me—
and used me for a comparison in a vain love;
55 for to me alone are praises due,   VI

e a la reina del regname degno,
per cui cessa onne fraude."
Dir li porò: "Tenne d'angel sembianza
che fosse del tu regno:
60 non me fu fallo, s'in lei posi amanza."

21

In quanto la natura [1]
e 'l fino insegnamento
han movimento de lo senno intero,
und'ha più dirittura
5   lo gran cognoscimento,
da nodrimento o da natura, quero;
se la gran canoscenza   I
dicess'om per ventura
che vèn più da natura
10   direbbe fallamento,
chè nessuna scïenza
senz'ammaestratura
non saglie in grande altura
per proprio sentimento.

15   Ma per nodrimento
om cresce in canoscenza,
che dà valenza d'ogni gio' compita;
però ha compimento
di bene in tal sentenza
20   senza fallenza persona nodrita;
adonqua, par che 'l segno   II
e la natura insieme
vivano ad una speme
in un sentire stando,
25   com'adovèn d'un legno

ch'a dui nomi s'attene

[1] Text: Salinari.

and to the Queen of this high realm,
through whom all fraud ceases."
I will be able to answer Him: "She looked like an angel
from your kingdom:
60 it was no fault in me to set my love on her."

21

    Since nature [1]
    and instruction
    are the origins of all knowledge,
    I inquire whence
5   knowledge has its greater
    cause—from nurture or from nature.
    If one should say   I
    that knowledge
    rather comes from nature,
10   he would speak in error,
    for no science
    would, without learning,
    ascend to great heights
    alone by its own desire.

15   But by study
    knowledge increases,
    which gives perfect joy.
    Thus, in this view,
    it is the learned man
20   who reaches perfect good, without deceit;
    wherefore it seems that learning   II
    and nature live
    together sharing one
    single hope, one desire;
25   as it happens with a ship

    that has two names

e pur una cosa ène
lo subbietto guardando.

Però provedimento
30   di conquistar convène
valor di bene   ciò è canoscenza;
se lo cominciamento
perseveranza tene,
cert'è che vène   a fine sua sentenza;
35   e la perseveranza   III
si mantèn per soffrire;
unde vole ubidire
ed ogne bene avanza;
adonqua per certanza
40   non si porìa compire
senza lo sofferire
alcuna incomincianza.

22

Lo vostro bel saluto e 'l gentil sguardo
che fate quando v'encontro m'ancide.
Amor m'assale e già non ha reguardo
s'elli face peccato over merzede,

5   chè per mezzo lo cor me lanciò un dardo
ched oltre in parti lo taglia e divide;
parlar non posso che 'n gran pene eo ardo
sì come quelli che sua morte vide.

Per li occhi passa come fa lo trono,
10   che fèr per la finestra de la torre
e ciò che dentro trova spezza e fende.

but remains one single thing,
considering the subject.

Wherefore it is fitting
30 to prepare for the conquest
of the good—that is, knowledge;
if the beginning
perseveres,
it is certain to reach its goal;
35 and perseverance   III
is upheld through suffering;
so it desires to obey
and acquires every good.
Therefore it is certain,
40 without suffering
there would be no end
to any beginning.

22

The handsome greeting and gentle look
you show me when I meet you kill me.
Love attacks me and does not care
whether he does me ill or good,

5 for he shot an arrow through the middle of my heart,
which cuts it up yet more and parts it.
I cannot speak because I burn with pain,
like one who sees his death.

It passes through my eyes, like a thunderbolt
10 that strikes through the window of a tower
and whatever it finds inside splits and smashes to pieces.

Remagno come statua d'ottono
ove vita nè spirto non ricorre,
se non che la figura d'omo rende.

23

Vedut'ho la lucente stella diana,
ch'appare anzi che 'l giorno rend'albore,
c'ha preso forma di figura umana,
sovr'ogn'altra mi par che dea splendore;

5 viso di neve colorato in grana,
occhi lucenti gai e pien d'amore;
non credo che nel mondo sia cristiana
sì piena di beltate e di valore.

Ed io da lo su' amor son assalito
10 con sì fera battaglia di sospiri
ch'avanti a lei di dir non seri' ardito:

così conoscess' ella i miei disiri,
chè, senza dir, di lei seria servito
per la pietà ch'avrebbe de' martìri.

24

A Bonagiunta da Lucca

Omo ch'è saggio non corre leggero,
ma a passo grada sì com vol misura:
quand'ha pensato riten su' pensero
infino a tanto che 'l ver l'asigura.

I am left standing like a statue of brass,
that holds neither the life nor the coursing spirit,
but only imitates the image, of a man.

23

I have seen the shining morning star,
that appears before the light of day
and has taken human form—
it seems to me to give more light than every other star;

5 face white as snow, colored with red,
eyes shining and gay and full of love—
I do not think in this world there's a Christian girl
so full of beauty and worth.

And I am assailed by love of her
10 with such a wild battle of sighs,
I would not be so bold, facing her, to say one thing.

If only she could so recognize my desires
that I, without speaking, might be comforted
by the pity she would feel for my suffering.

24

To Bonagiunta da Lucca

A wise man does not rush in thoughtlessly
but goes one step at a time, as prudence demands;
what he thinks he keeps to himself
till he is sure of the truth.

5 Foll'è chi crede sol veder lo vero
e non pensa che altri i pogna cura;
non se dev' omo tener troppo altero,
ma de' guardar su' stato e sua natura.

Volan ausel' per air di straine guise
10 ed han diversi loro operamenti,
nè tutti d'un volar nè d'un ardire.

Deo natura e il mondo in grado mise
e fe' dispari senni e 'ntendimenti:
perzò ciò ch'omo pensa non de' dire.[1]

[1] This is a reply to Bonagiunta's sonnet *Voi che avete mutata la mainera* (no. 16, above). It is possible to read this poem out of context so that the final line would have no pejorative meaning; in which case, as Contini points out, its theme is simply "prudence." The sonnet actually appears by itself, divorced from its original context and thus quite different in meaning, in several manuscripts.

5 A fool thinks he sees the truth alone
and never thinks someone else might strive for it.
A man should not think too highly of himself
but should consider his nature and condition.

Through the air fly birds of various kinds,
10 and their motions all are different,
not all are equally fierce, nor do all fly equally well.

God set degrees in nature and the world
and made unequal wits and intellects:
therefore, what the average man thinks he should not tell.[1]

GUIDO CAVALCANTI

(c. 1259–1300)

The poet was born in Florence to a rich and distinguished family. In 1300, the Guelphs having split into two factions and causing great civil disorder by their violent antagonism, Cavalcanti was exiled along with other leaders of both sides. (Dante at the time was one of the priors—chief magistrates—who ordered the banishment of the leaders.) Cavalcanti was recalled to Florence soon afterwards, and there he died at the end of August in that same year.

Dante was deeply devoted to Cavalcanti (who was at least six years his senior), calling him *"primo amico,"* his closest friend, and adopting into his own poetry the most distinctive features of Cavalcanti's style. From the time of their first meeting down to Guido's death, the poet was probably the most important influence on Dante, with respect to lyric poetry. Aside from the frequent citations in *DVE* and in numerous other places, the depth of Dante's devotion can be gauged from a reading of the *Vita Nuova* alone, which is dedicated to Guido.

The reasons for Dante's admiration are not hard to find. There had never been a poet like Guido before; and it was he—far more than Guinizelli—who set the future of the courtly tradition in Italy. What Contini puts forward as Dante's view holds good absolutely: ". . . if the stilnovist experiment must be reduced to a single initiative and a single name, it could not be anyone else's but Cavalcanti's."

It was he who most resolutely took a stand against what he considered the tortuousness, bombast, and vulgarity of Guittone's style; and it seems that it was from his influence that the attitude of the stilnovisti and of succeeding generations toward Guittone was formed. It is clear that Cavalcanti knew exactly what he wanted in the way of style: his poetry is far simpler in syntax, less periodic, more direct, and—insofar as it is freer of complex rhetorical formulations—more "natural" than Guittone's. On the other hand, while he rejected Guittone's rhetorical complications, he introduced other complications of a sort that Guittone never would have dreamed of: he formed his poetry out of other learned traditions—science and medicine, especially—that had not been considered "poetic" before. The heart, for example, as a poetic image is as old as poetry itself; but rarely, if ever, before Cavalcanti was it depicted so nonfiguratively—so scientifically, as the seat, not merely of the passions, but of specific medical processes.

It was not only out of his reaction to the negative ideal of Guittone that his "new style" was formed. His themes were carefully chosen out of the traditional repertory of the courtly lyric. Salinari has defined what he kept and what he left out:

"His themes and his sentimental situations do not differ from the themes and situations already hallowed by tradition; his theories on love, though they benefit from the logical clarity of a more subtle and original background in philosophy (especially Averroism), do not reveal new aspects of the phenomenon of love . . . Cavalcanti conceives [of love] as violent and sensual . . . Thus the possibility of an ideal and edifying love is excluded, and consequently such themes are excluded from Guido's lyric poetry . . . It cannot escape notice that the principal motifs which are basic to his poetry (love as a battle; tears, terror, sighs, and finally the death of the heart, as effects of love; the joy of love as a fleeting consequence of the illusion that there was pity in the eyes of the lady; the love that reaches through the eyes and penetrates into the heart) correspond exactly to the fundamental aspects of love according to his theory . . . Nor can one overlook Cavalcanti's rejection of a great part of the themes greatly in vogue in the troubadour tradition . . . Gone are the slanderers, those who discredit the honor of the beloved and create differences between the lovers; gone are the walks beneath the windows, the jealousy, the conversations with the beloved, the laments for the distance, the memories of meetings and of moments passed together, of endearments and quarrels. Gone

above all (except in some imitations in his youth) is every
analogy with the world of nature, of science, those analogies that
had been so dear to the Provençals, the Sicilians, and Guinizelli.
Gone are the roses, the flowers, and the precious gems, all the
delicate comparisons with which the courtly poets strove to
represent the beauty of the beloved lady; gone are the 'blond
tresses' and the 'clear visage' which, even in their generality, de-
lineated a concrete and material reality. Cavalcantian praise
rejects every earthly reference: the lady is beautiful, humble,
gentle—so beautiful that she cannot be described . . . The
Cavalcantian lady is deprived of face, of body, of any kind of
background. She, like all of Guido's figures, moves in a scene
without space and without colors . . ."

This passage, it should be noted, concerns itself exclusively
with Cavalcanti's "tragic style": everything in the courtly tradition that needs any kind of communal audience—especially a
court—to complete its meaning is left out; everything else that
does not require a specific setting is retained. The results are
disheartening. For this loss of "earthly reference" must mean
that love is no longer an ameliorative and integrative force. The
old "courtly love" could not have existed without a social setting: it integrated the lover with his class by fixing all his lusts
and aspirations on a class ideal. The recognition of his peers
was his reward. But once the objective setting—the court—is
dissolved, the ethical rewards of courtly love are canceled out,
and the only part of it that remains is the deprivation—an un-
rewardable suffering that has nothing to do with "courtliness"
any more. Courtly love without a court is a bad dream, sacrifice
without expectations. The lover has no prospect but extinction,
and the beloved lady no other rôle to play but that of La Belle
Dame sans Merci.

Now there are plenty of Cavalcanti's poems in which love is a
pleasant and unworrisome thing, especially when he composes
in one of the traditional genres that never had a courtly setting
—the *pastorela* (no. 33) for an obvious example. Cavalcanti
composed in many styles, including the old courtly style. But
when his songs are "tragic," that is, when they are concerned
exclusively with the inner experience of love, then the love they

tell about is irrational, debilitating, sterile—its destructive effect is carefully spelled out in his famous theoretical *canzone, Donna me prega.*

The lady, too, is denigrated, though in a quite subtle way. She is never denounced, all direct abuse being reserved for Love itself, rather than the lady. But in the absence of a court, once her beauty and virtue are no longer seconded by the belief of an exalted community, all her glory is tentative. She now becomes an absolutely empty screen on which the lover sees whatever Love, firmly seated in his heart, wants him to see. Nothing the lover says about her is reliable: her indescribable beauty; the voice preceding her, foretelling her celestial return; the star arising from her image announcing the lover's salvation—all these are visions arising from the lover's need, for Love uses the lover's native forces to enslave him, even his infinite longing. For the lover's soul, like all human souls, is magnetized by the infinite; but Love knows how to mislead it, through the senses, into thinking that the lady is its goal. And so it comes about that that infinite magnetism follows the track of all the common desires that propel the lover to the lady.

The lyrics that have this lady as their subject are quite different from those that focus on the poet's subjective experience of love, for the simple reason that they have to have some kind of setting. These lyrics that praise her beauty and beneficence accomplish this praise by celebrating her effect, and so there is always some trace of a secular scene in which she appears—a street, a voice, a witnessing citizenry that instantly recognizes her perfection; though these testimonies all are illusions too. But in the lyrics of the tragic style, there is no setting outside the boundaries of the lover's being, there is only an inner space full of violence and tension caused by the unrolling of physical processes.

Just as he reduced the thematic elements of the courtly tradition and thereby achieved a powerful, urgent-sounding message, so he reduced the stylistic elements, with a corresponding effect. Foster and Boyde, as they trace the effects of Cavalcanti's influence on Dante, specify Cavalcanti's chief devices: ". . . the independent status of the faculties, the consecutive clauses, the

use of snatches of direct speech . . . favourite words as *paura,*
pensoso . . . the technique whereby the *pensieri* . . . *spiriti,*
anima, core, are all personified as independent and autonomous
agents, and the lover has no integrated personality . . . consecutive clauses leading to a passage in direct speech to close the
frons . . ." Opposing this starkness of rhetoric and theme is a
dazzling skill in rhyme and versification—a love of technical
virtuosity that is inherent, and has remained intact, in the courtly
tradition. Thus the tension and multiple conflicts of the inner
life are reflected on the verbal surface.

The means by which Cavalcanti represents that inner experience is the most remarkable aspect of the new style. This
is the whole complex of the "spirits." These spirits had been
around earlier but had never played such a rôle in anyone's
poetry before; so prominent are they in Cavalcanti's, however,
that he himself wrote a wonderful parody of the whole works
(*Per gli occhi fere un spirito sottile*). What follows is the briefest
sketch of this proliferating system. (There is a good orientation
to the subject in Maurice Valency's *In Praise of Love.*)

These spirits are material substances, produced by the body.
Their function is to serve as a medium in various relations: between the senses and their objects; between the organs of the
body and the soul. They originate in the digestion of ordinary
food and undergo various degrees of refinement through heat,
depending upon the nature of their specific tasks.

The *spiritus naturalis,* the basic substance, is produced in the
liver. It is superheated in the heart, the lungs acting as a cooling
bellows to prevent scorching, and becomes the *spiritus vitalis,*
which brings warmth and motion to the organs and limbs. It is
further refined in the brain and becomes the *spiritus animalis.*
The spirit is an extremely volatile and rarefied substance and, in
its highest degree of refinement, as dematerialized as matter can
be without ceasing to be matter. It is this hot and airy stuff that
forms the nexus between all inner relations, such as that between
the senses and the intellect, and outer relations, such as that between the lover and the beloved lady.

Various spirits, formed from the *spiritus naturalis,* are crucial to all the operations of the senses. For example, visual spirits fly from the eye, strike the object, and return bearing its shape and color. In the same way, there are tactile, olfactory, auditory, gustatory spirits, each capable of returning with a special image. These fragmentary images are integrated by the common sense, the *sensus communis,* which is still a physical, not a mental, faculty: all these operations so far are common to men and animals.

This integrated image of spirits passes into the heart, where it is superheated and then borne to the first of the three cells of the brain, the imagination, which is the storehouse of such images. Then it passes to the middle cell, the reason *(vis aestimativa)*, where all of its accidents are abstracted—its color, its shape, its peculiar location in time and space, all of the traits of its secular appearance. Washed clean of every local and individualizing mark, it is no longer a visual image: in this abstract state it reveals its essence to the intellect. (On the rôle of the passive and active intellects in this operation, see the notes to *Donna mi prega*.) The spirit is now borne to the third and hindmost chamber, the memory. Out of this chamber the passage of the spirit continues downward to relay the intellect's judgment and command to the organs and sinews of growth and movement.

Now it can be seen why one of the deadly effects of love is caused by too much sighing, for sighs are exhalations of vital spirits: as they "flee" and "betray" the lover, he must become physically weaker, he may even die. Only a new influx of spirits issuing from the lady—a kindly look (the emission of visual spirits), a gentle smile (the emission of risible spirits)—or the return of his own fled spirits can save him now. Thus, in one sonnet *(Veder poteste)*, Cavalcanti describes the near death of his body: afflicted by the spirit of love, the soul was on the verge of despair and desired to flee:

> E po' sostenne, quando vide uscire
> degli occhi vostri un lume di merzede,
> che porse dentro al cor nova dolcezza.
> E quel sottile spirito che vede
> soccorse gli altri che volean morire,
> gravati d'angosciosa debolezza.

(But then it stopped, for it saw issuing
from your eyes a light of pity,
which rendered an unknown sweetness in my heart.
And this subtle spirit of my sight
rescued every other desiring to die,
borne down by languishing weakness.)

The sighs, as visual and auditory spirits, range widely through barriers and spaces that the body cannot traverse. They bring to the beloved lady an image of the poet's inner state, which she may then come to understand—if she wishes to, that is; and they bring back to him new tidings of the lady, a new influence of her nobility and power. Sometimes these spirits return with no clear image, weak and in great confusion, their very vagueness and disorder a reflection of something ineffable, something miraculous in the lady:

> Lagrime ascendon de la mente mia
> sì tosto come questa donna sente,
> che van facendo per li occhi una via,
> per la qual passa spirito dolente;
> che entra per li miei sì debilmente
> ch'oltra non puote color discovrire
> che il maginar vi si possa finire.
>
> (Cavalcanti, *I' prego voi*)

(Tears from the depths of my soul arise
so quickly when it feels this lady near,
that going forth they make a passage through my eyes,
through which a spirit issues, full of fear.
So feeble is it when it re-enters there,
it can reveal no color, no design,
which this imagination can define.)

(The most beautiful poem ever composed upon this image of the "pilgrim spirit" is the final sonnet of the *VN:* the sigh issues from the poet's heart, mounts up beyond the outermost heaven, drawn by a new understanding bestowed by Love, and comes to Beatrice in her splendor; once returned to the longing heart that sent it forth, it speaks so subtly that the poet cannot understand it, he knows only that it speaks of Beatrice. The image of her he can see, but the meaning of her glory is as yet beyond him.)

The system upon which this imagery is based is infinitely more complex than this little sketch could possibly suggest—the four humors, the four elements, the influences of the zodiac, and the various complexions of men find their places within it, and it is made to harmonize with Aristotelian and Averroistic epistemology. As a theory of knowledge it was invented in order to preserve the autonomy and supremacy of the intellect; that is, it sought to explain how the intellect could interpret sense stimuli without being subjected to them. For if the mind responded to material objects directly, it would be passive regarding them—they would be the stimuli, its act of understanding the response—and hence inferior to them (by the principles of this theory, the passive is inferior to the active).

In Cavalcanti's hands this system of spirits did great things. It enabled him to go against the current of conventional poetic usage and to find what he could believe in as the source, the spring of poetry, not yet descended through settlements and generations. And the way he found this source is the way of poets in every period, who seek the meaning of experience not so much in experience itself, as in the language that depicts it—just as great aesthetic movements arise when artists see new possibilities, not in the object, but in the resources of their art. Cavalcanti uses this medical theory of the spirits always to one purpose: the literalization of figurative language. This is a method followed by many another poet intent on redeeming the reference of "poetic" words.

It was through this system that Cavalcanti achieved what other late poets aspired to in vain: the complete desecularization of inner experience, and an objective system of describing it. The love relation now has no other setting than the inner life of the lover, and it unfolds according to the processes of that inner life, rather than any ethical or communal ideal. The inner experience of love now is no longer expressed in a pattern of conventional subjective assertions to an audience of assumed lovers who are supposed to recognize their own experience, but in terms of an autonomous process so organic and coherent that it can be "demonstrated." Nothing is needed but an inceptive stimulus: the lady, or rather the sight of the lady, sets the machinery going, and then it goes on in its own determined course. After that, there is not much else for the lady to do except to stand in as the goal of the searching spirits.

Nothing on earth, as a matter of fact, has much of a rôle to play outside the unrolling of the poet's inner experience. There is a certain subsecular nexus of communication from spirit to spirit, the public reality of both the lover and the lady being dissolved. Aside from that, the only other intimacy possible in this system—friends, enemies, the dearly beloved's residence, all the definitions of a community having vanished—is with the great cosmic process of the heavens, which have a somewhat analogous structure (as the intellect is to the spirits, so is the Creator to the intelligences of heaven) and exert a continual influence. This, too, is spelled out in *Donna me prega*. Poetic language has changed that larger context which every utterance needs to complete its meaning: its reference extends beyond the human circle to the cosmos.

Thus Cavalcanti was the most successful of all the late poets of the courtly tradition. He did what badly needed doing: he found a way to write effective love poetry without any secular setting. Through the imagery of the spirits, he was able to write of a love relation that needed no geographical, communal, or ethical realm —no messengers, no customs, no code. The inner life, the individuality, of the lover becomes the terrain of a condition. His spirits and faculties populate this condition. But what makes this innovation great—what makes all great innovations great— is that it gives to the tradition it acts upon a way to live on. It preserved as much of the courtly love tradition as could be, when there were no more courts.

The love relation in his poetry, for example, is still a relation between the lover and the image of a beautiful lady; but in the absence of an exclusive, self-defining audience, the image can no longer be ideal, tutelary, emblematic, "Lady Courtliness." The image is now materialized, consisting in part of spirits issuing from the lady, but mostly of the lover's own projected spirits returning to him in her likeness. This image does not vaguely "come to mind" now, but invades the lover's internal system through the organs of sense and eventually dominates it all the way to the intellect.

It is no longer possible for the poet to impersonate a lover and to cast the audience into various rôles—the friends and enemies are gone. But if impersonation now is obsolete, there is another, more fitting technique that Cavalcanti uses with great brilliance: he personifies the elements of a condition—the condition of love. He gives an urgent personality to the spirits and faculties in their inner scene—the spirits are afraid and run away, the soul grieves and longs to depart, the heart beholds a redeeming spirit approaching, the sighs go searching for help. In this way he dramatizes inner experience to the same extent as the earlier poets dramatized courtly experience. (This is just what other late poets—for example, Ulrich and Burkart—tried to do, with ludicrous effect.)

In the old courtly lyric, the singer would scan the various perspectives of the audience and depict his love from each point of view: in this way he revealed the ideal character of his love and proved the superiority of his noble conception to all those who mocked it. Now Cavalcanti, of course, could not do this, and he had to find another way, because some pattern of perspectives is essential to poetic language. As he changed the scene of poetry from the court to the inner world, he found a way, precisely suitable to this new scene, of making the reader's mind shift continually from one perspective to another.

His system of spirits, as we have noted, had the effect of materializing figurative language—images in the mind now are particles passing from chamber to chamber. At the same time, the conventional, figurative sense persists, for he was writing in the courtly tradition, where that language evolved. Thus, when the spirits fly in terror to the lady and render before her the figure of the poet sighing his life away, this is a way of expressing, in the language of medicine and physiology, the same thing contained in the old envoi, where the poet declared that his thoughts, or his heart, always wandered in search of the lady and dwelt with her—here, where he is, the world sees nothing but the shell of a man. The message, as such, is the same in both cases. What is different is that Cavalcanti has found a way of expressing this convention so that it comes forth as literally, unfiguratively, materially true—the doctrine of the spirits, after all, is not some sentimental effusion, it comes from Galen, and really sick people were treated in accordance with it. Sometimes they even recovered.

Cavalcanti's lines, therefore, are figurative statements denoting a real material process in the air; or purely denotative statements literalizing a figure of speech. The constant shifting of the reader's perspective between the scientific literalness and traditional figurativeness of Cavalcanti's language is the defining experience of his poetry. This is how he makes every line resound with perspective. Every time the reader is entranced by the movement of those tiny particles, he is snatched up by the recognition of the emotions they materialize; every time he reads these lines as standard effusions, he is wrenched back to see them in their guise as literal statements.

This experience of the literalness of figurative language does not occur in the courtly tradition before Cavalcanti; and out of this resolution of opposites a meaning is engendered that is new in the secular lyric genre: the theme of the astonishing relation between the soul's longings and the necessary processes of the material world. Neither realm abolishes the other, quite the contrary: the literalness of this spirituality corroborates it, proves that it is real and that it redeems reality. Above all, it confirms the sacred doctrine that the world was created for man—man comes forth as the glory of the world, for the world needs man, it is not sufficient unto itself in the blind processes that man's perception alone defines and signifies. Cavalcanti's imagery is altogether different from that of the traditional *Natureingang*, where the common ploy was to depict nature as reflecting or opposing the lover's emotional state. The relation in Cavalcanti's poems between the sentient lover and the atoms of his feelings is not one of reflection or opposition. Something quite different is conveyed: the sense of human intelligence transcending all these processes.

There is always the danger—and Cavalcanti never forgets it—that that intelligence can be engulfed by what it ought to transcend: in the "tragic" poems, love leads to ruination. But for all these dark shadows, Cavalcanti's poetry is incredibly optimistic and full of self-congratulation, quite in the vein of courtly song: in the earlier lyric, a representative of the courtly class sang about how good it felt to be on top of the pile; Cavalcanti celebrates the privileges of man—or rather of a very few gifted men, a small circle of poets—exalted above all things in the ordinary world. The tremendous, dwarfing presence of the Creator—the One who devised the world for man's pre-eminence—is pretty much excluded in this poetry: Cavalcanti's interest does not reach many orbits above the earth. His theme is the relation between the necessitarian sublunary world and man's redeeming presence in it, a relation already implied in the contrasting meanings of *spirit:* on the one hand, vision and understanding and a kinship with the eternal; on the other hand, the stuff concocted in the liver.

As we shift continually from one perspective to another, we become aware that this constant shifting is itself the final meaning of the poem, the experience it meant us to have: for that movement in our mind is a re-enactment of our duality; and it is already the fulfillment of our supreme purpose on earth: to see the world exactly and to spiritualize it—as when we are aware that the beauty of a beautiful sunset is caused by dust.

Cavalcanti's great service to the courtly lyric tradition was to save it through this literalization—to ground it in the rules of flux and thus to accredit its spirituality, when it was in danger of not being able to find a location in any sphere of life. His poetry is best understood in terms of this tradition. It is true that he often denounces love, but such denunciations are squarely in the tradition—how many poets before him sang that they were sighing their lives away and forsaking the highest things! Cavalcanti stresses this destructive aspect of love, its former ameliorative power having disappeared with the dissappearance of the courts, but not exclusively. The effect of the beloved lady sometimes leads the lover to look beyond the processes of love: "If you gaze upon this one, you will see her virtue ascended into heaven."

It is at this point, however, that Cavalcanti's vision fades; and yet, even in the terms of the theories he adopted, love had a redemptive power, which needed to be specified as precisely as its physical processes. For the beautiful image, once purified by abstraction, could lead the intellect to a vision of Beauty. But such a thought is hard to find in Cavalcanti, except as an unexamined corollary: he had no wish to follow this track, whereever it led. The only poet who did was the one who hailed him as the dearest friend.

Cavalcanti's vision, then, was pretty much confined to the sublunary world, the heavens being mostly a vast analogy to the inner life. But the temptation to read back from Dante is very great, especially in some passages. For example, Cavalcanti calls the lady *donna angelicata* in one lyric; in another, the thrice abstracted essence of the beloved announces his salvation. But however often passages like this can be adduced, Cavalcanti was not on the road that Dante followed. The phrase *donna angelicata* in its context simply means "angelic lady" and so it takes its place in the register of compliments at the disposal of courtly love poets since the beginning.

But it is tempting to stress the participial form and to see in the beloved what would amount to an angelicized lady, a forebear of Beatrice—though such an idea does not fit the context. Dante himself, in a famous passage in the *VN* (xxiv), took her name, Giovanna, and the season she was compared to (Spring, *Primavera*) and depicted an overwhelming concept: in the unrolling of his life, there was an analogous re-creation of the great order of salvation, for as Beatrice is his savior, so Giovanna re-creates Saint John, announcing her (*prima verrà*, "she will come first").

But, of course, this is all Dante's idea, it is none of Cavalcanti's, and to look for it in Cavalcanti is to misread and misprize him. He had nothing like this in mind. What he wanted to do, and what he did so wonderfully, was to revivify traditional courtly poetry, to make it fit the circumstances of belief in his generation. As such it was no different from the ambition of Guinizelli and of the Sicilians before him—and of many fine poets ever since the first "new generation." The special problem of these late poets, as we have observed, was that they were continuing a theme created for a scene that was gone, and they had only the inner life and the vast air as possibilities for a setting. What Dante did has nothing to do with them, nor were they concerned with what concerned him.

The best way to read a poem like *Fresca rosa novella*, for example, is to forget about Dante first of all, and to stay within the confines that the poet has marked out: the poem, the inner life, the universal analogy. Then there arises from the text itself —from the images and the verbal forms—a certain pattern, a continuous alternation between activity and passivity, between the emission and reception of transforming energy. It is this pattern that determines the passive form *angelicata*. It is this pattern, also, that gives the ending, with its reiterated *forza*, a dramatic and triumphant effect; and a retroactive resonance to the beginning. *Fresca rosa novella* comes to denote one elemental integrity—the repetition of the *-a* ending, apart from its grammatical necessity, has the effect of a ligature. These words now signify, not a thing with two attributes, but the integrity of a creature whose youth and miraculousness are of its essence—a new reality at the beginning and at the end of the worldwide process of spring.

In this personification and dramatic play of forces lies Cavalcanti's special gift. And it is instructive to see this in a poem like *Fresca rosa novella*, for that is one of his most joyous and least doctrinaire lyrics, not at all in the "tragic style," which is usually regarded as most characteristic, and to which most of this introduction has been devoted.

Text: Guido Favati, ed. *Guido Cavalcanti, le Rime*. Documenti di Filologia, 1. Milan and Naples: Riccardo Ricciardi, 1957; with some changes in punctuation.

Fresca rosa novella,
piacente Primavera,[1]
per prata e per rivera   I
gaiamente cantando,
5 vostro fin pregio mando a la verdura.

Lo vostro pregio fino
in gio' si rinovelli
da grandi e da zitelli
per ciascuno cammino;
10 e càntine gli augelli
ciascuno in suo latino
da sera e da matino   II
su li verdi arbuscelli.
Tutto lo mondo canti
15 (poi che lo tempo vène)
sì come si convene,
vostr'altezza pregiata;
chè siete angelicata criatura.

Angelica sembianza
20 in voi, donna, riposa;
Dio, quanto aventurosa
fue la mia disianza!
Vostra cera gioiosa,
poi che passa e avanza

25 natura e costumanza,   III
ben è mirabil cosa.
Fra lor le donne dèa
vi chiaman come sète:
tanto adorna parete

[1] *Primavera* (Spring) is an epithet given by Dante, alluding to this song, to
Cavalcanti's beloved lady, Giovanna. See *La Vita Nuova*, XXIV, 3.

New rose, miracle,
pleasing Primavera,[1]
through field and rivulets   I
gaily singing
5 I commend your excellence to everything becoming green.

Let your excellence
be sung anew in joy
by every man and boy
on every street;
10 and let the birds sing about it,
each in its latin,
evening and morning,   II
among the green bushes.
Let the whole world sing—
15 for spring comes forth—
as it is right,
of your exaltation:
for you are mortal made as angel.

The likeness of an angel
20 rests upon you, lady;
God, how lucky
was my desire!
Your joyous look,
as it surpasses

25 nature and everything we are used to—   III
it is a miraculous thing.
Among themselves the women call
you goddess, as you are:
so beautiful are you when you appear,

30 ch'eo non saccio contare;
   e chi poria pensare oltra natura?

   Oltra natura umana
   vostra fina piagenza
   fece Dio, per essenza
35 che voi foste sovrana:
   per che vostra parvenza
   vèr me non sia lontana;
   or non mi sia villana   IV
   la dolce provedenza!
40 E se vi pare oltraggio
   ch'ad amar vi sia dato,
   non sia da voi blasmato:
   chè solo amor mi sforza,
   contra cui non val forza nè misura.

                        26

   Biltà di donna e di saccente core,
   e cavalieri armati che sien genti,
   cantar d'augelli e ragionar d'amore
   adorni legni 'n mar forte correnti,

5 aria serena quand'appar l'albore,
   e bianca neve scender senza venti,
   rivera d'acqua e prato d'ogni fiore,
   oro e argento, azzuro 'n ornamenti,

   ciò passa la beltate e la valenza
10 de la mia donna e'l su' gentil coraggio,
   sì che rassembra vile a chi ciò guarda.

   E tant' à più d'ogn'altra canoscenza
   quanto lo cielo de la terra è maggio:
   a simil di natura ben non tarda,[1]

---

[1] Favati has: ". . . *ben om tarda*": "one longs (for one of such a nature) ."

30 I cannot describe it:
whose thought could reach beyond nature?

Beyond human nature
God created
your beauty, that you should be
35 in essence pre-eminent.
Therefore may your presence
be not beyond me,
or your gentle wisdom   IV
cruel to me.
40 And if it seems out of all degree
that I should be given to loving you,
do not blame me:
for it is Love alone that forces me
that no force can withstand, and no restraint.

26

Beauty of woman and the acquainted heart,
noble knights in arms,
singing of birds and talk of love,
fair ships running swiftly on the sea,

5   the serene air when the dawn comes up,
and white snow falling when no wind blows,
the water's shore and a field of every flower,
gold and silver, azure stones in ornaments

are surpassed, all, by the beauty and the worth
10   of my lady, and her gentle heart,
so that they all seem cheap to whoever regards them.

And she is greater than all in her wisdom,
as much as heaven is greater than earth:
the Good is not slow to come to its like.[1]

27

Chi è questa che vèn, ch'ogn'om la mira,
e fa tremar di claritate l'àre,
e mena seco Amor, sì che parlare
omo non può, ma ciascun sospira?

5　Deh! che rassembla quando li occhi gira!
dical Amor, ch'i' nol savria contare:
cotanto d'umiltà donna mi pare,
ch'ogn'altra vèr di lei i' la chiam'ira.

Non si porìa contar la sua piagenza,
10　ch'a le' s'inchin' ogni gentil vertute,
e la beltate per sua dea la mostra.

Non fu sì alta già la mente nostra,
e non si pose in noi tanta salute,
che propriamente n'aviam canoscenza.

28

Io non pensava che lo cor giammai
avesse di sospir tormento tanto,
che dell'anima mia nascesse pianto,
mostrando per lo viso agli occhi morte.
5　Non sentìo pace nè riposo alquanto
poscia ch'Amore e madonna trovai,
lo qual mi disse: "Tu non camperai,
chè troppo è lo valor di costei forte."
La mia virtù si partìo sconsolata,
10　poi che lassò lo core
a la battaglia ove madonna è stata:

I

27

Who is this one that comes, that each man gazes on,
that makes the air tremble with light
and leads Love along with her, so that no man
can speak, but each one sighs?

5   Oh, what she is like when she turns her eyes—
let Love tell it, I could not recount it.
She is a lady of such humility
I call every other woman fury, compared to her.

No one could recount her gracefulness,
10   for every noble virtue gives her homage,
and Beauty shows her forth as its goddess.

Our mind was never yet on such a height
nor did such grace ever dwell in us,
that we could have adequate knowledge of this.

28

I did not think my heart would ever
have such great torment from sighing
that tears would rise up from my soul—
and Death would take shape to all eyes on my face.
5   I have felt no peace or rest
since I found Love and my lady.
Love told me: "You will not escape,   I
the power of this one is too great."
All my forces withdrew in despair
10   and abandoned my heart
in the battle where my lady stood:

la qual degli occhi suoi venne a ferire
di tal guisa ch'Amore
ruppe tutt'i miei spiriti a fuggire.

15   Di questa donna non si può contare;
chè di tante bellezze adorna vene
che mente di qua giù no la sostene,
sì che la veggia lo 'intelletto nostro.
Tant'è gentil che, quand'io penso bene,
20   l'anima sento per lo cor tremare,
sì come quella che non può durare   II
davanti al gran valore ch'è in lei dimostro.
Per li occhi fère la sua claritate
sì, che quale mi vede
25   dice: "Non guardi tu questa pietate
ch'è posta invece di persona morta,
per dimandar merzede?" [1]
E non si n'è madonna ancor accorta.

Quando 'l penser mi vèn ch'i' voglia dire
30   a gentil core de la sua vertute,
i' trovo me di sì poca salute
ch'i' non ardisco di star nel pensero.
Amor, c'ha le bellezze sue vedute,
mi sbigottisce sì che sofferire
35   non può lo cor sentendola venire;   III
che sospirando dice: "Io ti dispero;
però che trasse del su' dolce riso
una saetta aguta
c'ha passato 'l tu' core e 'l mio diviso.
40   Tu sai, quando venisti, ch'io ti dissi:
poi che l'avei veduta,
per forza convenìa che tu morissi."

Canzon, tu sai che de' libri d'Amore
io t'assemplai quando madonna vidi;
45   ora ti piaccia ch'io di te mi fidi

[1] Pity has taken on his features; he has become the figure of Pity itself.

who advanced to strike
with her eyes, so that Love
put all my spirits to flight.

15 Of this lady nothing can be recounted,
for she comes adorned with such great beauty,
no memory here below can hold it
for the intellect to contemplate.
She is so gentle, when I think of her
20 I feel the soul of me trembling in my heart,
like a thing that could never survive   II
before the great power now revealed in her.
Her light strikes through the eyes so
that whoever sees me
25 says: "Do you not see Pity there,
come in the aspect of one who is dead,
to beg for mercy?" [1]
And my lady is not aware of all this yet.

When the thought comes to me to speak
30 of her virtue to gentle hearts,
I find myself so lacking in the grace,
I do not dare go on with the thought.
Love, who has seen her beauty,
terrifies me so, my heart,
35 feeling her approaching, cannot endure it;   III
Love, sighing, says: "I despair of you;
because from her sweet smile she drew
a sharp arrow
that has passed through your heart and shattered mine.
40 You know, when you came I told you,
since you had seen her,
it meant you would have to die."

Song, you know it was from the books of Love
I copied you, when I saw my lady;
45 now let me put my trust in you,

e vadi 'n guisa a lei ch'ella t'ascolti.
E prego umilemente a lei tu guidi
li spiriti fuggiti del mio core,
che per soverchio de lo su' valore   IV
50 eran distrutti, se non fosser vòlti;

e vanno soli senza compagnia
e son pien di paura.
Però li mena per fidata via:
e poi le di', quando le se' presente:
55 "Questi sono in figura
d'un che si more sbigottitamente."

29

O donna mia, non vedestù colui
che 'n su lo core mi tenea la mano,
quando ti rispondea fiochetto e piano
per la temenza delli colpi sui?

5   E' fu Amore che, trovando nui,
meco ristette, che venìa lontano,
en guisa d'un arcier presto soriano,
acconcio sol per uccider altrui.

E trasse poi de gli occhi tuoi sospiri
10 i quai mi saettò nel cor sì forte,
ch'i' mi partii sbigottito fuggendo.

Allor m'apparve di sicur la Morte,
accompagnata di quelli martiri
che soglion consumare altrui piangendo.

go to her, that she may hear you.
And I beg you humbly, lead to her
the fugitive spirits of my heart,
that the excess of her power   IV
50 would have slaughtered, had they not fled;

now they go alone, without company,
and full of fear.
Therefore, lead them by a safe way
and, when you have reached her, say:
55 "These are in the figure
of one who dies in terror."

29

O my lady, didn't you see him—that one
who was holding his hand on my heart
while I was answering you, all weak and speaking low
for fear of his blows?

5 He was Love, who, once he found us,
stayed with me, who had come from afar—
stayed, like a ready Syrian archer
poised intently to kill.

And then from those eyes of yours he drew sighs
10 that he shot so hard into my heart,
I withdrew in terrified retreat.

All of a sudden Death appeared before me then,
coming with those agonies
that have long consumed us, as we weep.

30

Veggio negli occhi de la donna mia
un lume pien di spiriti d'amore   I
che porta uno piacer novo nel core,
sì che vi desta d'allegrezza vita.

5 Cosa m'aven quand'i' le son presente,
ch'i' no la posso a lo 'ntelletto dire:
veder mi par de la sua labbia uscire
una sì bella donna, che la mente   II
comprender no la può, chè 'nmantenente
10 ne nasce un'altra di bellezza nova,
de la qual par ch'una stella si mova
e dica: la salute tua è apparita.

Là dove questa bella donna appare,
s'ode una voce che le vèn davanti;
15 e par che d'umiltà il su' nome canti
sì dolcemente, che s'i' 'l vo' contare,   III
sento che 'l su' valor mi fa tremare;
e movonsi nell'anima sospiri
che dicon: "Guarda, su tu costei miri,
20 vedra' la sua vertù nel ciel salita."

31

Donna me prega,   perch'eo voglio dire
d'un accidente,[1]   che sovente   è fèro,

---

[1] Cf. Dante, *VN*, xxv, 1: "Love does not exist in itself, like a substance, but
is an accident in a substance." An accident is that which, by its nature, belongs to another thing but is not an essential part of that thing (for example, color); it cannot exist separately.

30

In the eyes of my lady I see
a light full of spirits of love,   I
which bears to the heart a sweetness never known,
so that a joyous life awakens there.

5 Something happens to me when I am in her presence,
I cannot describe it to the intellect:
it seems to me that from her lips there issues forth
a lady so beautiful, the memory   II
cannot hold her, because at once
10 another is born of her, of unknown beauty,
from whom it seems a star arises
and says: "Your salvation is come forth."

There where this beautiful lady comes forth,
a voice is heard preceding her;
15 and it seems, moved by her humility it sings her name
so sweetly, that if I try to describe it,   III
I feel how her worth makes me tremble;
and in my soul sighs bestir themselves
which say: "Behold, if you gaze upon this one,
20 you will see her virtue ascended into heaven."

31

A lady asks me please to speak
of an accident [1] that is often cruel,

ed è sì altero   ch'è chiamato amore: [2]
sì che lo nega   possa 'l ver sentire.

5 Ed a presente   conoscente chero,
perch'io no spero   ch'om di basso core
a tal ragione porti conoscenza: I
chè senza   natural dimostramento
non ho talento   di voler provare
10 là dove posa, e chi lo fa creare,[3]
e qual è sua vertute e sua potenza,
l'essenza   poi ciascun suo movimento,
e 'l piacimento   che 'l fa dire amare,
e s'omo per veder lo pò mostrare.

15 In quella parte   dove sta memora
prende suo stato,   sì formato,   come
diafan da lome,   d'una scuritate
la qual da Marte   vène, e fa demora.[4]
Elli è creato   e da sensato   nome,
20 d'alma costume   e di cor volontate.
Vèn da veduta forma che s'intende,   II
che prende   nel possibile intelletto,
come in subietto,   loco e dimoranza.
In quella parte mai non ha possanza,
25 perchè da qualitate non descende;

---

[2] Contini points out that this refers to a popular etymology which takes the root of *amore* to be -*mor*-, thus relating it to the idea of death, or bitterness.

[3] Here the poet states the essential points of his "demonstration":

    l. 10: the seat of love and its origin (treated in strophe ii);

    l. 11: the power of love in relation to the soul's faculties (str. iii);

    l. 12: its essence and its effects (str. iv);

    ll. 13–14: the reason why it is called love and why it is not visible (str. v).

[4] The memory, in Aristotelian psychology, is one of the internal senses, that which stores up the images brought in by the external senses. The "part where memory is" therefore is the sensitive soul, the seat of the passions, which are aroused by the sight of external objects. As a diaphanous (transparent) body is transparent only when light passes through it—for the light makes its transparency actual—so love, which is a blind passion of the sensitive appetite, is actualized by an "obscurity"—a malign influence—from Mars touching the sensitive soul; it is therefore in this lower, sensitive, soul that love resides. Love arises from the pleasure which a perceived form excites in us; thus, for the birth of love it is necessary that an image enter into us

and so unmerciful, it is called love: [2]
to speak so that even one who denies it will sense the
    truth.
5 And now I speak to those who understand,
for I do not think that one whose heart is base
can follow such an argument: I
because unless I can use the methods of natural philos-
    ophy
I am unwilling to demonstrate
10 where it dwells and who created it, [3]
its influence and potency,
its essence, its effects,
the pleasure which gives it the name of love,
and whether it is visible.

15 In that part where the memory is
it comes into being, informed—as the diaphanous
by light—by a darkness
from Mars, and there it resides. [4]
It is created out of something seen,
20 the soul's disposition, and the heart's desire.
It comes forth from a form perceived and understood,   II
which takes its dwelling
in the possible intellect, as in its subject.
In that part Love has no force,
25 because the intellect is not derived from qualities,

through the senses: love "comes from a form perceived."
  However, something happens to this image in another part of the soul, a part that is beyond the carnal passions of the part where love arises and dwells. All the accidents—the visible qualities—that excite love are abstracted from the image in the memory. Thus freed from these material and temporal weights, the hidden essence is revealed and understood. This twofold process of abstraction and understanding is an intellectual activity. The active intellect (*intellectus agens*) abstracts the pure, intelligible idea; the passive or possible intellect (*intellectus passibilis*) perceives and understands. Therefore love, which responds to a "form perceived," can never affect that higher part, because the intellect does not originate in material "qualities" but "shines" in its perpetual understanding of the universals.

resplende   in sè perpetual effetto:
non ha diletto,   ma consideranza,
sì che non pote là gir simiglianza.[5]

Non è vertute,   ma da quella vène
30 ch'è perfezione,   che si pone   tale,
non razionale   ma che sente, dico.[6]
For di salute   giudicar mantene,
chè la 'ntenzione   per ragione   vale:
discerne male   in cui è vizio amico.

35 Di sua potenza segue spesso morte,   III
se forte   la vertù fosse impedita
la quale aita   la contraria via;
non perchè oppost'a naturale sia,
ma quanto che da buon perfetto tort'è,
40 per sorte   non pò dire om ch'aggia vita,
chè stabilita   non ha segnoria;
a simel pò valer quand'om l'oblia.

L'esser è quando   lo voler è tanto
ch'oltra misura   di natura   torna;
45 poi non s'adorna   di riposo mai.
Move, cangiando   color, riso in pianto
e la figura   con paura   storna;
poco soggiorna: ancor di lui vedrai
che 'n gente di valor lo più si trova.   IV
50 La nova   qualità move sospiri,
e vol ch'om miri   in un fermato loco,

[5] Favati: *sì che non pote largir simiglianza*, "so that it (the intellect) cannot
give forth a similitude," that is, cannot produce a concept of the experience
of sensual love, cannot know it. Favati, l. 19: *ed à sensato nome*.
[6] For Cavalcanti, love is a passion which comes, not from the rational faculty
of the soul, but from that faculty "which feels," that is, from the sensitive
soul, which is the form or "perfection" of the natural, organic body. Cavalcanti does not believe that the intellectual soul is the form of man, because
the intellect "shines in perpetual effect," it is always in act, independent of
the body. According to Bruno Nardi, in this departure from Aristotle's definition of the soul and in this apparent belief in the eternality and universality
of the intellect, Cavalcanti closely follows the doctrines of Averroës.
Love is an obscurity of the soul; it becomes a vice when it leads reason

but shines in perpetual effect;
it has no aptness for delight, it is pure contemplation,
so that no image can find a way to it.[5]

It is not a faculty of the soul, but derives
30 from the soul, which is the form of man—
not the rational soul, as I say, but that which feels.[6]
It deprives reason of well-being,
for now desire does the work of reason:
a man who befriends vice judges badly.
35 Death often follows from its power,   III
if that faculty should ever be impeded
which keeps open the path of life—
not that love is inimical to the body,
but insofar as a man has turned from the true good
40 he cannot be said to have any life,
for he has no stable mastery over himself;
and the same is true when a man forgets it altogether.

It truly exists when desire is so great
as to go beyond the limits of nature;
45 then it never knows the beauty of repose.
It moves—causing the lover's color to change—from
    smiles to tears,
and contorts the face with fear;
it never abides; and you will see
it most often in people of worth.   IV
50 This new quality arouses sighs

and makes one yearn for what he cannot reach,

and judgment astray. Death follows when the faculty which sustains life—the reason, according to one interpretation; the normal functioning of the body, in another—is impeded. On the other hand, love arises from a natural need and is not a vice unless it leads a man to turn from the true good. That is why the man who "forgets it altogether" is as much in danger as the one who is overwhelmed by it: because such a man repudiates his human needs and thus never attains that "stable mastery over himself" without which he can never contemplate, or accept, the truth. See Bruno Nardi, *Dante e la cultura medievale* (Bari, 1949), Chapter II.

destandos'ira, la qual manda foco [7]
(imaginar non pote om che nol prova),
nè mova   già però ch'a lui si tiri,
55 e non si giri   per trovarvi gioco,[8]
nè certamente gran saver nè poco.

De simil tragge   complessione sguardo
che fa parere   lo piacere   certo;
non pò coverto   star quand'è sì giunto.
60 Non già selvaggie   le beltà son dardo,
chè tal volere   per temere   è sperto: [9]
consegue merto   spirito ch'è punto.
E non si pò conoscer per lo viso   V
compriso,   bianco in tale obietto cade;
65 e chi bene aude,   forma non si vede; [10]
dunqu'elli meno che da lei procede.
For di colore, d'essere diviso,
assiso   in mezzo scuro luce rade.
For d'ogne fraude   dice degno in fede
70 che solo di costui nasce mercede.

Tu puoi sicuramente gir, canzone,
là 've te piace; ch'io t'ho sì adornata
ch'assai laudata   sarà tua ragione   VI
de le persone   c'hanno intendimento:
75 di star con l'altre tu non hai talento.

32

Pegli occhi fère un spirito sottile
che fa in la mente spirito destare,

---

[7] According to Nardi, the irascible faculty, which is aroused when the con-
cupiscent—the desiring—faculty is unable to have its object.
[8] Love is found in men of worth, because vulgar hearts are insensible to it. It
keeps the noble man intent on what he is excluded from, makes him forego
pleasure. Favati, l. 56: *cert' à mente.*

and thus arouses anger, which ignites fire [7]
(no man can imagine it who has not experienced it);
and does not want the lover to move, though he is drawn,
55 or seek to find some pleasure there; [8]
nor much, nor little, wisdom.

From one who is like the lover, Love draws out a look

that makes pleasure seem assured;
it cannot remain hidden when it has reached this point.
60 Vulgar beauty is not the arrow of Love,
for such desire is scattered by fear; [9]
but the spirit that is struck attains requital.
And it cannot be known by sight,   V
for there is only pallor in this object,
65 and—note this well—form itself is invisible; [10]
then all the more invisible is that which proceeds from it.
Without color, without essence,
dwelling in darkness it expunges the light.
Without deceit I say, and deserve belief:
70 from love alone is mercy born.

You may set forth in certainty, my song,
wherever it pleases you; for I have so provided you
that your reasoning will be praised abundantly   VI
by those who understand:
75 you have no wish to be with others.

32

Through the eyes a subtle spirit strikes
and causes another spirit to stir in the memory,

[9] Beauty apart from refinement—the raw beauty of a female body—never
arouses love; for love, in contrast to mere lust, is never turned off by fear.
[10] Love, which is aroused by physical qualities, cannot itself be seen; for, not
being a physical object, it has no color. For all its dangers, it is a source of
mercy and compassion.

dal qual si move spirito d'amare,
ch'ogn'altro spiritello fa gentile.

5   Sentir non pò di lu' spirito vile,
di cotanta vertù spirito appare!
Quest'è lo spiritel che fa tremare,
lo spiritel che fa la donna umile.

E poi da questo spirito si move
10   un altro dolce spirito soave,
che siegue un spiritello di mercede:

lo quale spiritel spiriti piove
chè di ciascuno spirit'ha la chiave
per forza d'uno spirito che'l vede.[1]

33

In un boschetto trova' pasturella   I
più che la stella bella al mi' parere.

Cavelli avea biondetti e ricciutelli
e gli occhi pien d'amor, cera rosata;
5   con sua verghetta pasturav' agnelli,   II
discalza, di rugiada era bagnata;
cantava come fosse 'nnamorata;
er' adornata di tutto piacere.

D'amor la salutai mantenente
10   e domandai s'avesse compagnia,
ed ella mi rispuose dolcemente   III
che sola sola per lo bosco gìa,

[1] The visual spirit is the first and the last in the sequence described here. The repetitions and the ridiculous neatness of the scheme indicate that Cavalcanti's intention is to make fun of the whole machinery of the spirits, in self-parody (contini).

from which arises the spirit of love—
which makes every other little spirit gentle.

5 A vulgar spirit could not feel
a spirit of such great subtlety—
this is the little spirit that makes one tremble,
the little spirit that makes the lady humble.

And then from this spirit issues forth
10 another sweet and gentle spirit,
upon which follows a little spirit of mercy:

and this little spirit rains down spirits,
for it holds the key to every spirit
by virtue of a spirit that perceives it.[1]

33

In a little grove I found a shepherdess, I
I thought she was more beautiful than the star.

Her hair was blond, in curls,
her eyes full of love, her color like the rose.
5 She pastured the lambs with her little staff, II
and, barefoot, was wet with dew;
and singing as though in love.
She was adorned with everything pleasant to look at.

Straight off I greeted her, meaning love:
10 and asked if anyone was with her,
and she answered me softly: III
she was going through the woods alone, alone,

e disse: "Sacci, quando l'augel pia
allor disia   'l me' cor drudo avere."

15 Po' che mi disse la sua condizione,
    e per lo bosco augelli audio cantare,
    fra me stesso diss'i': "Or è stagione   IV
    di questa pasturella gio' pigliare."
    Merzè le chiesi sol che di baciare
20 e d'abracciare se le fosse 'n volere.

    Per man mi prese, d'amorosa voglia,
    e disse che donato m'avea 'l core:
    menommi sott'una freschetta foglia   V
    là dov' i' vidi fior d'ogni colore;
25 e tanto vi sentio gioia e dolzore
    che'l dio d'amore   mi parea vedere.

and said: "Now listen: when the bird chirps,
my heart longs to have a friend."

15 When she told me of her heart's condition
and throughout the woods I heard the birds atwitter,
I said to myself, "Right now is the time   IV
to take my pleasure with this shepherd girl."
I asked her for the grace, if it pleased her,
20 to kiss her and hold her in my arms.

She took my hand with a longing to love
and told me she had given me her heart:
she led me where it was cool under leaves,   V
and I saw flowers of every color;
25 and felt such joy and sweetness there,
I thought I saw the god of love.

LAPO GIANNI

(c. 1250–1328 or later)

It is generally believed that the poet was a notary, born in Florence of the family of Ricevuti; this identification is not positive, however, and other figures have been proposed. He was a friend of Cavalcanti and Dante, both of whom name him in their poetry; Dante, moreover, praises him in *DVE,* I, xiii, as one of the three Florentine poets who achieved eloquence in the vernacular (the other two being Lapo's two friends).

Stilnovist themes and phrases abound in Lapo's poetry; but the love depicted has a mildness, and the lover's suffering a joyousness, that belong to the older poetry of the courtly tradition; this acceptance of Sicilian and Provençal conventions is reflected as well in his verse forms. Lapo combines these disparate elements with much skill.

Text: Contini.

34

Amor, eo chero mia donna in domino,
l'Arno balsamo fino,
le mura di Firenza inargentate,
le rughe di cristallo lastricate,
5   fortezze alte, merlate,
mio fedel fosse ciaschedun latino;

il mondo 'n pace, securo 'l cammino;
non mi noccia vicino;
e l'aria temperata verno e state;
10   e mille donne e donzelle adornate,
sempre d'amor pregiate,
meco cantasser la sera e 'l mattino:

e giardin fruttuosi di gran giro,
con grande uccelagione,
15   pien di condotti d'acqua e cacciagione;
bel mi trovasse come fu Absalone;

Sansone pareggiasse e Salamone;
servaggi di barone
sonar vïole, chitarre e canzone;
20   poscia dover entrar nel ciel empiro;

giovane sana allegra e secura
fosse mia vita fin che 'l mondo dura.

35

Sì come i Magi a guida de la stella
girono invèr le parti d'orïente
per adorar lo Segnor ch'era nato,

Love, I would like my lady in my power,
and the Arno exquisite perfume,
the walls of Florence silvered over,
the streets paved with crystal,
5   high, castellated fortresses,
every Italian my vassal,

the world in peace, the highway safe,
no neighbor harming me,
and the air mild in winter and summer;
10   a thousand women and girls adorned,
continually made beautiful, by love,
singing with me evening and morning;

and fruitful gardens of great extent,
with a great preserve of fowl,
15   full of fountains and streams and good game;
to find myself as handsome as was Absalon,

the equal of Samson and Solomon;
and the servants of a baron
playing viols, guitars, and songs;
20   then to be certain of entering the highest heaven;

A youthful, happy and secure
life as long as the world shall endure.

35

Just as the Magi, guided by the star,
turned toward the regions of the East
to adore the Lord newborn,

così mi guidò Amore a veder quella,
5   che 'l giorno amanto prese novamente[1]
ond'ogni gentil cor fu salutato.
I' dico ch'i' fu' poco dimorato,
ch'Amor mi confortava: "Non temere,
guarda com'ella viene umile e piana!"
10   Quando mirai un po' m'era lontana:
allora m'afforzai per non cadere;
il cor divenne morto ch'era vivo.
Io vidi lo 'ntelletto su' giulivo
quando mi porse il salutorio sivo.

36

Nel vostro viso angelico amoroso
vidi i belli occhi e la luce brunetta,
che 'nvece di saetta
mise pe' miei lo spirito vezzoso.

5   Tanto venne in su' abito gentile
quel novo spiritel ne la mia mente,
che 'l cor s'allegra de la sua veduta.
Dispose giù l'aspetto signorile
parlando a' sensi tanto umilemente
10   ch'ogni mio spirito allora 'l saluta.
Ora hanno le mie membra canosciuta
di quel segnor la sua grande dolcezza,
e 'l cor con allegrezza
l'abbraccia, poi che 'l fece virtuoso.

---

[1] The mantle of humility, of goodness; or the mantle of authority. In the last line, Contini has *salutario sivo,* "the balm of blessedness, well-being."

so Love guided me to behold that one
5   who put on anew that day the mantle [1]
wherein every gentle heart was blessed.
I say, I had not waited long
when Love comforted me: "Do not be afraid,
see how she comes forth meek and gentle."
10   When I had gazed a while, she was far from me:
then I had to gather up my strength not to fall;
my heart became dead, that was alive.
I saw the soul of her inclined toward me
when she held out her greeting.

36

In your face, like an angel's, full of love,
I saw your beautiful eyes and the dark light
that bore like an arrow
through my eyes a tender spirit.

5   This new spirit came in its gentle way
so far into my soul,
the heart rejoices at the sight of it.
It set aside its lordly aspect
and spoke to the senses with such humility,
10   it gives bliss to every spirit since that hour.
Every part of me knows now
the great sweetness of this lord,
and my heart embraces him
with joy, for he fills it with his power.

37

Dolc'è 'l pensier che mi notrica il core
d'una giovane donna che disia,   I
per cui si fe' gentil l'anima mia,
poiché sposata la congiunse Amore.

5 I' non posso leggeramente trare
il novo esemplo ched ella simiglia,
quest'angela che par di ciel venuta;
d'Amor sorella mi sembr'al parlare
ed ogni su' atterello è maraviglia: II
10 beata l'alma che questa saluta!
In colei si può dir che sia piovuta
allegrezza, speranza e gioi' compita
ed ogni rama di virtù fiorita,
la qual procede dal su' gran valore.

15 Il nobile intelletto ched i' porto
per questa gioven donna ch'è apparita,
mi fa spregiar viltate e villania;
e 'l dolce ragionar mi dà conforto
ch' i' fe' con lei de l'amorosa vita,   III
20 essendo già in sua nuova signoria.
Ella mi fe' tanta di cortesia
che no sdegnò mio soave parlare;
ond'i' voglio Amor dolce ringraziare
che mi fe' degno di cotanto onore.

25 Com'i' son scritto nel libro d'Amore
conterai, ballatetta, in cortesia,   IV
quando tu vederai la donna mia;
poi che di lei fui fatto servidore.

37

Sweet is the thought my heart nurtures
of a young woman it desires,   I
for whom my soul has made itself noble,
since Love made her one with him, his bride.

5   I cannot easily portray
the new image she resembles,
this angel who seems come from heaven;
to me she's like Love's sister when she speaks,
and her slightest motion is a miracle: II
10 The soul is blessed that she greets,
for we can see that laughter,
hope, and perfect joy have rained down upon that soul,
and every flowering branch of virtue,
which comes forth from her great goodness.

15 The noble thought that is mine
since this young woman has appeared
makes me scorn every base and vulgar thing;
and the sweet conversation I had with her—
being already in the new day of her power—   III
20 about the life of love gives me comfort yet.
She was so courteous to me,
she did not disdain my soft words;
wherefore I want to thank sweet Love,
who made me worthy of such honor.

25 How I am inscribed in the book of Love
you shall recount, my song, in courtesy,   IV
when you see my lady:
for I have become her man, and serve.

DANTE ALIGHIERI

(*1265–1321*)

The poet was born in Florence into a family of the lesser nobility, whose lineage he traced back to the time of the city's origin. Little is known about the circumstances of his youth, including his schooling. When he was eighteen he sent a sonnet to Guido Cavalcanti, who replied in kind, and from this exchange began his lifelong friendship with the older poet. He fought among the ranks of the nobility in the battle of Campaldino (1289), in which Florence won a great victory over Arezzo. Probably around this time he married Gemma Donati, with whom he had three sons and a daughter and perhaps more children: little is known about his family life, for he never speaks of it in his writings. His relation with Beatrice, from his first glimpse of her when he was nine to her death in 1290, is described in *VN*.

From 1295 on, he was active in the government of the Florentine commune; in 1300 he became a prior, one of the six guild representatives who held municipal governing power for a term of two months (he had become a member of the guild of apothecaries, which also included painters and artists). The events leading immediately to his exile began in 1301 with the coming of Charles of Valois, the brother of the King of France, Philip the Fair. Charles was invited into Italy by the Pope, Boniface VIII, as an ally in the struggle between the papal and imperial parties that raged everywhere, especially in Florence. There the ruling Guelf party was divided into two factions, the Blacks (aligned with the nobility and supporting the secular claims of the Pope) and the Whites (representing the rich middle class—the "fat people," the *popolo grasso*—and in their political views closely resembling the exiled imperial party, the Ghibellines). The Pope especially wanted Charles to pacify

Florence and promised to make him Emperor. Charles entered Florence, the Blacks (as Dante had feared) came into power and, by way of securing their control, exiled those they regarded as their enemies; Dante was among the first ones condemned, in 1302, at a time when he was absent from the city on a mission to the Pope. Though his official words and actions had always been free of partisanship (he had, as prior, concurred in the banishment of Cavalcanti, a White, his dearest friend), he had on several occasions resisted the intentions of the Pope, especially in the matter of Charles de Valois. He was never to return.

Early during his exile he joined in the efforts of the Whites to fight their way back into the city; but within a couple of years he quarreled with his fellow exiles (who included the Ghibellines as well) and dissociated himself from them entirely. In *Paradiso* XVII (68f), Cacciaguida, his illustrious ancestor, foretelling the events of Dante's life, proclaims: . . . *a te fia bello/averti fatta parte per te stesso* ("it shall be your glory to have made a party for yourself"). This period of utter isolation is the likeliest setting for the great *canzone* he wrote in exile, *Tre donne* (no. 49).

His wanderings brought him to many courts and to the dwellings of many different protectors throughout Italy in the ensuing years. His last hope of seeing a strong Emperor established, and therefore his last hope of return, vanished with the failure and death, in 1313, of Henry VII, the elected Emperor, whom Dante had exhorted to strike first of all against that fox, that viper, that infected sheep, Florence. Two years later Dante was offered a chance to return provided he accepted humiliation (internment and public penitence). He refused. His final residence was in Ravenna, where he died soon after finishing the last cantos of the *Paradiso*.

As a lyric poet Dante was well acquainted with the work of his predecessors. In the *DVE* he surveys the course of the vernacular lyric and the principles of its technique, finding much to admire among the troubadours, the trouvères, and the Sicilians, bluntly denouncing Guittone and his followers as vulgar and pretentious, praising some among the stilnovisti (including himself) as models of vernacular eloquence. In other places as well he assesses his own poetry by referring to what was done before him (for example, in the famous passages, *VN*, xxv; *Purgatorio*, XXIV, 49ff). It is therefore as a lyric poet whose songs are all rooted in the courtly tradition that he appears to us here: many things come to light in his songs if we shut out, for a while, the obliterating splendor of the *Commedia*.

Then we can see how his most famous lyrics are descendants of a venerable line. Among the *rime petrose*, for example, he took over and improved upon the sestina form of Arnaut Daniel; and in *Così nel mio parler* (no. 48) the outburst against love (or the beloved) and the dream of violent revenge continue a theme already sounded by Bernart de Ventadorn and often repeated later on (compare Friedrich von Hausen, Pt. I, no. 17). The imagery of the spirits as well as other stilnovist themes appear with greater precision and a greater range of meaning than ever before. The exchanges with Forese are in line with the songs of abuse that were written to delight both the court and especially the other poets of the court. Dante's lyrics scan every period of the courtly tradition and reflect themes and techniques characteristic of many different poets, including Guittone d'Arezzo, whose rectitude and astonishing rimes inspired him, despite his official attitude of contempt.

From his conscientious study he developed possibilities of meaning and expression that were unprecedented. No one before him, to take an obvious example, not even Cavalcanti, would have dreamed of claiming for his song the higher levels of meaning Dante assigns to three of his *canzoni* in the *Convivio* (see notes). However, one has to read the *Convivio* in order to perceive these meanings, for they leave no clues on the literal surface of the poems. We can look at certain other songs that have no other text but their own to speak for them; in these songs we can measure, in terms appropriate to the lyric tradition, the greatness of Dante's innovations. We can take, for example, Dante's treatment of the imagery of the *Natureingang* and the theme of "exile"—both standard topics of the courtly lyric—in *Io son venuto* (no. 46).

In all respects but one, it should be noted, the imagery of nature in this song is completely traditional. When a courtly poet compared himself to the condition of nature in winter or spring, he meant to say that his love was better than anything in the whole wide world outside the courtly circle in which he sang: in the spring all nature rejoices, the birds chirp cheerily, but he stays full of grief (or else he too rejoices, but for reasons that have nothing to do with the time of year), for the birds are creatures of the spring while he responds to the vicissitudes of a love that transcends all natural change. This is the meaning of Dante's song too, and the contrast between the circling of the year and the steadfastness of the lover is made all the more forceful by the constant alternation between "then" and "now" in every strophe, a constant shifting that takes place in nature, but never in the poet, whose love stays always in the present.

Now the courtly poet's "nature" referred to the fields and meadows just outside the castle walls, extending as far as the eye could see or a man could walk. It was outside the poet's circle, but still close by, its exclusion and proximity proving at once that the lover has risen above his own natural desires (for he is guided by an ethical ideal that is not found outside the circle of his friends, is not "natural"), and that he suffers for it, for those desires are immediate and strong. Between that ethical circle (the realm of nobility) and the fields outside (the realm of "nature") stand the poet's enemies (in the realm of "exile"), the vulgar ones, men who act like birds. Thus the three basic moral categories of courtly literature are arranged on a bounded plane extending from the singer to the hilltop in the window. (See the introductions to Heinrich von Morungen and Reinmar.)

But Dante's lyric stands out from this tradition by the vast amplitude of the natural setting: the conventional imagery of nature never extended so far. Dante compares his love not just to the little fringe of green around the courtly circle but to the whole created universe. The vertical dimension of nature begins (as the poem begins) with the heavens and descends without a breach to the upper atmosphere, the lower atmosphere, the surface, and finally the bowels of the earth; its horizontal dimension includes all the lands of Africa and Europe. At the end, after scanning the whole sublunary world, the poet declares, "Love is in me alone." This enlargement of the image of nature has momentous consequences, which we can best follow by thinking back, for a moment, to two other courtly poets, Walther and Neidhart, who also made great innovations in the tradition of the *Natureingang*.

The two German poets transformed the *Natureingang* by animating its elements and giving "nature" a dramatic horizontal spaciousness. Before them (and after them as well) "nature" —what one saw through the window—was only a metaphoric backdrop to set off the poet's nobility: the poet referred to nature, but he was never "in" it, or if he was, he got out of it and back into the court, the only true setting for his love, before the first strophe was over (for example, Jaufré Rudel, *Lanquan li jorn*). The effect of Walther's and Neidhart's innovations was that a scene having to do with love could now be acted out in a meadow or a hillside: "Nature" became more than a metaphoric image in their poetry, it was a dramatic setting (as it had always been in the *pastorela* but not in the *canzone*). Then the question inevitably arose: what is the effect of the setting upon the love that is dramatized within it? And both poets, for all their differences in technique and style, gave exactly the same answer: the natural setting made the love common and uncourtly, unfit for a noble man. Minne alone was true to his nature, a noble love that could retain its meaning and ethical value only within the confines of the court.

Now the effect of Dante's innovation is precisely the opposite of theirs: his "nature" is so enormous that no intimate scene could possibly be acted out within it. The literal statement of his poem is clear: there is no love anyplace, and no place for his love. And the reason is not simply that it is winter—indeed, one may more justly say that it is winter because the world is loveless—but that nature is no longer proportioned to human experience; it is boundless, mechanistic, too great to be framed by the windows of a hall, a realm of great eruptions and precipitations. The song scans every level of creation and finds no resting place: "A path that pleased me when the days were pleasant/ now has become a stream."

But there is another "place" that is missing here, not only a sweet meadow. All the other poets who used this imagery, including both Walther and Neidhart, meant to contrast the instinctual life of nature with the courtly life of love: in a conventional song the poet quickly turns from the hillside to confront the defining inhabitants of the court—the beloved, the friends, the enemies. If the song, like Dante's, had a winter setting, the poet would rejoice in the loveliness and warmth of castle chambers where, in the company of women, he could look out upon the storms that despoiled the hillside; or he could send a messenger to tell the lady that love had made him immune to the winter's rages, for the falling snow was like white and red and yellow flowers to him (Bernart de Ventadorn). The seasons come and go, as Bernart says, but his love stays the same; for his love has an interior setting, is sheltered from the cycling force of nature by the walls of the castle, the sympathy of friends, the remoteness of his beloved.

Now this decisive turning toward the court does not, and of course cannot, occur in Dante's poem: there is no court, no exalted community of any kind, that he can long for. This song, therefore, is truly unique: it departs from the conventional meaning of nature by denying the existence of an alternative realm of gentleness; and from the innovative meaning (of Walther and Neidhart) by denying the possibility of a sojourn anywhere else. It is this methodical scanning of heaven and earth from strophe to strophe that gives such force to the poet's astonishing declaration, "Love exists in me alone."

One may say this line is astonishing because it is strangely familiar: every reader of the courtly lyric has heard something like it many times before. "You *Minnesänger*," says Hartmann von Aue (Pt. I, no. 32), "you have to fail over and over again . . . but I shall boast that I know how to sing about love"—meaning that he alone, and not a single one of them, knows what love is. "Those who think that I am really here do not understand how my spirit is with her," says Bernart (*Pel doutz chan*)—meaning that these people "here," among whom I find myself, do not know what love is, that love is in me alone. It is a familiar line in the courtly tradition because it is exactly what the poet would say when he compared himself to his enemies, or when he found himself in "exile," the desolate region they inhabit.

We have already encountered the two conventional modes of the theme of "exile." In Hartmann it is the supreme service of love: "A man who goes into exile for love—there is a man who loves." The other treatment of this theme occurs frequently in Bernart. The wilderness of the ordinary world, outside the circle of friends, becomes a testing ground for the courtly lover: he may rediscover the pleasure of common lust and thus prove he is like his enemies—which is to say, like everyone else; or he may stay faithful to the one lady and thus prove he is no different in the wilderness from what he is surrounded by those who know him. In any case, whether exile is a service, a banishment, or a forsaking, the lover must make his way through a world in which no one can sympathize with his devotion. And when he keeps faith, he declares, distinguishing himself from his enemies, "Love is in me alone."

But this familiar line suddenly becomes astonishing in Dante's poem, because its frame of reference has nothing to do with enemies, or with any society, either gentle or vile. This platitude now expresses his reaction, not to those outside the courtly circle, but to "nature," an entirely new context, which is, in his conception, the whole world, all existence from the highest heaven to the bowels of the earth. The line takes on an unprecedented meaning, because he means what it says absolutely.

The climactic image in the *congedo* shows the poet full of love in a world of ice. Two venerable themes of the courtly lyric are united and, in union, transformed: the winter setting of the *Natureingang* has been enlarged till it coincides with the whole human world, and in this new dimension it becomes the supreme image of "exile." But, conveyed by this image, "exile" means something new. The universal ice has replaced the alien society—the vulgar, ordinary world—in which the lover had to dwell for a time: with the disappearance of enemies and friends, "exile" is no longer the condition of being outside some special circle, it is the unique, unrelievable, lifelong condition of the one man in whom love exists. His love defines him as an exile, because there is no home for it outside himself; there is no community because there is no love in the world.

There is no other moral or geographical reality but exile. Somewhere, it is true, there is a beloved lady, and he longs for her; but she is a *petra,* a stone: there is no love in her, and she has no secular residence in a joyous land. If his love is so intense now, he asks in the *congedo,* in the least propitious of seasons (it is winter, Venus is eclipsed, cold Saturn is in the ascendancy, the constellation under which the poet was born is now farthest from the sun), what must he be in the season of love? When spring returns to the world and the animals again gladly mate, he will be stone-cold dead, "a man of marble," at one with the world's essential ice. His love makes him an alien in this world. He shall never say, as Bernart says, "There where she is, it is Easter"; he can only say, Love is wherever he is, winter is everywhere else.

The only "setting" for true love now is neither a court nor any fellowship of gentle hearts, but the poet's heart alone. This severe separation between the inner and outer worlds is different from anything Cavalcanti or anyone else ever conceived of; for no matter how interior the setting in other late poets of the courtly tradition, it is still a common setting within an experienced, though nongeographical, community—a community of poets. The process that Cavalcanti describes in *Donna me prega,* for example, is a universal process that affects every noble life (the same may be said for the later German poets—see notes to Burkart von Hohenvels). Dante himself, when he writes in the stilnovist mode, celebrates this fellowship; for example, in his famous sonnet to Cavalcanti, *Guido, i' vorrei che tu e Lapo ed io* (no. 38).

But here the world is involved in a process of chrystallization, culminating in the "man of marble." There is no court for love, no gentle worldwide inner life, no stilnovist fellowship. Nor does the poet come forth as a model of devotion to the qualities that integrate a class or a community: he is the one shelter, the one "place" of all the love on earth and of all exalted meaning. He is in "exile," not because he needs to be tested before being readmitted into some inner circle of nobility, but because there is no such circle outside of himself, neither on earth nor in the atmosphere. There is no other condition possible for him *except* exile. He is doomed to be alone on earth, alone with love, which is absent everywhere else. Nothing like this total and unrelievable solitude—authenticated by the careful scanning of the whole world—ever appeared before this. From the astrological references in the first strophe, the poem has been dated December 1296. This means: "exile" was the essential setting of his poetry long before he was expelled from Florence and plunged into the lifelong horror of real exile.

His great lyric about exile is *Tre donne* (no. 49). Three ladies have "come around" his heart and wait with grave and stately patience "outside," till they can speak with Love, who dwells in the poet's heart. The ensuing conversation between Love and Justice is so exalted and prophetic, and at the same time so courteous and comforting, that the poet's experience of exile is transformed: he is not alone any more, he now shares a common misery with these other noble "exiles." At once he understands that if Justice and Love are in exile, then exile is the only honorable state; and so the poet's apparent humiliation is now revealed as his honor.

Thus, in contrast to *Io son venuto,* though Love still resides in him alone, the poet discovers in the midst of the world's desolation a courteous circle of significance, filled with justice and love. In the first *congedo* this noble sanctum is opened to certain other persons: the song is sent forth into the world, where it may find someone else who is a lover of virtue; if it does, it will reveal its full meaning to him and so fill him with longing for that ethical community which, in this world, can exist only in exile.

De Sanctis called this "the most beautiful allegorical *canzone* ever written," a judgment it is difficult to disagree with. However, it is worth remarking that these noble Beings, whose misery and certain triumph vindicate the poet in his exile, appear in a way that is unprecedented in allegory.

There are two ground rules that every allegory must conform

to, no matter how innovative it may be. One is set forth by Kenelm Foster in his excellent study of the poem:

> Pure allegory requires that a particular image represents a particular idea and nothing else; and this correspondence of image or idea presupposes a clear distinction between the two: in a word, that the idea shall be an abstraction from sense-data, and the image shall be a fiction invented or adapted to represent it.
> (*God's Tree*, p. 28)

It follows from this one-to-one relation between image and idea that the personification must be devoid of personality, or any localizing trait: all of its features and ornaments must be translations of the idea and its corollaries. In the *Psychomachia* of Prudentius (348–c. 410), Pride rides upon a horse which she had covered with a lion's skin, so that, appearing to ride on the mane of such a beast, she might make a more imposing figure: the horse (which resents its bit), the choice of the lion's skin, and above all the sham, are all direct translations of the idea and its consequences. The more gratuitous, personalizing detail not strictly related to the idea, the less allegorical the figure: instead of Gluttony, this gluttonous man (as in *Piers Ploughman*).

The other point concerns allegory as a literary form, to be distinguished from allegory as an exegetical method. This distinction is important, for allegory began as a method of interpreting sacred texts in order to bring their significance up to date, the method being to assign to the characters, objects, and events in the text meanings that are not determinable through the text alone: Dante's *Convivio* is an example of allegorical exegesis (see notes to nos. 41 and 42). Allegory as a literary form developed later, as a narrative in which meanings were assigned to invented (rather than already existing) figures. Every allegory (as literary form) is set inside an allegorical space that is explicitly distinguished from the ordinary waking world. And every object, no matter how everyday its appearance, takes on a predetermined meaning, is "allegorized," the moment it enters this space. We can see a beautiful example of this process of allegorization in the *Romance of the Rose*. In this dream vision, the Dreamer (the image of the young man sleeping in bed) enters a walled garden (the allegorical space), wanders around till he is shot by Love with five arrows, the first of which is called Beauty: from this point on the central figure ceases to be called the Dreamer (a name that could not have an allegorical significance corresponding to that of the other figures in the garden) and is henceforth called the Lover: the sleeper's image is allegorized, it no longer represents a man asleep in bed but an attitude toward experience. Whether it is a dream vision set inside a walled garden, a battle set in the human soul, an account of the senses set in a hunt, a morality set on a stage, a disquisition on learning set in a marriage feast of the gods—every allegory takes place in a special field full of folk, in which all of the figures act out their significance and react upon each other.

Considering these two definitive traits of the formal allegory— the severed ground and the one-to-one relation—we can see how Dante's *canzone* eludes us. There is no allegorical space, for one thing. This is no dream vision, nor do all of the figures occupy precisely the same space. The three ladies are "outside," Love is in the poet's heart, the poet is distinct from the others in the order of being—he is mortal, nonallegorical, under sentence of death in the Florentine commune. It is true that he shares a common ground of exile with them, but exile is not a marked-out place: it is, on the contrary, the desolate world. And this equation of "exile" with the condition of being in the ordinary world appears here not only as a theme in the tradition of courtly poetry; it has a special, painful meaning in this instance: "exile" means somewhere in Italy, outside Florence—only the paucity of facts concerning Dante's continual movement at this time prevents us from identifying the setting more specifically. Dante, and Love, and the three ladies are in exile in a literal as well as literary sense: they are in the world at large, outside the poet's defining settlement.

In this lyric, then, we have figures of abstractions wandering in the real world, the world of Dante's homelessness and humiliation, wherein he longs to return to the city he loves, his native Florence. With great skill Dante contrasts the abstract quality of these figures with the reality of his exile. In this we may see a great example of the use of performance time, which all courtly poets, but none more effectively than Dante, made the basic principle of the structure of their lyrics. If we view this poem as a performed song, reaching us line by line, strophe after strophe, then we see that in the first four strophes the question of time and setting is held in suspense—we set ourselves to hear a more or less regular allegory. But with the fifth strophe comes a sudden turn: all at once a geographical location is revealed—the actual world, Italy, sometime after 1302—and the entire poem is suddenly deallegorized: this is no allegory, for the time, the place, the very condition of exile, are all real. *They* are of "the eternal rock," immortal beings who can vindicate him in his disgrace; but he is bound to this time and this place. Thus the moment he takes comfort from the words of these figures, he reveals his separateness from them and his ultimate loneliness.

As the setting is not strictly allegorical, neither are the figures. For an allegorical image, as we have seen, is a visible translation of an abstraction and its corollaries. Thus we have "the self-regard of Idleness" (a young woman gazing continually into her mirror), "the plenitude of Nature" (a beautiful lady upon whose gown innumerable birds of every kind are embroidered), "the impersonality of Death" (a jaunty figure who calls upon Everyman like a brisk official of the civil service). But here, in Dante's *canzone,* the appearance and the behavior of the three ladies in their tattered clothes depict for us the miserable state of exile rather than the abstract idea of Justice. They come forth as beings who share the poet's suffering.

Our perspective on the vivid figure of Justice oscillates between our presumption of allegory and the poet's own reaction as to a real presence. It is apparently the poet's will that we never come to rest at one or the other point of view; for he describes them in a way that is at once allegorical in method, and antiallegorical in effect. They appear before him destitute, despoiled, unornamented; their appearance suggests the allegorical meaning, "Justice is despised and cast out of the city." But the poet makes their barrenness so thorough, that he finally deallegorizes them; for he denies them every allegorical appurtenance except their names. What then remains, when a figure is stripped of its allegorical dress? That figure without attributes who calls herself Justice is no different from any ordinary woman's image. The poet insists on that: he tells us that she is perceived as a woman *sol di sé,* by her body rather than her clothes, by her womanliness. And that is not mere poetizing, for the torn gown of Justice reveals "that part of her it is decorous not to name." Nor is that unnamable part strictly metaphorical (in contrast to the similar passage in strophe vi, where the secret part of a lady's body is a metaphor for the hidden meaning of the song) : for if this is strictly an allegory, or if the figures are strictly allegorical, then what is signified by "the unnamable part of Justice"? These ladies come forth, not as invented figures, but as images that really appear, that are personally and specifically visible, to the poet, to Dante in exile; as part of an experience that actually occurred to him somewhere—somewhere in time and under the sun.

But neither does he let us think of them finally as ordinary mortal images. In the momentous turning of the fifth strophe, at that point where the possibility of an allegorical space is suddenly and positively denied—in that instant he sets himself apart from these exiles. In the very words by which he reveals his common lot of exile with them and the comfort he takes in their dignity, he also reveals that his experience of exile is different from theirs, that his longing lights on a real city, Florence, the target of his eyes. He is a man involved in time in a way that distinguishes him from these noble exiles, Justice and Love: he is a man with a past and a future that articulate with the misery of his present state—a past that contains an injustice committed against him and also the possibility of some blame attaching to him, a future that contains the possibilities of death, forgiveness, companionship. But they, though they suffer now through time, are of the eternal citadel.

Thus the moment the poet takes comfort from their words, he puts himself in a new perspective regarding them: he stands apart, listening to their conversation. Their initial positions are changed. Love was in his heart, the three ladies outside; now Love and Justice face each other, and the poet, though he shares exile with them, is not really one of their company. Just as this change in perspective shows that his exile is real and not simply a literary theme, in the same instant it shows the meaning, the moral worth of the state of exile: it is the state of honor. The poet is vindicated. Though he appears to confess vaguely to some fault and to claim that he has done full penance for it (at the end of strophe v), and though he seems to make an outright appeal to be allowed to return (in the second *congedo*, which, it should be noted, is generally held to have been written later than the rest of the poem, witness the difference in versification), this humility and this appeal are expressed in the context of a vindicated and unshakable honor.

The lady who calls herself Justice, therefore, is indeed the figure of an abstraction, but she is not confined within an allegorical frame, nor is she endowed with allegorical traits. This woman who neither looks nor acts nor situates like an allegorical figure—she is really Justice, appearing to the poet. If she were otherwise, if she were simply an invention, then the vindication of the poet's exile would amount to self-serving and to a childish play of rhetoric.

She is an abstraction, but she is also an image, or a person. How she can thus be in two realms at once is explained in part by her description of the engendering of the other two ladies. Her daughter is engendered in a way that resembles, except for one crucial difference, the engendering of the Second Person: the Word of God is the *Imago* of God, His total and identical image. But in the case of Justice's engendering, the image is a descent; for that image is not the pure, abstract "word" of Justice, it is rather materialized, reflected in the Nile, a river of this earth that once flowed through Paradise. Since the image is thus involved in time and matter, it is of a lower order than that which engendered it. Though nothing is said about the origin of Justice herself, it is she who introduces the idea of an abstraction brought forth in matter.

An abstraction involved in time and matter which yet remains an abstraction and hence immortal—what an enormous contradiction; and yet it is precisely the description of the figure Dante sees and whose conversation with Love Dante attends. And this impossible contradiction bears the closest resemblance to a

greater contradiction, the greatest of all: for the Imago, too,
became involved in time and matter once descended to the mirror of the Virgin, and becoming flesh yet did not cease to be God.
He was God and man, divine Person and human person, and
he too bore injuries, though he was of the eternal rock; he too
was an exile, "despised by all and unregarded." And through that
supreme and joyful contradiction, He appeared to Man. Even
those who came after Him may have an image of his suffering
and resurrection, and may rejoice in His gift.

This strange situation in which a man is so intimate with an
abstraction that he is judged, vindicated, and comforted in its
presence, is inspired by it to the thrilling rediscovery of his own
dignity and the integrity of his entire past and present, though
it reveals much in particular about the mind of Dante, should
not really be so strange to us after all. It should rather be familiar
to us, not only because the great paradigm of this experience is
provided by the central event of human history, but also because it is precisely the situation in which abstractions exist
for us.

When, for example, we soar with pride or shrink with shame,
before what presence do we rise or crawl? Clearly we judge ourselves in the light of an ideal, a moral code, an ethical abstraction. But how does that abstraction exert its power over us? We
may say: it has assumed a face, and it looks at us.

Indeed, we may doubt whether abstractions ever have any
other existence for us. In our subjective discourse there is no real
difference in signification between the word *justice* and the lady
in her tattered dress, for the one is an audible, the other a visible
summoning of an abstraction that means much to us—though
there is a great difference in the implication of human involve-
ment. For the immortal ideal, unreflected in a human form, continually eludes us. We may even say that the more visible the
summoning of this ideal, the more intimate its effect. The face
and figure by which we bring the abstraction into our lives will
differ for each of us; for that image, in contrast to allegorical
figures, is always personal in the extreme. For one, it is the stern
face and pointing finger of a father; for another, the circle of a
community; for still another, a face of such extraordinary grace

that it becomes his "word" for every kind of order in which human love is not irrelevant, though he may not even be able to recall exactly when or where he saw that face. As the song and figure of Wordsworth's Solitary Reaper become the poet's "word" for the futility of man's efforts and the triumph of his spirit without becoming allegorical, something similar happens in every human being who wants his earthly life to transcend its moments: he envisages an abstraction—not, however, as an allegorical figure, but as an image capable of presence and effect. There is really no abstraction that is ever free of a figure in our minds. The "substances," "operations," and "accidents" in metaphysical discourse are all, in the final analysis, merely the hypostatization of grammatical terms (subjects, verbs, adjectives), which are themselves finally denominations of human postures and appearances. Thus, giving these abstract realities a face and figure is not formally different from giving them a name. These are not assigned images, as in an allegory: they are the presences abstractions assume for each of us so that we may have some experience of them; and judge, and be judged, by them. St. Augustine called this effective presence of a universal in our soul our *verbum*, our "word."

These images of moral abstractions are not less real for us than any of the other images that guide us every day, guardians of our identity—not less real than all the images by which we realize the past and aim toward the future. For the intimate objects of our experience are either actually present before us, or else they are absent and experienced as images: we care for what is in our arms, and we care for what is beyond our reach, the distant, the dead, the uncreated. The image enables us to experience what is gone forever, or has not come to pass, or cannot touch the ground. The three ladies are really present—like the personal past we remember, like the historical past we imagine, like the joys we anticipate or the accidents we dread, like deep sworn vows, like the sense of duty or the hope of return—like all the images that are a necessary condition of moral experience.

The three ladies are therefore not inventions, at least not as allegorical figures are. They are not part of any metaphor extended in allegorical space and time; they are rather images such as preserve each man's identity. Once seen in this light, their kinship with another nonallegorical figure will be revealed: the courtly poet's lady. For it was through the figure of this beautiful lady that the courtly man could respond with all his faculties to an abstract and indefinable ideal and be justified. She was the embodiment of courtliness—the "embodiment" in a literal and secular sense: she was not simply a visualization of some moral category, but a real person. The lady whom the poet praises for her beauty, grace, and conversation—he could call her *Cortezia,* as he sometimes does, without any allegorical intention. Quite the contrary, he longs for her body; the proof of his courtliness is that all of his physical passion is focused on her and not on any common woman. Thus his love for her was the proof of his commitment to the ideal of a noble life. However, though she is real, she is distant, as distant from the lover, almost, as the ideal itself. He could never be of her company; but in his loneliness and exile he beheld her image and marveled at this miracle, that his heart could be filled and comforted by what his eyes could not perceive—that his heart could see what his eyes could not (for example, Heinrich von Morungen, Pt. I, no. 26). This image of the lady was the lover's "word" for courtliness. It kept him the same from day to day, guided him in all his choices—I would not do one thing to displease my lady, he says again and again—and made all the moments of his days coherent. Just so, the ladies in Dante's *canzone* appear before his heart, and his past and present life is justified, its integrity affirmed.

But, of course, there are enormous differences between these three ladies and the ladies of the lyric tradition—differences that suggest the greatness of Dante's genius. Those courtly ladies are, with rare exceptions, emblematic, conventional: it is no accident that they all look alike, being depicted according to a rhetorical prescription for feminine beauty, for they were not meant to be the unique objects of private desires but representations of everything a courtly man should love—*any* courtly man. When a poet names his lady's "unnamable parts," it is not because he wants to individualize her by his passion, but because he is now aping his enemies, being deliberately uncourtly. Otherwise, when they come forth in courtly mode, they are distant, impersonal, monumental, devoid of all qualities except a brilliant, signifying visibility.

But the poet's experience in *Tre donne* is entirely personal and intimate. The ladies appear to him alone, just as Love is in his heart alone. The "matter" of this song is not the theme of "exile," but *his* exile, something that happened only to him. Others were banished, but the glorification of his exile sheds no light on theirs. He is not one of them, he broke with them, and their misery has no dignity. He speaks for himself alone, not as the representative of any class or party; indeed, he strongly suggests that no one else in the world shares his commitment to justice and love. Thus we can see how the song is both aligned with, and different from, the courtly lyrics that preceded it. It is, like them, a song of self-justification; but the great difference is that the poet is not vindicated by any audience or group of peers. He is justified by the circle of abstractions, the one community with which he feels any intimacy. It is this purely spiritual community that confirms the poet's identity and worth by sharing with him the dignity of exile and a prophetic sense of merit. Never has there been such an inhabited solitude. Neither the troubadours nor the stilnovisti ever created a song that transcends all human place. In fact, Dante annihilates the very idea of exile, for the defining community is in exile with him.

Besides the courtly lyric, there are other words that Dante's song causes to resound in our ears. Boethius, whom Dante revered and named an exile (*Paradiso,* X, 124ff), lay in prison, falsely accused; a beautiful and noble lady appeared before him and taught him to regard his misfortune in a better light; and her words were a triumph over their common suffering, for she too was an exile and abused:

> While I ruminated these things with myself . . . methought I saw a woman stand above my head, having a grave countenance, glistening clear eye, and of quicker sight than commonly Nature doth afford; her color fresh and bespeaking unabated vigour, and yet discovering so many years, that could not at all be thought to belong to our times; her stature uncertain and doubtful, for sometime she exceeded not the common height of men, and some-

time she seemed to touch the heavens with her head, and if she lifted it up to the highest, she pierced the very heavens, so that she could not be seen by the beholders . . .

(Loeb Classical Library translation)

It is clear that Dante, in his banishment, looked back to this other great exile who had inspired him to the love of philosophy. If we assume the inspiration of Boethius, we may again measure the uniqueness of Dante's song. The Lady Philosophy, with her quick sight and ranging stature, is a carefully invented allegorical figure, every one of her attributes a perfect visualization of the idea; but the suffering women who wait around the heart of Dante are "poor in dress and ornament," present and unsignifying images. This song is no *consolatio,* for the poet does not depict himself as blinded by false values: he is, and was from the beginning, in the right. It was only the value of exile itself that he did not understand; Justice and Love reveal the dignity of his outcast state, not by instructing him, but by sharing the same misery.

The Consolation of Philosophy is not intended as a work of self-justification. Though Boethius declares he was falsely accused, his purpose is not to vindicate himself but to show how Philosophy led him beyond the instability of fortune to the understanding of true felicity: the question of his guilt or innocence is not a central issue. But Dante's poem records his vindication. And that is why Justice and her daughters cannot be allegorical figures. For the circumstances illuminated by their words are unique, not universal; but an allegory cannot exist except on a universal plane: it is a blueprint of a basic human experience—of the experience of secular, aristocratic love, for example, as in *The Romance of the Rose*—an abstract paradigm transcending circumstances. If the intention of Dante's poem had been to define the inevitable consequences of unwavering rectitude, for example, then allegory might have been a suitable form for it. But this poem sets forth the vindication of Dante's rectitude, and no one else's, in the events of 1302 in Florence.

In this personal and unique context, no allegorical figure could have the authority to vindicate him, for such an invented figure would only express the will of the poet who invented it. The only

possible objective judgment in this instance can come from
Drittura, from Justice, Rectitude, itself. And it speaks here.
having appeared before Dante in the same mode in which all
abstract moral realities appear to a man and define his present
state. "Here we are nymphs and we are stars in heaven," say the
four cardinal virtues in the scene where Dante is judged
(*Purgatorio,* XXXI, 106). *Drittura* is Dante's "word" for Justice.

In the *Convivio* Dante briefly distinguishes between the "allegory of poets," made up of invented figures and confrontations,
and the "allegory of theologians," in which the signifying persons and events are all historical. From this point of view we
may again judge how inadequate is the term "allegorical *canzone*" when applied to Dante's poem. For *Tre Donne* cannot fit
into either definition. It is not composed according to the allegory
of poets, because the figures come forth as women really perceived rather than as invented figures; nor according to the allegory of theologians, because these women appear only to the
eyes of the poet—it is the proof of his rectitude that they appear
to him alone; nor do the elements in this song point, one-to-one,
beyond themselves to another meaning: they refer only to Dante's
life in exile.

Because Love is in his heart—Love, being image and abstraction at once, is of the same reality as the three ladies—the exile
finds himself in the company of Justice; and in the presence of
this new community he comes to understand that he is vindicated, and that his exile is his honor. The traditional theme of
"exile" is thus exactly reversed. The lover's exile now marks
neither a great service for love nor a failing in his devotion, nor
in any case a separation from the ethical realm in which he is
truly at home: the lover's exile proves the total degradation of
the community that exiled him. Thus exile becomes the only
place where he can be true to himself, the place of honor, the
sojourn of love and justice. Dante has taken the courtly lyric
along a certain line to the utmost point. The original setting of
the lyric was a circle of mobility in a court; with the stilnovists
the lyric moved out of the court and was set in a common inner
life among a community of poets; with Dante, the very idea of a

setting is rejected, and the song becomes completely personal, the justifying presences essentially abstract and subjective. The lady named Justice is Dante's "word"—his own knowledge and experience, his awareness, his image, of a universal. In this song, the meaning of his exile is revealed by his word for Justice and his word for Love: he judges and vindicates himself according to his own understanding of Justice and Love.

Moved as he is by their courteous and prophetic discourse, the poet yet burns with longing for the "sweet target" of his eyes, the beloved city that is morally ruined. For that is where he would like to belong, not here in exile. But that can never be. He is, in fact, despite the feeble hope that the song may find someone who is a lover of virtue, in the permanent and defining condition of exile. Every poet of the courtly tradition was defined by some sort of class; the poet of *Tre donne* is defined by exile, by the condition of being full of love and in the company of justice in the midst of an endless desolation. This new setting, with the suppression of every kind of secular audience, has a momentous effect: the song can express things never heard before. The essential form of the courtly lyric—the dialogical relationship between poet and audience—remains intact in Dante's poetry; but for the first time, through the spiritualization of the audience, it is capable of making a completely personal statement, of expressing feelings and a point of view uncorroborated by any group or by any rhetorical or poetical tradition.

This is something new on earth: a poet and a lover who attends the discourse of noble and suffering abstractions, who longs to return to the city of his birth, who finds himself more truly in exile and despair than in any other state. It is something new, and it will be followed by other things never conceived of before. To look forward, finally, to the *Commedia:* these abstractions will remain as real as they are here, only their secular appearance will become still more specific, still more secular and personal, until they assume the images of persons who once actually lived.

Text: Michele Barbi, ed. *Rime,* in *Le Opere di Dante,* testo critico della Società Dantesca Italiana. Florence: R. Bemporad, 1921; reprinted 1960.

Guido, i' vorrei che tu e Lapo ed io [1]
fossimo presi per incantamento
e messi in un vasel, ch'ad ogni vento
per mare andasse al voler vostro e mio;

5 sì che fortuna od altro tempo rio
non ci potesse dare impedimento,
anzi, vivendo sempre in un talento,
di stare insieme crescesse 'l disio.

E monna Vanna e monna Lagia poi [2]
10 con quella ch'è sul numer de le trenta [3]
con noi ponesse il buono incantatore, [4]

e quivi ragionar sempre d'amore;
e ciascuna di lor fosse contenta,
sì come i' credo che saremmo noi.

39

Per una ghirlandetta
ch'io vidi, mi farà   1
sospirare ogni fiore.

I'vidi a voi, donna, portare
5 ghirlandetta di fior gentile,

---

[1] Guido Cavalcanti, Lapo Gianni.
[2] The ladies of Guido and Lapo respectively.
[3] In *VN*, vi, Dante says that he wrote "an epistle in the form of a *sirventes*" in which he celebrated the sixty most beautiful women in Florence as an accompaniment to his praise of Beatrice, whose name "did not allow itself to stand at any other number but nine." Who the lady in this sonnet might be, therefore, is uncertain.
[4] Perhaps Merlin.

Guido, I wish that you and Lapo and I [1]
could be taken by magic
and put in one boat, which in any wind
would run the sea at your sweet will and mine,

5   so that no storm or any bitter weather
would hinder us,
but living always with a single will
would increase our wish to be together.

And then that Monna Vanna and Monna Lagia [2]
10   and she who is at the number thirty [3]
could be put with us by that kind enchanter, [4]

there to talk always of love;
and that each lady would be happy,
as I think we would be.

Because of a garland
I once saw, every flower   I
will make me sigh.

I saw you, Lady, wearing
5   a garland of sweet flowers,

e sovr'a lei vidi volare
un angiolel d'amore umile;   II
e 'n suo cantar sottile
dicea: "Chi mi vedrà
10   lauderà 'l mio signore." [1]

Se io sarò là dove sia
Fioretta mia bella a sentire,[2]
allor dirò la donna mia
che port' in testa i miei sospire.   III
15   Ma per crescer disire
mia donna verrà
coronata da Amore.

Le parolette mie novelle,
che di fiori fatto han ballata,
20   per leggiadria ci hanno tolt'elle
una vesta ch'altrui fu data: [3]   IV
però siate pregata,
qual uom la canterà,
che li facciate onore.

40

Amore e 'l cor gentil sono una cosa,
sì come il saggio in suo dittare pone,[1]
e così esser l'un sanza l'altro osa
com'alma razional sanza ragione.

5   Falli natura quand'è amorosa,
Amor per sire e 'l cor per sua magione,

---

[1] That is, Love, who appears in line 17.
[2] These lines could also be translated: "If I am where she could hear me."
[3] Either: They (the verses) are to be sung to a melody already given to other poetry; or: They have formed a *ballata* of the flowers in the garland worn by Fioretta.
[1] Guido Guinizelli, *Al cor gentil*.

and above it I saw flying,
all mild, an angel of love   II
in his melodious song
declaring, "Who sees me
10 will praise my lord." [1]

If I am there to hear
my beautiful, my Fioretta singing,[2]
I shall say my lady
wears my sighs upon her head.   III
15 But my lady will come forth,
to increase desire,
crowned by Love.

My young verses,
having made of flowers a ballata,
20 have put on for its grace
a garment given to another: [3]   IV
so I pray you,
honor him
who sings this song.

40

Love and the gentil heart are one thing,
as the wise one sets forth in his poem,[1]
and one can be without the other only
as much as the rational soul without reason.

5 Nature creates them both when it is turned toward love—
Love as the lord, the heart as his mansion

dentro la qual dormendo si riposa
tal volta poca e tal lunga stagione.

Bieltate appare in saggia donna pui,
10 che piace a li occhi sì, che dentro al core
nasce un disio de la cosa piacente;

e tanto dura talora in costui,
che fa svegliar lo spirito d'Amore.
E simil face in donna omo valente.

41

Voi che 'ntendendo il terzo ciel movete,[1]
udite il ragionar ch'è nel mio core,
ch'io nol so dire altrui, sì mi par novo.
El ciel che segue lo vostro valore,
5 gentili creature che voi sete,
mi tragge ne lo stato ov'io mi trovo.
Onde 'l parlar de la vita ch'io provo,
par che si drizzi degnamente a vui:
però vi priego che lo mi 'ntendiate.
10 Io vi dirò del cor la novitate,
come l'anima trista piange in lui,
e come un spirto contra lei favella,
che vien pe' raggi de la vostra stella.

Suol esser vita de lo cor dolente
15 un soave penser, che se ne gia
molte fïate a' piè del nostro Sire,
ove una donna glorïar vedia,

I

[1] This lyric describes how the thought of a new lady replaces the thought of
Beatrice, now dead and in heaven, as the ruling power in Dante's soul. There
is an elaborate allegorical interpretation in *Convivio*, II: the new woman
represents Philosophy; the third heaven, the realm of rhetoric; the rays, the
works of the rhetoricians, especially Boethius' *De consolatione Philosophiae*

wherein he abides and sleeps
sometimes a short while, sometimes long.

Then beauty comes forth in a lady who is wise,
10 so pleasing to the eyes that in the heart
a desire is born for that beautiful thing;

and lasts so long, sometimes, in the heart,
it makes the spirit of Love awaken.
In woman's heart a man of worth brings forth the same
awakening.

41

You who by understanding move the third heaven,[1]
hear what is spoken in my heart,
for I cannot tell it to any other, it is so strange.
The heaven that moves to your power,
5 noble creatures that you are,
draws me into this state.
Thus it seems my words about the life   I
I now experience should rightly be addressed to you:
therefore I beg you, hear me.
10 I shall tell you of the marvel in my heart—
how my sad soul weeps in it,
and how a spirit coming on the rays
of your star disputes with her.

The life of my grieving heart used to be
15 a gentle thought, that would go
many times to the feet of our Lord,
where it would see in glory a lady

and Cicero's *De amicitia,* which moved Dante to love philosophy. The opening lines are addressed to the angelic intelligences that guide the heavens in
their courses; the third heaven is that of Venus. On these indwelling spirits,
see the note to line 43f of Guinizelli's *Al cor gentil* (no. 20). Lines 12–13 here
refer to the influence of the planet Venus.

di cui parlava me sì dolcemente
che l'anima dicea: "Io men vo' gire." [2]
20 Or apparisce chi lo fa fuggire [3]   II
e segnoreggia me di tal virtute,
che 'l cor ne trema che di fuori appare.
Questi mi face una donna guardare,
e dice: "Chi veder vuol la salute,
25 faccia che li occhi d'esta donna miri,
sed e' non teme angoscia di sospiri."

Trova contraro tal che lo distrugge
l'umil pensero, che parlar mi sole
d'un'angela che 'n cielo è coronata.
30 L'anima piange, sì ancor len dole,
e dice: "Oh lassa a me, come si fugge
questo piatoso che m'ha consolata!"
De li occhi miei dice questa affannata: III
"Qual ora fu, che tal donna li vide!
35 e perché non credeano a me di lei?
Io dicea: 'Ben ne li occhi di costei
de' star colui che le mie pari ancide!'
E non mi valse ch'io ne fossi accorta
che non mirasser tal, [4] ch'io ne son morta."

40 "Tu non se' morta, ma se' ismarrita,
anima nostra, che sì ti lamenti,"
dice uno spiritel d'amor gentile; [5]
"ché quella bella donna che tu senti,
ha transmutata in tanto la tua vita,
45 che n'hai paura, sì se' fatta vile!
Mira quant'ell'è pietosa e umile,   IV
saggia e cortese ne la sua grandezza,
e pensa di chiamarla donna, omai!
Ché se tu non t'inganni, tu vedrai

[2] His thought used to ascend to heaven and witness the glory of Beatrice
there; then he would long to die, so that he could be with her. Cf. the last
sonnet in *VN*.
[3] What takes place in these lines is described in *VN*, xxxvff. "It" in line 20
and the following lines refers to the thought of Beatrice; "this one" (23) is

of whom this thought would speak to me so sweetly,
my soul would say, "I want to go there." [2]

20 Now someone appears who makes it flee [3]   II
and rules me with such power,
my heart trembles, as all may see.
This one makes me look upon a woman,
and says: "Whoever wants to see bliss,
25 let him gaze into this lady's eyes,
if he does not fear the anguish of sighs."

This humble thought that used to speak to me
of an angel crowned in heaven
meets an adversary that destroys it.
30 The soul weeps, it still grieves so for that thought,
and says, "Alas, how it flees,
this one full of pity that consoled me."
This my troubled soul speaks of my eyes: III
"What a time that was, when such a lady saw them!
35 And why would they not believe me!
I told them, 'Surely in those eyes of hers
stands the one who kills all like me.'
And it did not avail that I was watchful
lest they gaze on such a woman; [4] and now I am dead."

40 "You are not dead, but only bewildered,
O our soul, who so lament,"
says a gentle spirit of love; [5]
"for that beautiful lady whose effect you feel
has so transformed your life,
45 you are afraid, you have grown so weak.
See how she is humble and full of pity,   IV
in her greatness wise and courteous,
and now think only of calling her your lady from this
            time forth.
For if you do not err, you will see

---

the "someone" that drives the thought away. The "humble thought" (28) is,
again, the thought of Beatrice.
[4] The new woman.
[5] The new thought speaks, addressing the soul.

50 di sì alti miracoli adornezza,
    che tu dirai: 'Amor, segnor verace,
    ecco l'ancella tua; fa' che ti piace.' "

    Canzone, io credo che saranno radi
    color che tua ragione intendan bene,
55 tanto la parli faticosa e forte.
    Onde, se per ventura elli addivene
    che tu dinanzi da persone vadi   V
    che non ti paian d'essa bene accorte,
    allor ti priego che ti riconforte,
60 dicendo lor, diletta mia novella:
    "Ponete mente almen com'io son bella!" 6

42

    Amor che ne la mente mi ragiona 1
    de la mia donna disïosamente,
    move cose di lei meco sovente,
    che lo 'ntelletto sovr'esse disvia.
5   Lo suo parlar sì dolcemente sona,
    che l'anima ch'ascolta e che lo sente
    dice: "Oh me lassa, ch'io non son possente
    di dir quel ch'odo de la donna mia!"
    E certo e' mi conven lasciare in pria,   I
10 s'io vo' trattar di quel ch'odo di lei,
    ciò che lo mio intelletto non comprende;
    e di quel che s'intende
    gran parte, perché dirlo non savrei.
    Però, se le mie rime avran difetto
15 ch'entreran ne la loda di costei,

6 If they cannot grasp your deeper meaning, let them at least take note of
your surface beauty, the beauty of your ornamentation.
1 In *Convivio* III Dante sets forth the allegorical meaning of this poem: he
extols philosophy (in the figure of the lady) and dedicates himself to it.
Note the important reference to this *canzone* in *Purg.* II, 112.

50 beauty of such exalted wonder,
 you will say, 'O Love, my true lord,
 behold your handmaid—do as you will.' "

Song, I believe they will be few
 who truly understand your meaning,
55 so subtle and hard are your words.
 Therefore, if you, by chance, should come   v
 before those to whom, as it seems,
 your meaning is not clear,
 I beg you then find new strength
60 and tell them, O my new delight,
 "Take note, at least, how beautiful I appear." [6]

42

Love, who in my mind discourses [1]
 fervently of my lady,
 often puts forth such things concerning her,
 the intellect loses its way with them.
5 His speaking sounds so sweet
 that my soul, as she concentrates and feels the effect,
 says, "Alas, that I am not able
 to speak forth what I hear about my lady."
 And surely I must first give up—   I
10 if I wish to treat of what I hear of her—
 what my intellect does not understand;
 and a great part
 of what it understands, for I could not express it.
 Therefore, if my verses are not adequate
15 that undertake the praise of her,

di ciò si biasmi il debole intelletto
e 'l parlar nostro, che non ha valore
di ritrar tutto ciò che dice Amore.

Non vede il sol, che tutto 'l mondo gira,
20 cosa tanto gentil, quanto in quell'ora
che luce ne la parte ove dimora
la donna, di cui dire Amore mi face.
Ogni Intelletto di là su la mira,
e quella gente che qui s'innamora
25 ne' lor pensieri la truovano ancora,
quando Amor fa sentir de la sua pace.

Suo esser tanto a Quei che lel dà piace,   II
che 'nfonde sempre in lei la sua vertute
oltre 'l dimando di nostra natura.[2]
30 La sua anima pura,
che riceve da lui questa salute,
lo manifesta in quel ch'ella conduce: [3]
ché 'n sue bellezze son cose vedute
che li occhi di color dov'ella luce
35 ne mandan messi al cor pien di desiri,
che prendon aire e diventan sospiri.[4]

In lei discende la virtù divina
sì come face in angelo che 'l vede;
e qual donna gentil questo non crede,
40 vada con lei e miri li atti sui.
Quivi dov'ella parla, si dichina
un spirito da ciel, che reca fede
come l'alto valor ch'ella possiede
è oltre quel che si conviene a nui.
45 Li atti soavi ch'ella mostra altrui   III
vanno chiamando Amor ciascuno a prova

[2] That is, true Wisdom lies beyond the power of the human intellect.
[3] Literally, the body; allegorically, "the moral effects of philosophy" (Foster and Boyde, II, 178).
[4] On sighs, see introductory note to Cavalcanti.

let the infirm intellect be blamed,
and our speech, which does not have the power
to recount all that Love speaks forth.

The sun that circles the entire world never sees
20 a thing so noble as in that moment
when it lights the region where she dwells,
the lady of whom Love makes me speak.
Every intelligence above beholds her,
and men and women here who love
25 still find her in their thoughts
when Love lets them feel what his peace is like.

Her being is so loved by the One who gives her being   II
that he continually pours his power into her
beyond what our nature demands.[2]
30 The pure soul of her
reveals in what it governs [3]
that she receives this blessedness from Him:
for in her beauty are such things seen,
the eyes of those who receive her light
35 send messengers full of longing to the heart,
that draw in air, becoming sighs.[4]

Divine power descends into her
as it descends into an angel that beholds Him;
and whatever noble lady will not believe this—
40 go with her and contemplate her acts.
There, where she speaks, a spirit
descends from heaven bearing witness
that her high worth
goes beyond what is allotted us.
45 The graceful acts that she reveals   III
rival each other calling Love

in quella voce che lo fa sentire.
Di costei si può dire:
gentile è in donna ciò che in lei si trova,
50 e bello è tanto quanto lei simiglia.
E puossi dir che 'l suo aspetto giova

a consentir ciò che par maraviglia;
onde la nostra fede è aiutata: [5]
però fu tal da etterno ordinata.

55 Cose appariscon ne lo suo aspetto
che mostran de' piacer di Paradiso,
dico ne li occhi e nel suo dolce riso,
che le vi reca Amor com'a suo loco.
Elle soverchian lo nostro intelletto,
60 come raggio di sole un frale viso:
e perch'io non le posso mirar fiso,
mi convien contentar di dirne poco.
Sua bieltà piove fiammelle di foco,   IV
animate d'un spirito gentile
65 ch'è creatore d'ogni pensier bono;
e rompon come trono
l'innati vizii che fanno altrui vile.
Però qual donna sente sua bieltate
biasmar per non parer queta e umile,
70 miri costei ch'è essemplo d'umiltate!
Questa è colei ch'umilia ogni perverso:
costei pensò chi mosse l'universo.

Canzone, e' par che tu parli contraro
al dir d'una sorella che tu hai; [6]
75 ché questa donna, che tanto umil fai,
ella la chiama fera e disdegnosa.

[5] The visible miracle of the lady's beauty helps us to believe in the invisible miracles in the Christian faith; philosophy points to wonders beyond those it is able to reveal. Cf. lines 55f.
[6] Referring to an earlier *canzone*, *Voi che savete ragionar d'Amore*, in which he denounced the lady's cruelty and disdain. He now attributes this error to his faulty understanding.

in a voice that causes him to wake.
This can be said of her:
nobility in woman is whatever one discovers in her,
50 and beauty is what resembles her.
And it can be said, her aspect helps

us to accept what seems miraculous;
wherefore our faith is strengthened: [5]
thus she was appointed from eternity.

55 In her aspect things appear
that image the joys of Paradise,
in her eyes, I mean, and her sweet smile:
Love leads them there as to his realm.
These things overcome our intellect
60 as a ray of sunlight eyes that are weak;
and because I cannot gaze on them continually
I must be content to speak little of them.
Her beauty rains down flames of fire   IV
alive with a gentle spirit
65 that is creator of all good thoughts;
and like a thunderbolt they shatter
the inborn vices that make us vile.
Therefore whatever lady hears her beauty
blamed for not appearing humble and serene,
70 let her gaze upon this one who is the form of all humil-
          ity.
It is she who restores humility to everyone who turns
          away:
He conceived her, Who moved the universe.

Song, it seems you speak contrary
to the words of one of your sisters; [6]
75 for this lady, whom you make out to be so humble,
your sister calls cruel and disdainful.

Tu sai che 'l ciel sempr'è lucente e chiaro,
e quanto in sé non si turba già mai;
ma li nostri occhi per cagioni assai
80 chiaman la stella talor tenebrosa.
Così, quand'ella la chiama orgogliosa,   V
non considera lei secondo il vero,
ma pur secondo quel ch'a lei parea:
ché l'anima temea,
85 e teme ancora, sì che mi par fero
quantunqu'io veggio là 'v'ella mi senta.
Così ti scusa, se ti fa mestero;
e quando pòi, a lei ti rappresenta:
dirai: "Madonna, s'ello v'è a grato,
90 io parlerò di voi in ciascun lato."

43

"I' mi son pargoletta bella e nova,
che son venuta per mostrare altrui   I
de le bellezze del loco ond'io fui.

I' fui del cielo, e tornerovvi ancora
5 per dar de la mia luce altrui diletto;
e chi me vede e non se ne innamora
d'amor non averà mai intelletto,   II
ché non mi fu in piacer alcun disdetto
quando natura mi chiese a colui
10 che volle, donne, accompagnarmi a vui.

Ciascuna stella ne li occhi mi piove
del lume suo e de la sua vertute;
le mie bellezze sono al mondo nove,
però che di là su mi son venute: III
15 le quai non posson esser canosciute
se non da canoscenza d'omo in cui
Amor si metta per piacer altrui."

You know how the sky is always clear and shining
and never in itself grows dark;
and yet our eyes, for many reasons,
80 sometimes say the stars are vague.
Just so, when your sister calls her proud,   V
she considers her, not according to the truth,
but only according to what the lady seemed to her:
for my soul was afraid,
85 and is still afraid, so that everything
I see seems cruel when she perceives me.
In this way excuse yourself, if you need to.
And when you can, present yourself to her;
you will say: "My Lady, if it is your will,
90 I will speak of you everywhere."

43

"I am a lovely young girl, a miracle
come to reveal to men   I
a little of the beauty of the place whence I have come.

"I have come from heaven and shall go there again
5 to give to others pleasure of my light;
and whoever sees me and does not fall in love
will never have intelligence of love,   II
because no part of beauty was denied me
when Nature begged me of Him
10 who desired, Ladies, to make me your companion.

"Every star rains into my eyes
of its influence and light;
my beauty is a miracle in this world,
for it has come to me from high above;   III
15 and cannot be understood
but by the understanding of a man in whom
Love comes to dwell through someone's beauty."

Queste parole si leggon nel viso
d'un angioletta che ci è apparita:
20 e io che per veder lei mirai fiso,
ne sono a rischio di perder la vita;
però ch'io ricevetti tal ferita
da un ch'io vidi dentro a li occhi sui,
ch'i' vo piangendo e non m'acchetai pui.

IV

44

Chi udisse tossir la mal fatata [1]
moglie di Bicci vocato Forese,
potrebbe dir ch'ell'ha forse vernata
ove si fa 'l cristallo, in quel paese.[2]

5 Di mezzo agosto la truove infreddata:
or sappi che de' far d'ogni altro mese.
E non le val perché dorma calzata,
merzé del copertio c'ha cortonese.[3]

La tosse, 'l freddo e l'altra mala voglia
10 non l'addovien per omor ch'abbia vecchi,
ma per difetto ch'ella sente al nido.

Piange la madre, c'ha più d'una doglia,
dicendo: "Lassa, che per fichi secchi
messa l'avre' 'n casa del conte Guido!" [4]

[1] This sonnet and the one following are addressed to Forese Donati, nick-named Bicci Novello, a close friend of Dante and a relative of Dante's wife; he died in 1296. In *Purgatorio* XXIII, 48ff, Dante finds him among the circle of the gluttons.
[2] It was believed that rock crystal came from the freezing of water in very cold regions.
[3] *Cortonese* is a pun, referring at the same time to Cortona—that is, she is covered with a bed covering from Cortona—and to *corto*, "short." So *coper-toio*, in this same line, has an obscene meaning. Cf. *Decameron*, IV, 10.
[4] That is, for a small dowry I could have married her off to one of a powerful and noble family.

These words can be read in the face
of an angel come forth here;
20 and I, who gazed intently to see her,
now am in danger of losing my life;   IV
because I got so great a wound
from one I saw within her eyes,
that I go weeping now, and have known no peace since
       then.

44

Whoever heard the unlucky wife of Bicci,[1]
also called Forese, coughing,
might say she'd spent the winter
in the land where crystal is made.[2]

5 You would find her in the middle of August frozen:
now guess how she must do the other months.
And it doesn't do her any good to sleep with stockings on,
because what covers her falls short.[3]

The coughing, the cold, the other ills
10 come on her not because she's got the humors of old age—
but because of what she feels is missing in the nest.

Her mother weeps, who has more griefs than one,
and says, "Alas, it would have cost dry figs
to get her in Count Guido's house among the best." [4]

45

Bicci novel, figliuol di non so cui,
s'i' non ne domandasse monna Tessa,[1]
giù per la gola tanta roba hai messa,
ch'a forza ti convien torre l'altrui.

5 E già la gente si guarda da lui,
chi ha borsa a lato, là dov'e' s'appressa,
dicendo: "Questi c'ha la faccia fessa
è piùvico ladron negli atti sui."

E tal giace per lui nel letto tristo,[2]
10 per tema non sia preso a lo 'mbolare,
che gli appartien quanto Giossepp' a Cristo.

Di Bicci e de' fratei posso contare
che, per lo sangue lor, del male acquisto
sanno a lor donne buon cognati stare.[3]

46

Io son venuto al punto de la rota[1]
che l'orizzonte, quando il sol si corca,
ci partorisce il geminato cielo,[2]
e la stella d'amor ci sta remota[3]
5 per lo raggio lucente che la 'nforca

[1] Forese's mother. Monna = Ma donna.
[2] Forese's father, Simone.
[3] In other words, they neglect them, because they are able to pay for pleasures elsewhere.
[1] That is, the revolution of the stars and planets.
[2] When the sun goes down, the constellation of the Twins arises.
[3] Venus cannot be seen now because of the sun's rays.

45

Young Bicci, son of I don't know who,
unless I ask Monna Tessa,[1]
you've crammed so much stuff down your throat already,
you have to lift from others now.

5 And already people who have money in their pocketbooks
watch out for him when they see him coming,
and say, "That one with his face cut up—
a notorious thief, to judge by his looks."

And one man lies in bed whom worry seizes,[2]
10 afraid Forese will be caught in the act—a man
who has as much to do with Bicci as Joseph had with Jesus.

Of Bicci, knowing the stock from which he derives,
and his brothers I can say, they use their illicit gains
to be good brothers-in-law to their wives.[3]

46

I have come to that point on the wheel [1]
when the horizon, as the sun goes down,
brings forth for us the twinned sky,[2]
and the star of love is taken from our sight [3]
5 by the shining ray that rides

sì di traverso, che le si fa velo;
e quel pianeta che conforta il gelo   I
si mostra tutto a noi per lo grand'arco
nel qual ciascun di sette fa poca ombra: [4]
10 e però non disgombra
un sol penser d'amore, ond'io son carco,
la mente mia, ch'è più dura che petra
in tener forte imagine di petra.

Levasi de la rena d'Etïopia
15 lo vento peregrin che l'aere turba,
per la spera del sol ch'ora la scalda;
e passa il mare, onde conduce copia
di nebbia tal, che, s'altro non la sturba,
questo emisperio chiude tutto e salda;
20 e poi si solve, e cade in bianca falda   II
di fredda neve ed in noiosa pioggia,
onde l'aere s'attrista tutto e piagne:
e Amor, che sue ragne
ritira in alto pel vento che poggia
25 non m'abbandona; sì è bella donna
questa crudel che m'è data per donna.

Fuggito è ogne augel che 'l scaldo segue
del paese d'Europa, che non perde
le sette stelle gelide unquemai; [5]
30 e li altri han posto e le lor voci triegue
per non sonarle infino al tempo verde,
se ciò non fosse per cagion di guai;
e tutti li animali che son gai   III
di lor natura, son d'amor disciolti,
35 però che 'l freddo lor spirito ammorta:
e 'l mio più d'amor porta;
ché li dolzi pensier non mi son tolti

[4] Saturn, with its icy influence, exerts its maximum effect now as it proceeds along the great arc of Cancer, in which the rays of each of the seven planets strike the earth perpendicularly (thus each casts the shortest shadow).
[5] Ursa Major, the Great Bear, always visible in the northern hemisphere.

across and makes a veil before it;
and that planet which gives the cold its power   I
is all revealed to us along the great arc
wherein each of the seven casts the shortest shadow: [4]
10 and yet my mind does not let go
a single thought of love, and such thoughts burden me,
for my mind is firmer than stone
in holding tight to an image of stone.

From the sands of Ethiopia, that the sphere
15 of the sun is burning now, rises up
the pilgrim wind that darkens the air;
rises up, crosses the sea and brings a mass
of cloud so great that, unless another wind should scat-
    ter it,
it covers over and encloses our hemisphere;
20 and then dissolves and falls in white flakes   II
of frigid snow and in wearisome rain,
so that all the air grows sad and weeps:
and Love, who spreads
his nets out in the air on the wind that rises,
25 does not depart from me, so beautiful a lady
is this cruel one given me as lady.

Fled from the lands of Europe, which never lose
sight of the seven icy stars,[5]
is every bird that follows the warmth;
30 and all the others have set a pause upon their voices
and will not sound them till the green season,
except to lament;
and all the animals that by their natures   III
gladly mate now are untied from love,
35 for the cold deadens their spirit:
and yet my spirit is filled still more with love,
for these sweet thoughts are not taken away,

né mi son dati per volta di tempo,
ma donna li mi dà c'ha picciol tempo.[6]

40 Passato hanno lor termine le fronde
   che trasse fuor la vertù d'Arïete [7]
   per adornare il mondo, e morta è l'erba;
   ramo di foglia verde a noi s'asconde
   se non se in lauro, in pino o in abete
45 o in alcun che sua verdura serba;
   e tanto è la stagion forte ed acerba,
   c'ha morti li fioretti per le piagge,
   li quai non poten tollerar la brina:
   e la crudele spina
50 però Amor di cor non la mi tragge;
   per ch'io son fermo di portarla sempre
   ch'io sarò in vita, s'io vivesse sempre.

   Versan le vene le fummifere acque
   per li vapor che la terra ha nel ventre,
55 che d'abisso li tira suso in alto;
   onde cammino al bel giorno mi piacque
   che ora è fatto rivo, e sarà mentre
   che durerà del verno il grande assalto; [8]
   la terra fa un suol che par di smalto,
60 e l'acqua morta si converte in vetro [9]
   per la freddura che di fuor la serra:
   e io de la mia guerra
   non son però tornato un passo a retro,
   né vo' tornar; ché, se 'l martiro è dolce,
65 la morte de' passare ogni altro dolce.

   Canzone, or che sarà di me ne l'altro
   dolce tempo novello, quando piove
   amore in terra da tutti li cieli,

IV

V

[6] That is, she is young.
[7] The sun is in the sign of the Ram at the vernal equinox.
[8] From the waters and exhalations of the earth come winds and torrents.
[9] The waters are stagnant, still.

or given me, with the turning of the seasons,
but a lady gave them to me who has lived few seasons.[6]

40 The leaves have passed their time
that were brought forth by the power of the Ram [7]
to adorn the world, and the grass is dead;
branches green with leaf are lost for us
except in laurel, pine, or fir,
45 or in another that holds its verdure;
and the season is so bitter and severe   IV
it has killed the little flowers in the field
that were not able to withstand the frost:
and yet Love does not draw
50 out the cruel thorn from my heart,
for I am determined to bear it ever
while I live, though I live forever.

The fountains pour forth the fumey waters
from the vapors that the earth has in its bowels,
55 which it draws up into the air from the abyss;
wherefore a path that pleased me when the days were
                    pleasant
now has become a stream, which will remain as long
as the great assault of winter lasts; [8]
the earth has formed a crust that looks like stone,   V
60 and the dead water turns to glass [9]
for the cold that locks it in:
and yet I have not turned
back one step from the struggle,
nor shall I turn; for if this suffering is sweet,
65 death must surpass all sweet.

Song, what will become of me in that other
sweet new season, when love
rains down upon the earth from all the heavens,

quando per questi geli   VI
70 amore è solo in me, e non altrove?
Saranne quello ch'è d'un uom di marmo,[10]
se in pargoletta fia per core un marmo.

47

Al poco giorno e al gran cerchio d'ombra
son giunto, lasso, ed al bianchir de' colli,
quando si perde lo color ne l'erba: I
e 'l mio disio però non cangia il verde,
5 sì è barbato ne la dura petra
che parla e sente come fosse donna [1]

Similemente questa nova donna
si sta gelata come neve a l'ombra;
ché non la move, se non come petra,   II
10 il dolce tempo che riscalda i colli,
e che li fa tornar di bianco in verde
perché li corpre di fioretti e d'erba.

Quand'ella ha in testa un ghirlanda d'erba,
trae de la mente nostra ogn'altra donna;
15 perché si mischia il crespo giallo e 'l verde   III
sì bel, ch'Amor lì viene a stare a l'ombra,
che m'ha serrato intra piccioli colli [2]
più forte assai che la calcina petra.

---

[10] Man of marble: in other words, a lifeless man. It has been suggested (by
Zingarelli, Mattalia, Contini, and others) that this song as well as the other
rime petrose would have been subjected to an allegorical exegesis in the
Convivio, the *petra* representing the intellectual difficulties encountered by
the poet when he turned to the pursuit of philosophy.
[1] This lyric is a *sestina;* on the form, see section on Arnaut Daniel in
Lyrics of the Troubadours and Trouvères (Doubleday, 1973). The "hard
stone" in line 5 is, of course, the lady. Note that the winter setting changes
to spring in the following strophes.
[2] What this line refers to is not known.

if even in the middle of this ice VI
70 love is in me alone, and nowhere else?
It will be with me as with a man of marble,[10]
if in that young girl there is still a heart of marble.

47

To the short day and great circle of shadow
I have come, alas, and to the whitening of the hills
when the color is lost in the grass; I
and yet my desire stays green,
5 so rooted is it in the hard stone
that speaks and senses as though it were a woman.[1]

She stays frozen, this new woman,
as snow stays frozen in shadow;
nor is she stirred more than a stone II
10 by the sweet season that warms the hills
and changes them from white to green
as it covers them with flowers and grass.

When on her head she wears a garland of grass
she draws out of our mind every other woman;
15 because her blond curls mix with the garland's green III
so beautifully that Love comes to rest in their shadow,
who holds me fixed between small hills [2]
more firmly than mortar fixes stone.

La sua bellezza ha più vertù che petra,[3]
20 e 'l colpo suo non può sanar per erba;
ch'io son fuggito per piani e per colli,   IV
per potere scampar da cotal donna;
e dal suo lume non mi può far ombra
poggio né muro mai né fronda verde.

25 Io l'ho veduta già vestita a verde,
sì fatta ch'ella avrebbe messo in petra
l'amor ch'io porto pur a la sua ombra: V
ond'io l'ho chesta in un bel prato d'erba,
innamorata com'anco fu donna,
30 e chiuso intorno d'altissimi colli.

Ma ben ritorneranno i fiumi a' colli,
prima che questo legno molle e verde
s'infiammi, come suol far bella donna,   VI
di me; che mi torrei dormire in petra
35 tutto il mio tempo e gir pascendo l'erba,
sol per veder do' suoi panni fanno ombra.

Quandunque i colli fanno più nera ombra,
sotto un bel verde la giovane donna   VII
la fa sparer, com'uom petra sott'erba.

48

Così nel mio parlar voglio esser aspro [1]
com'è ne li atti questa bella petra,
la quale ognora impetra
maggior durezza e più natura cruda,
5 e veste sua persona d'un dïaspro [2]

[3] On the magical power of precious stones, see notes to Guido Guinizelli, no. 20 above. *Erba,* "grass," in line 20 means medicinal herbs.
[1] *Aspro* means at once "harsh," "bitter," and "harsh-sounding."
[2] According to the medieval lapidaries, jasper kept whoever carried it from harm.

Her beauty has more power than precious stone [3]
20 and her blow cannot be healed by grass;
and I have fled through plains and hills IV
to escape, if I could, such a woman;
but against her light I can find no shadow
from hilltop, wall, or branch of green.

25 Once I saw her dressed in green,
looking as though she could instill in stone
the love I bring even to her shadow; V
wherefore I have wanted her in a beautiful field of grass,
as much in love as ever any woman;
30 and all around, the field shut in by towering hills.

But the rivers will run back to the hills
before this wood all wet and green
takes fire—such is the way of a beautiful woman— VI
for me; who would be willing to sleep on stone
35 my whole life and feed on grass
just to see where her dress casts a shadow.

Whenever the hills cast the blackest shadow,
beneath her lovely green this young woman VII
makes it vanish, as a stone is made to vanish under grass.

48

I want to be as grating in my words [1]
as that beautiful stone in her deeds,
who every moment petrifies and takes on
greater hardness and a harsher nature,
5 and arms her body with jasper,[2]

tal, che per lui, o perch'ella s'arretra,
non esce di faretra I
saetta che già mai la colga ignuda:
ed ella ancide, e non val ch'om si chiuda
10 né si dilunghi da' colpi mortali,
che, com'avesser ali,
giungono altrui e spezzan ciascun'arme;
sì ch'io non so da lei né posso atarme.

Non trovo scudo ch'ella non mi spezzi
15 né loco che dal suo viso m'asconda;
ché, come fior di fronda,
così de la mia mente tien la cima.
Cotanto del mio mal par che si prezzi
quanto legno di mar che non lieva onda;
20 e 'l peso che m'affonda II
è tal che non potrebbe adequar rima.
Ahi angosciosa e dispietata lima
che sordamente la mia vita scemi,
perché non ti ritemi
25 sì di rodermi il core a scorza a scorza,
com'io di dire altrui chi ti dà froza?

Ché più mi triema il cor qualora io penso
di lei in parte ov'altri li occhi induca,
per tema non traluca
30 lo mio penser di fuor sì che si scopra,
ch'io non fo de la morte, che ogni senso
co li denti d'Amor già mi manduca;
ciò è che 'l pensier bruca III
la lor vertù, sì che n'allenta l'opra.³
35 E' m'ha percosso in terra, e stammi sopra
con quella spada ond'elli ancise Dido,
Amore, a cui io grido
merzé chiamando, e umilmente il priego;
ed el d'ogni merzé par messo al niego.

³ This passage could also be translated: "that is, the force of these teeth
gnaws on my mind and thus slows down its action."

because of which, or just because she ducks,
no arrow ever came   I
from quiver that could strike her where she's bare;
but she can kill—no use putting armor on
10 or running away from her killing blows,
which, as if they had wings,
strike flesh and break every weapon to pieces;
so that I don't know what to do with her and can't
        defend myself.

I find no shield she does not shatter,
15 no place to hide from her look;
because, like the flower on the stalk,
she takes hold on the summit of my soul:
she seems as worried by my suffering
as a ship by a sea that lifts no wave;
20 and a burden founders me   II
no poetry is equal to.
O fearful and pitiless rasp
that silently grates away my life,
why don't you refrain
25 from gnawing through my heart from crust to crust,
as I from telling who it is that gives you power?

For my heart trembles more—whenever I think
of her being where someone else's eyes could see her—
for fear lest my thought
30 shine out and be discovered,
than I tremble for death, which is already
eating, with the teeth of Love, all my senses;
I mean, my thought feeds   III
on their vitality and thus slows down their action.[3]
35 Love has struck me to the ground, and now stands over
                me
with that same sword he used to murder Dido,
and I cry out to him
calling for mercy, and humbly beg him,
and he looks dead-set against all mercy.

40 Egli alza ad ora ad or la mano, e sfida
   la debole mia vita, esto perverso,
   che disteso a riverso
   mi tiene in terra d'ogni guizzo stanco:
   allor mi surgon ne la mente strida;
45 e 'l sangue, ch'è per le vene disperso,   IV
   fuggendo corre verso
   lo cor, che 'l chiama; ond'io rimango bianco.
   Elli mi fiede sotto il braccio manco
   sì forte, che 'l color nel cor rimbalza:
50 allor dico: "S'elli alza
   un'altra volta, Morte m'avrà chiuso
   prima che 'l colpo sia disceso giuso."

   Così vedess'io lui fender per mezzo
   lo core a la crudele che 'l mio squatra!
55 poi non mi sarebb'atra
   la morte, ov'io per sua bellezza corro:
   ché tanto dà nel sol quanto nel rezzo
   questa scherana micidiale e latra.
   Ohmè, perché non latra   V
60 per me, com'io per lei, nel caldo borro?
   ché tosto griderei: "Io vi soccorro";
   e fare' l volentier, sì come quelli
   che ne' biondi capelli
   ch'Amor per consumarmi increspa e dora
65 metterei mano, e piacere'le allora.

   S'io avessi le belle trecce prese,
   che fatte son per me scudiscio e ferza,
   pigliandole anzi terza,
   con esse passerei vespero e squille: [4]
70 e non sarei pietoso né cortese,
   anzi farei com'orso quando scherza;
   e se Amor me ne sferza,   VI
   io mi vendicherei di più di mille.

[4] Terce is the third canonical hour (9 A.M.); vespers, the sixth and next-to-last hour.

40 Again and again he lifts his hand and menaces
    my feeble life, this unholy one
    who holds me stretched out
    on my back on the ground, too weary to move:
    then shrieks rise in my mind,
45 and my blood, that was dispersed in my veins,
    fleeing, courses back   IV
    to my heart, that calls it back; and I am left white.
    He wounds me under my left arm
    so badly, the pain surges up in my heart again:
50 then I say, "If he lifts his hand
    again, Death shall lock me up
    before the blow comes down."

    Would that I could see him cleave
    the heart of that cruel woman who tears mine to pieces;
55 then death would not be a black
    thing to me, who run toward death for her beauty,
    because she strikes as hard in the sun as in the shade,
    this thief, this murderous cutthroat.
    O why does she not howl   V
60 for me, as I for her, in the burning pit?
    because I'd cry out, right away, "I'll help you!";
    and I would, willingly; into that
    yellow hair
    that Love curls up and makes golden to ruin me
65 I would put my hand; and then she'd love me.

    Once I had those lovely tresses in my hand
    that have come to be my whips and scourges,
    grabbing them before terce
    I'd keep hold of them through vespers and the evening
              bell; [4]
70 and I would not be courteous or merciful,
    but like a bear at play;
    and though Love whips me with them now,   VI
    I'd take revenge a thousand times.

Ancor ne li occhi, ond'escon le faville
75 che m'infiammano il cor, ch'io porto anciso,
guarderei presso e fiso,
per vendicar lo fuggir che mi face;
e poi le renderei con amor pace.

Canzon, vattene dritto a quella donna
80 che m'ha ferito il core e che m'invola
quello ond'io ho più gola,   VII
e dàlle per lo cor d'una saetta:
ché bell'onor s'acquista in far vendetta.

49

Tre donne intorno al cor mi son venute,[1]
e seggonsi di fore;
ché dentro siede Amore,
lo quale è in segnoria de la mia vita.
5 Tanto son belle e di tanta vertute,[2]
che 'l possente segnore,
dico quel ch'è nel core,
a pena del parlar di lor s'aita.
Ciascuna par dolente e sbigottita,   I
10 come persona discacciata e stanca,
cui tutta gente manca
e cui vertute né beltà non vale.
Tempo fu già nel quale,
secondo il lor parlar, furon dilette;
15 or sono a tutti in ira ed in non cale.
Queste così solette

[1] These figures are difficult to interpret and were obviously meant to be
(see vi). What is clear from the description of the "births" in ii and iii is
that the three figures, considered together, represent a descent. Pietro di
Dante regarded them as the representations, respectively, of distributive justice, human justice, and positive law (laws that are enacted); this is still
the consensus of critics and scholars. On the "kinship" of love and justice in
Dante's thought, see *De Monarchia*, I,11ff, for example: "As greed, however

And then into those eyes, where the sparks fly out
75 that inflame my murdered heart,
   I would look deep, without moving,
   to take revenge on her for fleeing me;
   and when she gave me love, I would give her peace.

   Song, go straight to that lady
80 who has hurt my heart and robs me
   of what I most hunger for,   VII
   and put an arrow through her heart: attack!
   for sweet honor is won through getting back.

49

   Three ladies have come around my heart [1]
   and sit outside;
   for Love sits within,
   who has the lordship of my life.
5 They are so beautiful and of such great dignity, [2]
   that mighty lord—
   I mean him in my heart—
   must struggle with pain to speak with them.
   Each one seems afraid and full of grief,   I
10 like someone driven out and weary,
   without people,
   whom beauty and nobility do not avail.
   There was a time,
   from what they say, when they were loved;
15 now they are despised by all, and unregarded.
   Thus, all alone, they

slight, obscures the habits of justice, so charity or joy in righteousness refines
and enlightens it" (translated by Herbert W. Schneider, Liberal Arts Press
edition). The three ladies are represented as suffering exile at this moment
of human history. Dante's own exile, therefore, becomes a precious mark of
honor and righteousness.
[2] Foster and Boyde translate *vertute* as "dignity," the outward sign of virtue.

venute son come a casa d'amico;
ché sanno ben che dentro è quel ch'io dico.

Dolesi l'una con parole molto,
20 e 'n su la man si posa
come succisa rosa:
il nudo braccio, di dolor colonna,
sente l'oraggio che cade dal volto;
l'altra man tiene ascosa
25 la faccia lagrimosa:
discinta e scalza, e sol di sé par donna.[3]

Come Amor prima per la rotta gonna II
la vide in parte che il tacere è bello,
egli, pietoso e fello,
30 di lei e del dolor fece dimanda.
"Oh di pochi vivanda," [4]
rispose in voce con sospiri mista,
"nostra natura qui a te ci manda:
io, che son la più trista,
35 son suora a la tua madre, e son Drittura; [5]
povera, vedi, a panni ed a cintura."

Poi che fatta si fu palese e conta,
doglia e vergogna prese
lo mio segnore, e chiese
40 chi fosser l'altre due ch'eran con lei.
E questa, ch'era sì di pianger pronta,
tosto che lui intese,
più nel dolor s'accese,
dicendo: "A te non duol de gli occhi miei?"
45 Poi cominciò: "Sì come saper dei, III
di fonte nasce il Nilo picciol fiume
quivi dove 'l gran lume
toglie a la terra del vinco la fronda: [6]

---

[3] That is, not in her clothes or ornaments.
[4] Only few are capable of true love.
[5] Thus Justice is the sister of Venus, the mother of Love.
[6] The Nile was believed to be one of the four rivers of the Earthly Paradise.

have come as to the house of a friend;
for they know well, the one I speak of is within.

One puts her deep grief into words
20 and rests her head on her hand
like a cut rose:
her naked arm, a column of grief,
feels the rain that falls from her eyes;
the other hand conceals
25 her weeping face:
barefoot, ungirt, only in herself does she appear
a lady.[3]

When Love first through the torn gown   II
saw that part of her it is decorous not to name,
in pity and anger he
30 asked about her and about her grief.
"O food of the few," [4]
she answered, her voice mixed with sighs,
"our kinship sends us here to you:
I, the most sorrowful,
35 am sister to your mother, and I am Justice; [5]
poor, you see, in dress and ornament."

When she had made herself known and recognized,
grief and shame seized
my lord, and he asked
40 who the other two with her might be.
And she, who was so poised to weep,
heard him and was in that instant
set on fire with yet more grief,
saying: "Do you feel no pity for my eyes?"
45 Then began: "As you must know,   III
the Nile springs from its source as a little river:
there where the enormous light
is kept from earth by the osier leaf,[6]

Line 48 can also be translated, as in Foster and Boyde, "There where the
great light takes the osier leaf from the earth."

sovra la vergin onda
50 generai io costei che m'è da lato
e che s'asciuga con la treccia bionda.

Questo mio bel portato,
mirando sé ne la chiara fontana,
generò questa che m'è più lontana."

55 Fenno i sospiri Amore un poco tardo;
e poi con gli occhi molli,
che prima furon folli,
salutò le germane sconsolate.
E poi che prese l'uno e l'altro dardo,[7]
60 disse: "Drizzate i colli:
ecco l'armi ch'io volli;
per non usar, vedete, son turbate.
Larghezza e Temperanza e l'altre nate   IV
del nostro sangue mendicando vanno.
65 Però, se questo è danno,
piangano gli occhi e dolgasi la bocca
de li uomini a cui tocca,
che sono a' raggi di cotal ciel giunti;[8]
non noi, che semo de l'etterna rocca:
70 ché, se noi siamo or punti,
noi pur saremo, e pur tornerà gente
che questo dardo farà star lucente."

E io, che ascolto nel parlar divino
consolarsi e dolersi
75 così alti dispersi,
l'essilio che m'è dato, onor mi tegno:

ché, se giudizio o forza di destino
vuol pur che il mondo versi

---

[7] A traditional image; compare Ovid, *Met.*, i, 468–471. Foster & Boyde accept
the interpretation that one arrow is the love of goodness; the other, hatred
of evil.
[8] Mortals are subject to malign astral influence.

on the virgin wave
50 I brought forth this one at my side,
   who wipes her tears with her golden hair.

   This my beautiful child
   gazing on her image in the clear spring
   brought forth the one who is further from me."

55 Sighs made Love somewhat slow to talk;
   and then with wet eyes
   that before were discourteous,
   he greeted his despairing kin.
   And then he grasped the one arrow and the other,[7]
60 and he said: "Raise up your heads:
   behold the weapons I meant to use:
   see, they are black from disuse.
   Generosity and Temperance and the others born   IV
   of our blood go begging.
65 But though this is calamity,
   let the eyes weep and the mouths lament
   of those it touches,
   for they are bound beneath the rays of such a fir-
             mament—[8]
   but we are not, we are of the eternal rock:
70 for, though we bear injuries at this time,
   we shall eternally *be,* and a generation shall return
   that shall make this arrow brightly shine."

   And I, who hear in these divine words
   such noble exiles
75 comfort each other and tell their grief,
   I hold my exile for an honor:

   for if judgment or the force of destiny
   truly wants the world to change

i bianchi fiori in persi,[9]
80 cader co' buoni è pur di lode degno.
E se non che de gli occhi miei 'l bel segno   V
per lontananza m'è tolto dal viso,
che m'have in foco miso,
lieve mi conterei ciò che m'è grave.[10]
85 Ma questo foco m'have
già consumato sì l'ossa e la polpa
che Morte al petto m'ha posto la chiave.
Onde, s'io ebbi colpa,
più lune ha volto il sol poi che fu spenta,
90 se colpa muore perché l'uom si penta.

Canzone, a' panni tuoi non ponga uom mano,
per veder quel che bella donna chiude: [11]
bastin le parti nude; [12]
lo dolce pome a tutta gente niega,
95 per cui ciascun man piega.   VI
Ma s'elli avvien che tu alcun mai truovi
amico di virtù, ed e' ti priega,
fatti di color novi,
poi li ti mostra; e 'l fior, ch'è bel di fiori,
100 fa' disïar ne li amorosi cori.

Canzone, uccella con le bianche penne;
canzone, caccia con li neri veltri,
che fuggir mi convenne,[13]
ma far mi poterian di pace dono.   VII
105 Però nol fan che non san quel che sono:
camera di perdon savio uom non serra,
ché 'l perdonare è bel vincer di guerra.

[9] That is, make evil triumph over good.
[10] His exile is painful only because it keeps him from seeing his beloved Florence.
[11] That is, do not reveal your meaning to the common crowd.
[12] That is, the literal sense.
[13] The wars between the Blacks and the Whites have caused his exile. See introduction.

the white flowers into dark,[9]
80 it is yet worthy of praise to fall with the good.
And were it not that the beautiful target of my eyes   V
is rapt by distance from my sight—
this is what has set me on fire—
I would hold this heaviness for light.[10]
85 But this fire has
already so consumed my bones and flesh,
Death has put his key to my breast.
And even if some blame was mine,
the sun has circled several moons since that has ceased
                to be,
90 if it is true blame dies when a man repents.

Song, let no man put his hand to your dress
to see what a beautiful lady hides: [11]
let the visible parts be enough; [12]
deny to everyone that sweet fruit
95 for which every man stretches out his hand.   VI
But if it ever happens that you find someone
a lover of virtue, and he entreats you,
put on new colors,
then show yourself to him; and make the flower that is
                outwardly fair
100 be longed for in hearts that love.

Song, go hawking with the white wings,
song, go hunting with the black hounds
that I have had to flee,[13]
though they could make me the gift of peace.   VII
105 They do not do so because they do not know what I am:
a wise man does not lock the chamber of forgiveness,
for to forgive is sweet victory in war.

50

Io sono stato con Amore insieme
de la circulazion del sol mia nona,
e so com'egli affrena e come sprona,
e come sotto lui si ride e geme.

5 Chi ragione o virtù contra gli sprieme,
fa come que' che 'n la tempesta sona,
credendo far colà dove si tona
esser le guerre de' vapori sceme.

Però nel cerchio de la sua palestra
10 liber arbitrio già mai non fu franco,
sì che consiglio invan vi si balestra.

Ben può con nuovi spron punger lo fianco,
e qual che sia 'l piacer ch'ora n'addestra,
seguitar si convien, se l'altro è stanco.[1]

[1] That is, if our devotion to one lady is worn out, we can devote ourselves to
another. This sonnet is a reply to one addressed to Dante by Cino da Pistoia,
Dante, quando per caso s'abbandona (below, no. 61). There Cino had posed
the question whether a man, if his love has no hope of fulfillment, can love
someone else.

50

I have been together with Love
since my ninth circling of the sun,
and know how he spurs and bridles,
and how everyone in his power laughs and groans.

5 Whoever calls up reason or virtue against him
acts like one who makes noises in a storm,
thinking he can make the collisions
of the vapors, up there where it thunders, less.

Thus within the circle of his arena
10 free will was never free,
so that reason bends its bow in vain there.

He can always prick the flank with new spurs, there is no
doubt;
and whatever pleasure leads us now,
we must follow, if the other is played out.[1]

GIANNI ALFANI

(fl. c. 1300)

The poet has never been clearly identified. Only seven songs of his are known, all of them *ballate* except for one sonnet addressed to Guido Cavalcanti. Echoes of Cavalcanti and Dante in his lyrics are numerous.

Text: Contini.

Guato una donna dov'io la scontrai,
che cogli occhi mi tolse
il cor, quando si volse
per salutarmi, e nol mi rendéo mai.

I

5 Io la pur miro là dov'io la vidi,
e veggiovi con lei
il bel saluto che mi fece allora;
lo quale sbigottì sì gli occhi miei,
che gl' incerchiò di stridi
10 l'anima mia, che li pingea di fora
perchè sentiva in lui venire umile
un spirito gentile
che le diceva: [1] "Omai
guata costei, se non tu ti morrai!"

II

15 Amor mi vien colà dov'io la miro,
amantato di gioia
nelli raggi del lume ch'ella spande;
e contami che pur conven ch'i' moia
per forza d'un sospiro,
20 che per costei debbo far sì grande,
che l'anima smarrita s'andrà via.
Ah bella donna mia,
sentirai tu che guai!
Che te ne 'ncresca quando li udirai!

III

25 Tu se' stata oggimai sette anni pura,
danza mia nova e sola,
cercando 'l mondo d'un che ti vestisse; [2]
ed hai veduto quella, che m'imbola
la vita, star pur dura

IV

[1] Refers to the soul.
[2] Meaning, perhaps, with music, or with a reply (which would explain why the song is *sola*, 1. 26). *Danza* means *ballata*.

51

I am gazing on a lady, standing where I saw her,
who, with her eyes, bore away
my heart, when she turned
to greet me, and never gave it back.   I

5 I gaze on her always, here where I saw her;
with her—there—I see again
the beautiful greeting she gave me then;
which so terrified my eyes
my soul encircled them   II
10 with screams—screams my soul sent forth
when she saw descending on that greeting gently
a noble spirit,
which told her,[1] "Never
look on her, or you will die!"

15 Love comes to me, here where I gaze on her,
cloaked with joy
in the rays of her light;
and tells me I must die
from the force of a sigh   III
20 for her so great,
my bewildered soul will flee.
O my beautiful lady,
what lamentation you will hear—
may it fill you with pity to hear it.

25 You have gone seven years unclothed,
O my new and lonely song,
seeking through the world for one to dress you,[2]
and have seen her who steals
my life away stay obdurate,   IV

30 e non pregare alcun che ti coprisse.
    Però ti conven gire a lei pietosa
    e dirle: "I' son tua cosa,
    madonna; tu che sai,
    fa ch'io sia ben vestita di tuo' vai."

35 "Se tu mi vesti ben, questa fanciulla,
    donna, uscirà di culla." [3]   V
    "E' saprò s'i' serrai
    alcuna roba vaia; sì l'avrai." [4]

52

Ballatetta dolente,
va mostrando il mi' pianto   I
che di dolor mi cuopre tutto quanto.

    Tu te n'andrai imprima a quella gioia
  5 per cui Fiorenza luce ed è pregiata;
    e quetamente, che no le sia noia,
    la priega che t'ascolti, o sconsolata;   II
    poi le dirai affannata
    come m'ha tutto infranto
 10 il tristo bando che mi colse al canto.

    S'ella si volge verso te pietosa
    ad ascoltar le pene che tu porti,
    traendo guai dolente e vergognosa,
    lei pingi come gli occhi miei son morti   III
 15 per li gran colpi e forti
    che ricevetter tanto
    da' suoi nel mi' partir, ch'or piagne in canto.

---

[3] The music or reply will make the *ballata* complete.
[4] Presumably it is the lady who speaks in the last two lines.

30 not beseeching anyone to cover you.
   Therefore in your wretchedness you must make your way
   to her and say: "I am your concern,
   my lady; you who know,
   let me be clothed with your robe of vair."

35 "If you clothe it well, this child
   shall come forth, lady, from the cradle." [3]   V
   "I shall see whether I have in keeping
   any robe of vair, and you shall have it." [4]

52

Grieving *ballatetta*,
go forth, show my sorrow,   I
for I am overwhelmed by grief.

You shall go first to that joy
5 by which Florence shines and is glorified;
   and gently, lest you vex her,
   beg her hear you, O disconsolate;   II
   then, tell her, in dismay,
   how I am broken
10 by the sad exile that fell on me without warning.

If she turns toward you full of pity
to hear of the suffering you bear,
lamenting in grief and shamefastness
picture for her how my eyes are dead   III
15 from the great blows
   they got so often
   from her eyes when I parted, that now, singing, you weep.

Poi fa sì ch'entri nella mente a Guido,[1]
perch'egli è sol colui che vede Amore,[2]
20 e mostrali lo spirito d'un strido
me trae d'angoscia del disfatto core;
e se vedrà 'l dolore
che 'l distrugge, i' mi vanto
ched e' ne sospirrà di pièta alquanto.

IV

[1] Guido Cavalcanti.
[2] That is, understands it.

Then find your way into the mind of Guido,[1]
for only he sees Love,[2]
20 and show him the spirit that draws forth
a scream from the anguish of my shattered heart;   IV
and if he sees the grief
destroying it, I declare
he will sigh with some compassion.

DINO FRESCOBALDI

(*c. 1271–1316*)

Frescobaldi was born in Florence, the son of a prosperous merchant and banker who was also a poet. He was highly regarded in his day. His poetry draws a great deal from Cavalcanti and Dante; he tries very hard for effect, introducing unusual conceits and elaborate periods, but the strain is too noticeable.

Text: Salinari.

53

Un'alta stella di nova bellezza,
che del sol ci to' l'ombra la sua luce,
nel ciel d'Amor di tanta virtù luce,
che m'innamora de la sua chiarezza.

5 E poi si trova di tanta ferezza,
vedendo come nel cor mi traluce,
c'ha preso, con que' raggi ch'ella 'nduce,
nel firmamento la maggior altezza.

E come donna questa nova stella
10 sembianti fa che 'l mi' viver le spiace
e per disdegno cotanto è salita.

Amor, che ne la mente mi favella,
del lume di costei saette face
e segno fa de la mia poca vita.

Donna, da gli occhi tuoi par che si mova
un lume che mi passa entro la mente;
e quando egli è con lei,[1] par che sovente
si metta nel disio ched i si trova.

5 Di lui v'appare una figura nova
che si fa loba e trovasi possente,
e signoria vi ten sì aspramente,
ch'ogni ferezza al cor par che vi piova.

[1] The soul.

53

A high star of miraculous beauty,
whose light darkens the sun's image in our eyes,
shines in the heaven of Love with such power,
it fills me with love by its splendor;

5   and then becomes so proud,
seeing how it pierces my heart with its light,
it has taken, with those rays it sends down,
the highest place in the firmament.

Now in the form of a lady this new star
10   shows she is displeased I go on living;
and through such great disdain she has risen up.

Love, who speaks to me in my mind,
makes arrows of her light
and a target of my lingering life.

54

Lady, from your eyes it seems a light
comes forth and enters my soul;
and this light, when it is with her,[1] often seems
to unite with the desire already there.

5   From this a strange figure comes forth,
that turns into a she-wolf, finding herself in power
and holds dominion there so cruelly
every torment seems to rain into my heart.

Pietà non v'è nè merzè nè calere,
10   perchè si fa crudel com'ella puote
e disdegnosa della vita mia.

Li spiriti, che nol posson soffrire,
ciascun si tien d'aver maggior virtute
qual può dinanz' a le' partirsi via.

55

Quest'altissima stella, che si vede
col su' bel lume, ma' non m'abandona:
costei mi die' chi del su' ciel mi dona
quanto di grazia 'l mi' 'ntelletto chiede.

5   E 'l novo dardo che 'n questa man siede
porta dolcezza a chi di me ragiona:
in altra guisa Amor sa che persona
non fedì mai nè fedirà nè fiede.[1]

Per che merzè aver così mi piace
10   con questa nuova leggiadria ch'i' porto,
dove mai crudeltà neuna giace.

Entro 'n quel punt'ogni vizio fu morto
ch'io tolsi lume di cotanta pace,
ed Amor sa ched io 'l ne feci accorto.

56

Per gir verso la spera la finice
si scalda sì, che poi accende fiamma

---

[1] Love does not arise through cruelty ("the other way").

Pity is not there, or kindness, or concern,
10 for she makes herself cruel—she knows the way—
and disdainful of this life of mine.

The spirits cannot endure this,
but some imagine they have greater power
because, when she approaches, they can run away.

55

This highest star, which is known
by its beautiful light, never abandons me:
he gave it to me who from his heaven gives me
every grace my intellect desires.

5   And the marvelous arrow poised in her hand
brings sweetness to all who speak of me:
Love knows, by any other way he never struck,
does not strike, will not strike the heart.[1]

Therefore, to have kindness greatly pleases me,
10 and gives me this new bliss;
and nowhere is cruelty lurking.

Every vice in me was killed that instant
I drew the light of such great peace.
And Love knows I have acquainted him with this.

56

Flying toward the light the phoenix
grows so hot the fire flares

in loco ov'ella infiamma,
sì che natura vince vita allora.
5   Così per veder che 'l meo pensier dice,
mi mena Amor verso sì fatta fiamma,   I
che 'l cor già se ne 'nfiamma,
tanto che Morte lui prende e colora,
de lo suo frutto altero ch' innamora.
10 Tant'è cocente, che chi 'l sente chiaro
trova radice d'ogne stato amaro.

Egli'l mi par sentir già nella mente,
venuto per vertù d'est'ugelletta
la quale uom non alletta,
15 nè altro, fuor ch'Amor, che·llei 'ntenda.
Ferr' ha spicciato sì, possibilmente,
chè, dentro stando, tempera saetta,   II
onde poi insaetta
le mie virtù sì che 'l martir m'apprenda.[1]
20 Ed io, che temo nel finir m'offenda,
chero Pietate al cui richiamo i' sono,
ed a costei nel mi' finir perdono.

Di ciò che la mia vita è nimistate,
lo suo bello sdegnar qual vòl la mira,
25 priegol, poi che mi tira

in su la morte, che mi renda pace.
Chè mi mostra un pensier molte fiate,
il qual, d'ogni altro più, in dolor gira,   III
com'io le sono in ira,
30 sì che tremando pianger me ne face.
Lo spirito d'amor che nel cor giace,
per confortarmi mi dice: "Tu dèi
amar la morte per piacer di lei."

Allor ch'i' odo che per su diletto
35 e' mi conven provar qual falso punto
───────────────
[1] These lines in strophe II are obscure; the text follows Contini.

that burns it up—
and nature vanquishes life.

5 Just so, beholding her my thought speaks to me about,
I am led by Love toward a flame so great   I
my heart burns all at once
for that proud fruit by which he makes me love,
and death seizes my heart and gives it his color.
10 So mighty is that flame, whoever truly feels it
finds the root of every bitterness.

It seems to me I feel Love already come
into my soul through the effect of that young girl,
that bird no man who desires her
15 can lure, only Love;
who has shaped some metal,
and, poised in my mind, he sharpens it into an arrow,   II
and with it strikes
my spirits, and I am seized with pain.[1]
20 And I, fearing injury when all is done,
call on Pity, my last appeal,
and on the point of death forgive that one.

Since my life is agony,
I beg that beautiful disdain of hers toward everyone
25 that might admire her, since that is what draws me

toward death, to give me peace.
For many times a thought, which above
all others finds its way to pain, reveals to me   III
how I am held in scorn,
30 and makes me, trembling, weep.
The spirit of Love that lies in my heart
says, to comfort me: "You should
love death, to please her."

Since I hear that for her delight
35 I must suffer that unnatural end

ov'i' son quasi giunto,
sì che mi mostra un doloroso affanno,
dico che mosse fuor del su' intelletto
l'ardente lancia che m'ha così punto   IV
40 dritto nel fianco appunto,
ed in qual loco ov'e' sospiri stanno;
li quali sbigottiti or se ne vanno
davanti a quella per merzè di cui,
poi ch'io la vidi, innamorato fui.

45 Deh, canzonetta, i' vo' che tu celata
tenghi costei con le parole c'hai,
ovunque tu girai;   V
perchè mi par ch'a torto faccia offesa,
non voglio, tua cagion, ne sia ripresa.

which I have almost reached—
for death already lets me see its racking toil—
I say that it was from her mind the burning lance
shot forth that now has pierced   **IV**
40 the exact center of my heart,
where my sighting spirits dwell;
which, terrified, now flee
before her, for whose grace I,
when I saw her, fell in love.

45 Alas, *canzonetta,* I command you,
in your verses let her stay unnamed
wherever you may go;   **V**
for I think she has injured me unjustly
and do not want her, you bearing witness, blamed.

CINO DA PISTOIA

(c. 1270–c. 1337)

The poet studied law in his native city of Pistoia and at the University of Bologna. From 1303 to 1306 he was under sentence of exile, as a Black. He was a distinguished jurist; a teacher of law at Siena, Perugia, Naples, and Florence; and the author of several highly praised legal treatises. He was a champion of Henry VII and the imperial cause—one of his many ties to Dante, who extols him in *DVF*.

Although he reveals several distinctive characteristics of the *dolce stil novo*—especially the concentration upon the internalized image of the distant lady—he has no interest in its pretensions to objectivity or its doctrinaire bias. As a result, his lyrics often seem personal and confessional. Because of this emphasis on personal sentiment, as well as his constant themes of solitude, longing, and grief, he is generally regarded as a formative influence on Petrarch, who, in fact, held him in high esteem.

Text: Guido Zaccagnini, ed. *Le Rime di Cino da Pistoia*. Biblioteca dell' "Archivum Romanicum," ser. I, vol. 4. Geneva: Leo S. Olschki, 1925; with some changes in punctuation.

Degno son io ch'i' mora,
donna, quand'io vi mostro
ch'i' ho degli occhi vostri Amor furato;
chè, certo, sì celato
5   mi venni al lato vostro,
che non sapeste quando n'uscì fòra;
ed or, perchè davanti a voi m'attento   I
mostrarlo in vista vera,
ben è ragion ch'i' pera,
10   solo per questo mio folle ardimento;
ch'i' dovea innanzi, poi che così era,
soffrirne ogni tormento,
che farne mostramento
a voi, ch'oltra natura sète altera.

15   Ben sono stato s astioso,
ch'i' ho servito quanto
mostrar vèr me disdegno vi piacesse:
ma, se non vi calesse
di mie follie, per tanto
20   dèe stare il vostro cor non disdegnoso;
chè questo Amor, ch'allotta vi furai,   II
per se stesso m'ancide
e dentro mi conquide,
sì che sovente mi fa trarre guai:
25   questa preda dal cor vita divide

che dentro a lui menai.
Donna mia, unque mai
così fatto giudicio non si vide.

Di mio ardir non vi caglia,
30   donna, chè vostr'altezza
mover non si conven contr'uom sì basso:

I deserve to die,
lady, whenever I let you see
that I kidnapped Love from your eyes;
because I hid so well
5   making my way to your side,
you never knew when he came away;
and now, because in your presence I attempt   I
to show the authentic face of Love,
it is right that I should perish
10 for this wild recklessness;
since I stole him, I should
suffer all his torments
before I make a show of him
to you, who are beyond the bounds of nature proud.

15 I have, in truth, been so wild,
I have deserved as much
disdain as it might please you to let me see.
But if my foolish deeds
do not touch you, still
20 your heart should not remain disdainful;
for that same Love, whom I stole from you that time,   II
kills me all on his own,
overpowers me within,
makes me continually lament:
25 this prey I led into my heart

tears its life away.
My lady, never
was there seen such punishment.

Do not mind my recklessness,
30 Lady, for it does not fit
your dignity to act against a man so low:

lasciatemi andar, lasso!
ch'a finir mia gravezza
fo con la morte volentier battaglia.
35 Vedete ben ched i' non ho possanza: III
dunque il mio folleggiare
piacciavi perdonare,
non per ragion, ma vincavi pietanza;
chè fa ben la vendetta da laudare,
40 e per regnare avanza
segnor, che perdonanza
usa nel tempo che si può vengiare.

58

Un'alta ricca rocca e forte manto
volesse Dio che monte ricco avesse,
che di gente inimica non temesse,
avendo un'alta torre d'ogni canto;

5 e fosse d'ogni ben compita, quanto
core pensare o lingua dir potesse,
e quine poi lo dio d'amore stesse
con li amorosi cori in gioia e in canto!

E poi vorrei che nel mezzo sorgesse
10 un'acqua vertudiosa d'amor tanto,
che lor, bagnando, dolce vita desse;

e perchè più fedele 'l mio cor vanto,
vorrei che 'l confalon fra quei tenesse
chi porta di soffrir più grave ammanto.

let me go—alas!
for to put an end to my suffering
I go willingly in battle against Death.
35 You see quite well I have no force.   III
Then let it please you
to forgive my foolishness,
not for cause, but—let Pity win you over;
because a lord takes glorious revenge
40 and makes his lordship great,
who pardons
when he could retaliate.

58

Would that God desired a high majestic citadel,
and very strong, upon a lordly mountain,
that would fear no enemies,
with a lofty tower at every corner;

5   and would be supplied with every good
the heart could think of or the tongue express;
and then that the god of love would dwell there
with hearts that love, in joy and song.

And then in the center I would like springing
10 forth a water with such potency in love,
it gave those bathing there a sweet life;

and I'd like him to bear the gonfalon—
since I boast mine is the truest heart—
who wears the heaviest mantle of martyrdom.

59

Io guardo per li prati ogni fior bianco,
per rimembranza di quel che mi face
sì vago di sospir ch'io ne chieggo anco.

E mi rimembra de la bianca parte [1]
5 che fa col verdebrun la bella taglia,
la qual vestio Amore
nel tempo che, guardando Vener Marte,
con quella sua saetta che più taglia
mi die' per mezzo il core:
10 e quando l'aura muove il bianco fiore,
rimembro de' begli occhi il dolce bianco
per cui lo mio desir mai non fie stanco.

60

Oimè, ch'io veggio per entr'un pensero
l'anima stretta ne le man d'Amore,
e legata la tien nel morto core,
battendola sovente, tant'è fero!

5 Onde la Morte chiama volentero
traggendo guai per lo gran dolore;
chè sente de li suoi colpi spess'ore,
quando avanti si volge per lo vero,

per tragger li miei spiriti d'erranza,

[1] "The white part" and "the dark green" are variously interpreted as referring to the dress or, more likely, the eyes (compare l. 11) of Selvaggia. It has also been suggested that these lines refer as well to the party of Selvaggia, who was a White.

59

I look through the fields at every white flower
in remembrance of that flower, which makes
me so long to sigh, I beg to see it more.

It reminds me of the white part [1]
5   that makes up, with the dark green, the lovely mode
which Love was wearing
that time when, Venus and Mars gazing down,
with the arrow that cuts deepest
he struck me through the heart:
10 and when the breeze moves the white flower,
I remember the lovely white of her beautiful eyes,
wherefore my desire never dies.

60

Alas, in a thought I saw
my soul held tight in the hands of Love,
who kept it bound in my dead heart,
beating it often, so cruel is he.

5   Wherefore it willingly calls on Death,
groaning and groaning in pain;
for many times it feels his blows
when Death—truly, Death comes forth

to draw my spirits from the error

10   là 've li mena Amor, quando ragiona
        di quella donna che la mente vede;

        ma la vertute de la sua persona
        non lassa mover per altra certanza
        color che son ne l'amorosa fede.

                        61

        Dante, quando per caso s'abbandona
        lo disio amoroso de la speme
        che nascer fanno gli occhi del bel seme
        di quel piacer che dentro si ragiona,

5   i' dico, poi se morte le perdona [1]
        e Amore tienla più de le due estreme,[2]
        che l'alma sola, la qual più non teme,
        si può ben transformar d'altra persona.

        E ciò mi fa dir quella ch'è maestra
10   di tutte cose,[3] per quel ch'i' sent'anco
        entrato,[4] lasso, per la mia fenestra.

        Ma prima che m'uccida il nero e il bianco,
        da te, che se' istato dentro ed extra,
        vorre' saper se 'l mi' creder è manco.[5]

[1] Either the soul (line 7) or hope (line 2).
[2] Variously interpreted: the Fates (Contini); heat and cold (Foster and Boyde).
[3] Probably, as Foster and Boyde suggest, Experience.
[4] Love.
[5] The last three lines are deliberately ambiguous, referring both to the condition of love (for example, the "black and white" of the new lady's eyes) and to events in Florence and in the lives of the two poets: both were in exile at this time, and so knew what it was to be "inside and outside" their beloved city, for both were deeply involved in the conflicts of the Blacks and the Whites. See Dante's reply above, *Io sono stato con Amore insieme*, no. 50. The text of this sonnet of Cino's is that established by Michele Barbi.

10   Love leads them to, whenever he discourses of
that Lady my mind beholds;

but the force of her person
will let none move toward any certainty
who belong to the faith of Love.

61

Dante, when the longing of love
comes to abandon hope—
hope that the eyes bring forth from the sweet seed
of that beauty which opens in the mind—

5   then I say: if death spares her,[1]
and Love rules her more than the two extremes,[2]
the soul, alone now and afraid no more,
can turn to another person.

And she who is mistress in all things [3]
10   makes me say this, because of One I feel again [4]
entered, alas, at my window.

But before I am killed by the black and the white,
Dante, I would like to learn from you, who have been
inside and outside, whether my belief is wrong.[5]

62

Io fui 'n su l'alto e 'n sul beato monte,
ove adorai baciando il santo sasso;
ed in su quella pietra caddi lasso,
ove l'onestà pose la sua fronte,

5   e ch'ella chiuse d'ogni vertù 'l fonte
quel giorno che di morte acerbo passo
fece la donna de lo mio cor, lasso!
già piena tutta d'adornezze conte.

Quivi chiamai a questa guisa Amore:
10   "Dolce mio iddio, fa che qui mi traggia
la morte a sè, chè qui giace 'l mio core."

Ma poi che non m'intese 'l mio Signore,
mi dipartii, pur chiamando Selvaggia;
l'alpe passai con voce di dolore.

62

I was on the high and blessed mountain
where I worshipped, kissing the holy tomb;
and fell, weary, upon that stone
where the noblest laid her forehead

5   and there closed off the fount of every virtue
that day, alas, the lady of my heart,
already perfect in glorious merits here,
took the bitter step to death.

There I called in this manner on Love:
10   "Let Death draw me to himself,
my sweet god, for here lies my heart."

But since my lord did not hear me,
I went away, always calling Selvaggia.
I passed over the mountain, voicing grief.

Selected Bibliography

Barbi, Michele. *Life of Dante,* tr. Paul G. Ruggiers. Berkeley and Los Angeles: University of California Press, 1966.

Bowra, M. "Dante and Arnaut Daniel," *Speculum,* 27 (1952), 459–474.

Contini, Gianfranco. *Poeti del Duecento.* 2 vols. Milan and Naples: Riccardo Ricciardi, 1960.

de Boor, Helmut. *Die höfische Literatur* (Helmut de Boor, Richard Newald, *Geschichte der deutschen Literatur von den Anfängen bis zur Gegenwart,* Vol. 2). 7th ed. Munich: C. H. Beck, 1966.

Der deutsche Minnesang, ed. Hans Fromm. Darmstadt: Wissenschaftliche Buchgesellschaft, 1961.

Dronke, Peter. *The Medieval Lyric.* London: Hutchinson, 1968; New York: Harper & Row, 1969.

———. *Medieval Latin and the Rise of European Love-Lyric.* 2 vols. Oxford: Oxford University Press, 1965–66.

Foster, Kenelm. *God's Tree; Essays on Dante and Other Matters.* London: Blackfriars, 1957.

Foster, Kenelm and Patrick Boyde, eds. *Dante's Lyric Poetry.* 2 vols. Oxford: Clarendon Press, 1967.

Frank, István. *Trouvères et Minnesänger.* Saarbrücken, West-Ost-Verlag, 1952.

Goldin, Frederick. *The Mirror of Narcissus in the Courtly Love Lyric.* Ithaca: Cornell University Press, 1967.

Jackson, W. T. H. *The Literature of the Middle Ages.* New York: Columbia University Press, 1960.

Jones, George F. *Walther von der Vogelweide.* New York: Twayne, 1968.

Kolb, Herbert. *Der Begriff der Minne und das Entstehen der höfischen Lyrik.* Tübingen: Niemeyer, 1958.

Kuhn, Hugo. "Zur inneren Form des Minnesangs," in *Der deutsche Minnesang.*

———. *Minnesangs Wende.* 2d ed. Tübingen: Niemeyer, 1967.

———. "*Minnesang* and the Form of Performance," in *Formal Aspects of Medieval German Poetry,* ed. Stanley N. Werbow. Austin & London: University of Texas Press, 1969.

Mohr, Wolfgang. "Minnesang als Gesellschaftskunst," in *Der deutsche Minnesang.*

Monaci, Ernesto. *Crestomazia italiana dei primi secoli.* Rome, Naples, Città di Castello: Società Editrice Dante Alighieri, 1955.

Moret, André. *Les débuts du lyrisme en Allemagne (des origines à 1350).* Travaux et Mémoires de l'Université de Lille, 27. Lille, 1951.

————. "Qu'est-ce que la Minne? Contribution à l'étude de la terminologie et de la mentalité courtoises." *Études Germaniques,* 4 (1949), 1–12.

Nardi, Bruno. *Dante e la cultura medievale.* Bari, 1942; 2d ed. 1949.

Salinari, Carlo, ed. *La poesia lirica del Duecento.* Turin: Unione Tipografico, 1951.

Sayce, Olive, ed. *Poets of the Minnesang.* Oxford: Clarendon, 1967.

Singleton, Charles. *An Essay on the Vita Nuova.* Cambridge: Harvard University Press, 1949.

Tervooren, Helmut. *Bibliographie zum Minnesang und zu den Dichtern aus "Des Minnesangs Frühling."* Berlin: Erich Schmidt, 1969.

Valency, Maurice. *In Praise of Love.* New York: The Macmillan Company, 1958.

Wehrli, Max, ed. *Deutsche Lyrik des Mittelalters.* Zürich: Manesse, 1955.